The Cockapoo Handbook

2ⁿᵈ Edition

BY

LINDA WHITWAM

ISBN: 978-1659903645

Acknowledgements

My sincere thanks to the dedicated breeders, owners and canine experts for sharing their extensive knowledge and enthusiasm for the lovable Cockapoo. This book, the 15th in The Canine Handbook series, would not have been possible without them.

Specialist Contributors:

JESSICA SAMPSON

REBECCA GOINS

KAROL WATSON TODD

PAT POLLINGTON

JEANNE DAVIS

JULIE SHEARMAN

JACKIE STAFFORD

Other Contributors:

Special thanks also to: The British Cockapoo Society, American Cockapoo Club, The Doodle Trust, IDOG International, Dave and Linda Zarro, Diana Hoskins, Eileen Jackson, Mary Gosling, Dr Sara Skiwski, Ann Draghicchio, Arleen Stone King, Beth Ratkowski, Caroline Littlewood, Judy and Greg Moorhouse, Mike Payton, Nigel and Julie Houston, Stacy Robinson, Tiff Atkinson, and Karol Watson Todd's puppy parents.

(Full details appear at the back of the book)

Contents

Author's Notes:

1. This book has been written in British English, except where North Americans have been quoted and the original American English has been preserved.

2. "He" and "she" are interchanged to make the book relevant to all owners.

1. Meet The Cockapoo

The Cockapoo has been known and loved in North America since the 1950s. More recently, it has shot through the canine ranks to become one of the most common dogs in the UK, as well being increasingly seen in countries across the world. You won't go far without spotting one of these lively, friendly dogs; they are everywhere.

The Cockapoo - also known as the Cockerpoo, Spoodle (if you're in Australia) and even Cockadoodle - is the original designer dog, and is the result of crossing a Cocker Spaniel with a Poodle. The Cockapoo is not a purebred or pedigree, but a hybrid or crossbreed, and over the last couple of decades, crossbreeds have exploded in popularity.

Nobody knows the exact origins of this crossbreed and whether it happened by accident. But these days, Cockapoos are definitely born by design – and with three great attributes: their *"hypoallergenic"* coat, manageable size and happy temperament. The Cockapoo also gets along with everything and everybody, and has earned a well-deserved reputation as an excellent all-round family pet.

FACT 〉 *According to Kennel Clubs on both sides of the Atlantic, there is no such thing as a non-shedding dog! All dogs shed a little.*

Many allergy sufferers DO live perfectly well with Cockapoos, but there is no cast-iron guarantee you won't have a reaction - every dog is different, every human is different. See **Chapter 4. Cockapoos for People with Allergies** for more details.

Most Cockapoos have a soft, low-shedding wavy coat, *pictured,* unless they have a coat like their Spaniel parent or ancestor, in which case, they will shed to some extent. How much it sheds varies from one dog to another. However, as the typical Cockapoo coat loses hardly any hair, regular brushing and trips to the grooming parlour are a must – unless you learn to clip the dog yourself.

Unfortunately, the coat's hypoallergenic trait (which means *"less likely to cause an allergic reaction"*) has led to some unscrupulous breeding to cash in on the craze – but none of this is the fault of the dog. If you haven't got your puppy yet, make sure you spend the time to find a reputable, ethical breeder who health tests her dogs.

 Cockapoos come in various sizes, shapes and colours as well as with different coat types, but one thing is generally agreed – an ugly Cockapoo has yet to be born! Do your research BEFORE you view, as the sight of a litter of cute Cockapoo pups will almost certainly be too hard to resist.

The Cockapoo Club of Great Britain says: "The coat type of the Cockapoo will vary as characteristics are inherited from both the Poodle and the Cocker Spaniel. There may even be some variety within a litter. The three possible coat types are a tight curly coat, a loose wavy/ringlet coat and a straighter coat.

"An experienced breeder will be able to advise you what the likely coat type of a puppy will be from their Cocker Spaniel/Poodle mix, and when the puppies are just a few weeks old, it is possible to see the coat type starting to develop. The texture of the Cockapoo coat usually consists of dense, soft or silky fur, unlike the coarser fur found on many dogs, and all three coat types of the F1 Cockapoo will be low-shedding/dander with low-allergen qualities."

The second outstanding feature of the Cockapoo is his excellent temperament. These dogs are intelligent, easy to train and eager to please, affectionate and loyal, have a sunny disposition and get along well with other dogs and people - from children to the elderly. Given sufficient exercise and mental stimulation, Cockapoos are relatively uncomplicated and suitable for first-time owners. They excel at agility and other canine competitions where they are physically and mentally challenged and can be trained to a high level. Their intelligence, even-tempered nature and love of humans mean that they make excellent therapy, service and assistance dogs – one of the few crossbreeds to be trained in this manner.

In order to better understand your Cockapoo, it helps to understand what went into his or her genetic make-up, so let's take a look at the parents and ancestors.

....

Cockers and Poodles

A Cockapoo is the result of mating a Cocker Spaniel with a Poodle. The size, and to some extent, temperament and energy levels, of a Cockapoo depends on which types of Cocker Spaniel and Poodle he or she was bred from, and which parent - if any - the puppy favours.

The ancestors are one of three types of Spaniel. The English Cocker Spaniel could either be a show type *(pictured, above)* or a working type *(pictured, below).* And although the Kennel Club does not distinguish between show and working Cockers, there are some big differences between the strains.

The English Show Cocker is the largest of the three types and is characterised by a domed head, long ears and a thick, wavy coat.

Working Cockers were bred to find and flush game birds out of dense undergrowth. They are smaller, typically with shorter legs and a long, slim body. They are more athletic with a shorter coat, ears set higher on the head and a slightly shorter muzzle.

Cockapoos from working Cockers usually have higher energy drives and exercise requirements than show Cockers; after all, they are used to running for hours on end on a shoot. Like all dogs bred to do a job, they need mental stimulation, as they have to use their brains out in the field, and love a challenge. A bored Cockapoo can result in mischief.

The third type is the American Cocker Spaniel *(pictured overleaf),* which is slightly smaller than its British cousins. The main differences are the shorter muzzle, longer ears and shape of the head. The American Cocker's coat is denser and longer than the English, but it still retains that silky texture.

Referred to simply as the *"Cocker Spaniel"* in the US, they were bred predominantly as companions and for the show ring and most have a calm, sweet disposition with lower energy requirements than many English Cockers.

Spaniels are one of the oldest breeds of dog - they have certainly been known for hundreds of years. Originally called the *"Cocking Spaniel,"* the breed took its name from the woodcock, which it was specifically bred to flush out.

Classed in the Gundog Group in the UK, they are the smallest breed in the Sporting Group in the US. In the late 1800s, the Cocker was recognised in the UK as a separate breed from the larger Field and Springer Spaniels.

The trademark characteristic of all three types of Spaniel is the constantly wagging tail; these are happy dogs with a great desire to please their owners. They are affectionate and enthusiastic and enjoy learning, with scent work being high on their agenda.

All Spaniels love using their noses. If your Cockapoo has retained a lot of Spaniel instinct, teach the Recall before you let him or her run free, or you will last see them disappearing into the distance with their nose to the ground on the scent of a small furry critter or bird! Cocker Spaniels are listed in the top 20 of 110 dogs tested for psychologist Stanley Coren's Intelligence of Dogs List.

The other breeds that make up the Cockapoo are the Poodle — usually the Toy or Miniature. We may think of the Poodle prancing around a show ring with elaborate hairstyles, but people often forget that the Poodle was bred as a water dog in Germany, where it was known as the Pudelhund. The word *"Pudel"* comes from Low German "pudeln" or "puddeln" meaning "to splash in water," similar to the English word puddle, and *"Hund"* means dog in German.

The first Poodles were all Standards, bred as gundogs for hunting duck and sometimes upland birds. In the 17th century, the Poodle was regarded as the best of all hunting dogs, when it was used to trap ducks in the marshes of Europe, and then to retrieve them from reed beds and water.

The original Poodle clip was designed for practical reasons. The hair was left long in pompoms to keep the chest, loins and joints warm in icy water and give a bit more buoyancy, and the topknot on the head was tied with a coloured ribbon so hunters could easily identify their dogs — a far cry from the modern show ring! The Miniature and Toy Poodles were later bred down from the Standard.

FACT 〉 *Apart from its unique appearance, the Poodle has two other outstanding features: the unique wool coat and intelligence. Yes, the Poodle has beauty AND brains! After the Border Collie, this is the most intelligent canine on the planet, according to the Intelligence of Dogs List.*

The non- or low-shedding qualities of the breed's unique wool coat have led to the Poodle becoming the Number One choice for dam or sire when it comes to creating hybrid puppies. And today there are oodles of Doodles and piles of Poos in the canine world.

All Poodles — even small ones - like to run, play and swim, and exercise is a necessity for their happiness. They excel at agility and obedience classes, being both athletic and highly intelligent.

The breed has a reputation for being intuitive, i.e. picking up on their owner's moods. Because of this, some Poodles do not respond well to stress, loud noises or extremely boisterous households.

Breeders on Cockapoos

A number of Cockapoo breeders and owners have kindly given their time to share their experiences in this book. This is what they said, starting in the UK:

Pat Pollington, of Polycinders Cockapoos, Devon, has been breeding dogs for 35 years and Cockapoos for 11. She said: "My Cockapoos are from show strain parents. We believe the show strain Cockapoos are calmer, less energetic, more of a family pet. The working Cockapoos are more hyperactive and need a family that is very active and like walking all the time.

"The working Cockapoo needs to be exercised more than the show Cockapoo. The show strain Cocker Spaniels are bred for the show ring so they are more relaxed, whereas the working Cocker Spaniels are bred to work all day and do a job, i.e. beating, picking up and working on farms, so they like to be on the go a lot. Both strains have lovely temperaments, if bred from the right parents. They are brilliant with children.

"Every Cockapoo wants to be a lapdog and sleep on your lap, but unfortunately they grow to be a touch too big! Every time a Cockapoo needs telling "NO," they give you the big soppy Cockapoo eyes and it is impossible to not give them a big cuddle. They love other dogs and they make brilliant family pets."

Pictured is Pat's three-month-old F1 pup, Lucy, enjoying a walk in the countryside.

"They fit into everyone's lifestyle. If you like walking a lot, they will love that too, but if you fancy a pyjama day watching movies, they will join you on the sofa and enjoy the snacks with you! They are very good at training. If you put your time into a Cockapoo, you will have a well-behaved, trained, loyal and loving family pet.

"The Cockapoo is a very special breed thanks to its fantastic coat. We have had many Cockapoos go to people who are extremely allergic and they have never had any problems. They are just over the moon because they never believed they would be able to own their own dog. If you buy from the right parents, you will have a Cockapoo with a long, wavy, shaggy coat that's the softest thing you can touch. They are low to non-moulting."

Karol Watson Todd, KaroColin Cockapoos, Lincolnshire: "Our Cockapoos are bred from both working and show Spaniels, and I find adult show Cockers to be lazier and less biddable! The working stock is more honest and eager to please in attitude.

"With the puppies, those from show Spaniels do not always get on as well together, while puppies from working Cockers are better at co-operative play from the beginning. I make my own rag toys and working puppies will take an end each and have a great game, while show Cocker puppies will try to get the other puppy to release the toy. It's very interesting!

"Even though people think puppies from show Cockers require less exercise, I haven't found this to be true. I also find that working puppies simply need more mental stimulation, rather than exercise. I always pop a Kong-style toy into my puppy packs for this reason."

Julie Shearman, Crystalwood Cockapoos, Devon: "We breed from show Spaniels. We have found them to be slightly calmer and needing a little less exercise, so better suited to family life. The typical temperament is loving, loyal, intelligent, energetic and fun with a happy disposition, and the most appealing thing is their affection towards people."

Jackie Stafford, Dj's Cockapoo Babies, Texas, US: "Cockapoos are the best family dogs that there are. They are loving, kind and the smartest of all hybrids. They are unique because they are very smart and yet happy-go-lucky at the same time. They are happy in their owner's lap all the time and are always looking to their owner for ways to please them. They are sweet and loving, yet playful and energetic for a moderate timespan. They live to please their owners and the only fault in their temperament is the possibility of separation anxiety."

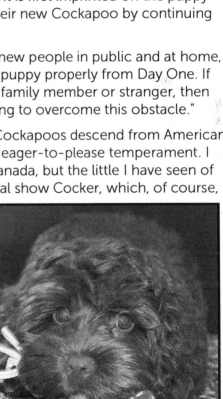

Jeanne Davis, Wind Horse Offering, Maryland: "The typical Cockapoo temperament? Wonderful! Smart, great companions and easy to train. I breed from working Spaniels and I do find there is a difference in temperament between them and other Spaniels. I find working Spaniels are more serious and show Cockers like to be pampered a bit more."
Photo courtesy of Jeanne.

Rebecca Mae Goins, MoonShine Babies Cockapoos, Indiana: "Most of our Cockers, Poodles and Cockapoos are from the heavy-coated show type, but we do have a few that are more towards the working type. The working type does seem to require more exercise and be harder to keep in a home setting, unless the family is very active.

"The typical Cockapoo temperament is very loyal and loving to their family and very smart; easy to train to become a perfect loving family pet. They also do very well as therapy and service dogs. The Cockapoo is very playful and can be comical and a true joy to be around. The temperament is first imprinted on the puppy when it is still with the breeder, and the new family has to help their new Cockapoo by continuing with the training and socialisation.

"If you see a Cockapoo that is happy and loves to play and meet new people in public and at home, then the breeder and family did their jobs well and socialised the puppy properly from Day One. If you see a Cockapoo that is overly shy or aggressive with either a family member or stranger, then he was not properly socialised and will require professional training to overcome this obstacle."

Jessica Sampson, Legacy Cockapoos, Ontario, Canada: "All our Cockapoos descend from American Cocker Spaniels. We chose them for their calm, affectionate and eager-to-please temperament. I have not had a lot of experience with working Spaniels here in Canada, but the little I have seen of them, I have noticed they have a lot more energy than your typical show Cocker, which, of course, would be needed for working in the field.

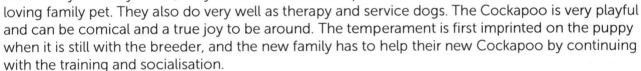

"The typical Cockapoo is a happy, merry dog that knows no stranger. They are very intelligent and eager to please. Also, they have the unique gift of being able to sense one's emotional state and are extremely forgiving. The forgiving nature makes the Cockapoo unparalleled as a family dog and has also made it one of the top picks as a therapy dog, especially when children are involved - particularly those with autism.

"I would say that the best and most appealing thing about the Cockapoo is that it is loving and eager to please, and thus easily trained."

Pictured relaxing at home with a favourite toy is Jessica's F2 chocolate stud Karl.

Sizes

As well as the different coat colours and parentage, there are other factors to consider when considering a Cockapoo; namely size and F numbers. The size and weight of a Cockapoo depends on which type of Poodle went into his or her make-up. The most popular sizes of Cockapoo are Toy and Miniature, bred – unsurprisingly - from Toy and Miniature Poodles. The sizes are:

❧ A **Teacup** (seen in the US) is less than six pounds in weight and under 10 inches in height

❧ A **Toy** Cockapoo weighs less than 12 pounds and can reach 10 inches in height, but has a sturdier build

❧ A **Miniature** ranges from 13 to 18 pounds and stands 11 to 14 inches high

❧ A **Standard** or **Maxi** Cockapoo (bred from a Standard Poodle) is less common and weighs more than 19 pounds. It stands at least 15 inches high

These sizes and weights are not written in stone. If you are considering a Cockapoo puppy, find out exactly what the parent breeds are and ask to see both parents, if possible. This will give you a good idea of the size of the adult dog.

"Teacup" varieties of many different breeds and hybrids have sprung up in the US and are miniaturised versions of the original breed. There have been some recorded health issues with Teacups, notably regarding adverse effects on the dog's skeleton. I am currently not aware of any documented issues with Teacup Cockapoos. However, there is anecdotal evidence of health problems and shortened lifespans with some Teacup Poodles (which is not a breed recognised by the Kennel Clubs). Whatever size of Cockapoo you get, the important thing is to check the health history and certificates of the parents.

F Numbers Explained

The Cockapoo is a crossbreed, not a purebred (North America) or pedigree (UK). It is the product of crossing two breeds of dog: the Cocker Spaniel and the Miniature, Toy or Standard Poodle.

Because the Cockapoo is a crossbreed or hybrid, you cannot get Kennel Club or AKC registration papers with your dog - although if the parents are purebred dogs, they should have registration papers. If this is the case, ask to see the documents and take details. You should always find out about your dog's parents and ancestry because, provided you care for him well, genes will play a major role in your dog's future health. Cockapoos bred from healthy parents are robust dogs with a good lifespan - 10 to 15 years; even longer in a few cases.

FACT ❯ *In the canine world, F numbers have nothing to do with photography or Formula One motor racing. They describe the generation of a crossbreed dog. The F comes from the Latin filius (son) and means "relating to a son or daughter."*

❧ An F1 Cockapoo is a first generation cross. One parent is a pure Cocker Spaniel and the other is a pure Poodle, so 50% Spaniel and 50% Poodle

That's simple enough and many of today's Cockapoos are F1 crosses with two pure breed parents. While this cross often throws a loose, wavy coat, it can occasionally throw tighter curls, or a straighter, shedding coat like the Spaniel. Many experts believe that this first-generation cross benefits from *"hybrid vigour,"* i.e. the first cross between two unrelated purebred lines is healthier and grows better than either parent line.

❧ An F2 Cockapoo is second generation. It is generally a cross between two F1 Cockapoos, so is still 50% Cocker Spaniel and 50% Poodle

❧ An F3 Cockapoo is the offspring of an F2 parent when the other parent was F2 or higher

- ❖ Further down the line there are also *"multigenerations."* The idea behind multigenerations is that breeders can more reliably produce a Cockapoo to type with a low-shedding coat and consistent features

NOTE: The F numbers are worked out by always adding one to the lowest number. While an F2 could be the offspring of two first-generation doodles (F1 x F1), it could also be the product of an F1 x F2 or higher (bigger) number cross.

- ❖ Then we get on to the Bs - the B stands for *"Backcross"* to one of the parent breeds — normally the Poodle (so when a Cockapoo is bred with a Poodle). This is usually done to increase the possibility of a low shedding coat. It is not common practice for breeders to backcross to a Spaniel, so a typical F1B Cockapoo will be one-quarter Spaniel and three-quarters Poodle.

An F2B is the result of an F1 Cockapoo bred to a Cockapoo backcross (F1B). Although three generations in the making, F2Bs are technically second-generation dogs.

All clear? No, well, we're moving on anyway...!

··

Hybrid Vigour

Hybrid Vigour (Vigor in the US), scientific name **heterosis,** is the theory, when applied to dogs, that **the first cross between two unrelated purebred lines is healthier and grows better than either parent line.** Note that this only applies to first generation or F1 crosses.

Also, the theory only applies to F1 crosses from healthy parents. Obviously, if both the Cocker and Poodle have hereditary eye conditions, luxating patellas or hip dysplasia, there is every chance the Cockapoo will inherit - or at the very least be a carrier of - these diseases.

On the Institute of Canine Biology website, Carol Beuchat PhD says: "Mating related animals makes it more likely that offspring will inherit two copies of the same gene."

She says this can cause *"inbreeding depression"* and a loss of: "The collection of traits that affect reproduction and lifespan, such as fertility, offspring size, pre- and post-natal mortality, maternal care, resistance to disease, and general *"vigor and vitality."*

"These effects have been documented in many thousands of studies and in all manner of organisms and although there is much yet to be learned about it, there is no debate about the fact that it is a real phenomenon in both wild and domestic animals."

Interestingly, Dr Beuchat adds that the parent dogs don't even have to be of different breeds, they can be two dogs of the same breed, but with completely unrelated bloodlines. She adds: "Many long-time dog breeders understand heterosis and use it to good effect in their breeding programs." www.instituteofcaninebiology.org/blog/the-myth-of-hybrid-vigor-in-dogsis-a-myth

If true, a deliberately chosen healthy purebred sire and dam can give an F1 crossbreed puppy the advantage of *hybrid vigour — or robustness.* Genetics is a complicated science, and there are also

more variables with hybrids like the Cockapoo. Physical appearance, size, colour and coat are just some of the inconsistencies.

Although many families with allergies live perfectly happily with Cockapoos, no breeder can categorically say that you will NOT be allergic to their dogs. Allergies vary from one person to the next and the odds are that even the other littermates didn't turn out exactly the same as your puppy. Spending time with the individual puppy is the way to find out.

A University of California, Davis study tracked 24 genetic disorders in more than 27,000 dogs. It revealed that the prevalence of 13 of the diseases was roughly the same in purebred dogs as it was in mixed breed dogs. However, 10 disorders were more common in purebred dogs, and just one was more common in mixed breeds. The study also found that purebred dogs that shared a similar lineage (bloodline) were more susceptible to certain inherited disorders.

Read the findings at: www.ucdavis.edu/news/purebred-dogs-not-always-higher-risk-genetic-disorders-study-finds

 As scientists can't yet completely agree on the topic, it's impossible for any breeder to 100% guarantee that his or her Cockapoo pups have hybrid vigour. The best thing you can do is check the health screening certificates of the parent dogs.

Breed Standard

Although you cannot get Kennel Club or AKC registration papers with your dog, you can register him or her with one of the Cockapoo clubs in your country (see back of book for details).

Breed clubs for purebred dogs have a written set of guidelines that govern how all dogs of that breed should look and move and what sort of temperament they should have. This blueprint is called a **Breed Standard** and it ensures that all dogs of the same breed conform.

The Breed Standard is registered with the Kennel Club or AKC and all approved breeders produce dogs that conform to these guidelines. They are then allowed to register their puppies with the Kennel Clubs and receive a family tree certificate for the puppy - this is called a pedigree.

However, in the past it has also led to some breeders using a very narrow gene pool to breed for certain exaggerated traits — for example the very flat nose on a Bulldog — and sometimes this has led to health issues. It's fair to say that the Kennel Club in the UK has relaxed some of the breed standards and, along with the breed clubs, is making great strides to improve the health of pedigree (purebred) dogs.

Because the Cockapoo is a crossbreed, there is no Kennel Club or AKC Breed Standard. The Cockapoo Club of Great Britain (CCGB) promotes a "**breeding standard**" - rather than a breed standard — which promotes ethical breeding and allows for variations in appearance. The CCGB says that *"healthy and fit for purpose"* should be the main consideration for Cockapoo breeders. The American Cockapoo Club does have a written Breed Standard, and this is it:

The American Cockapoo Club Breed Standard

General Appearance. Cockapoos have a sturdy, squarely-built appearance. The length from the body measured from the breastbone to the rump is approximately the same-to-slightly longer than the height from the highest point of the shoulder to the ground. He stands up well at the shoulder on straight forelegs with a top line that is level-to-slightly sloping toward moderately-bent hindquarters. He is a dog capable of great speed and endurance, combined with agility. The body must be of sufficient length to permit a straight and free stride. Cockapoos should never appear low and long, or tall and gangly, but should always be in proportion.

Size and Weight. Size of Cockapoos can be influenced by either parent's recent background. Adult dogs 10" at the shoulder or less are toy size. Dogs 11"-14" at the shoulder are considered mini size, and those 15" at the shoulder and over are standard size. Cockapoo size is judged by their height, not their weight.

Two dogs that are the same size can vary considerably in weight depending both on their overall build and whether one is fat or thin. Weights of individuals will depend on the factors explained above. To give a general idea of weight, a toy would ideally weigh under 12 pounds, a Mini 13-20 pounds and a Standard 21 pounds and up.

Head, Expression. Large, round, well-set, well-spaced eyes with a keen, soulful, endearing and intelligent expression. The color of the eyes should be dark brown on dogs with black noses. Brown dogs have brown noses. Dogs with light-colored noses may have lighter (i.e.: greenish, hazel) eyes. The eyes should not have a droopy appearance.

Hair should be scissored back so as not to obstruct the eyes or vision. The ears should hang fairly close to the head, starting above the eyes and hanging to well below eye level. They should be well-feathered, but never erect or carried up over the head. Ideally the bottom of the ears should be level with the beard. The skull is moderately rounded but not exaggerated, with no tendency towards flatness.

Bite. Aligned bite, with neither over- nor under-bite. Level bites (incisors striking edge to edge) are acceptable, but scissors bite (lower incisors striking just behind the uppers) is preferred.

Neck, Top Line, Body. The neck rises strongly from the shoulders and arches slightly as it tapers to join the head. Carried high and with dignity, the neck is never pendulous (no throatiness - skin tight). The top line is level-to-slightly sloping toward the hindquarters. The chest is deep and moderately wide, with well-sprung ribs, its lowest point no higher than the elbow.

Tail. The tail is set on line with the back and carried on line with the top line or higher; when the dog is in motion the tail action is merry. The tail can be left long or docked like the parent breeds; both are acceptable. The tail should be well feathered and full coated when left long. If not docked, the tail is to be curled up over the back and left long, never shaven. If docked, tail should be no more and no less than 4 inches. **(NOTE: It is illegal to dock a Cockapoo's tail in the UK and Europe).**

Forequarters. The shoulders are well laid back, forming an angle with the upper arm of approximately 90 degrees, permitting easy movement and forward reach. When viewed from the side with the forelegs vertical, the elbow is directly below the highest point of the shoulder blade. Forelegs are parallel, straight, with strong pasterns. Legs should be set close to the body.

Front dew claws can be left or removed; back dew claws should be removed. Feet should be in balanced proportion with the dog; however, the feet should be compact, with arched toes and turn neither in nor out.

Hindquarters. When viewed from behind, the legs are parallel when in motion and at rest. Moderately angled at the stifle, and clearly defined thighs. When standing, the rear toes should be behind the point of the rump.

Coat Types. As with many other breeds, Cockapoos have three different coat types. There is the tight curly coat, the medium curl, and the flat coat. While we strive for the medium curl, all three coat types are acceptable. It is very common to see all three types within the same litter of pups. This can happen with 1st, 2nd, 3rd (etc). generation litters.

Coat length. The Cockapoo's coat should be clipped all over in a *"teddy bear"* type cut of about 2-3 inches. The top of the head should be the same length as the body. If the tail is docked, the hair on the docked tail should be the same length as the body. A Cockapoo should never be shaven. They should have facial hair and a beard; all flowing into each other and trimmed no longer than 4 inches. The ears should be trimmed straight across and even with the bottom of the beard. The face should never be shaven. If the dog is not being shown, then a shorter or longer coat is allowed. Just remember to keep the eyes clear of fur and keep them well brushed.

Color and Markings. Any solid color; parti color (two or more solid colors, one of which must be white); phantom (brown, black or silver body with contrasting color on legs, under tail, eyebrows, side of face, inside ears); sable (may be black, brown, brindle, changing to silver, silver/gold mix, red, brown, other, all with darker points); tri-color (parti color with white base and tan markings over each eye, on the sides of the muzzle/cheeks, on the underside of the ears, on all feet and/or legs and optionally on the chest). Merle and/or roan are also acceptable colors.

The nose and rims of eyes should be one solid color. Brown colored dogs may have brown noses, eye rims, lips, dark toenails and dark amber eyes. Black, blue, gray, cream and white dogs have black noses, eye rims and lips, black or self-colored toenails and very dark eyes. In light-colored dogs, the liver-colored nose is quite common.

Owners on Cockapoos

Ann Draghicchio, owner of F1 Toby and F1b Winston adds: "I believe they are a good first-time dog. They were super easy to potty train - both were quick to be bell-trained - and are great to cuddle with. They have a good energy level, but mine don't necessarily require multiple walks daily."

"Although any puppy requires a lot of work, I feel like these were a nice mix of work and reward for your efforts. Winston chewed a hole in a leather recliner and has since chewed a few other leather items. Even though we don't give him rawhide, he seems to love that smell and texture. We would redirect and say *"no"* if we saw him chewing. Otherwise we would use a bitter apple spray to deter him. Toby, on the other hand, did not chew anything that I recall." *Winston (left) and Toby are pictured enjoying the sunshine.*

"One thing that has surprised us is Toby's anxiety. He is a bit more energetic than Winston and sometimes anxious. That being said, the majority of Cockapoos I have been around have been on the more laid-back side."

Tiff Atkinson, owner of four-year-old F1 Dolce says: "Dolce's temperament is very playful, loving, and easy going. Just as much as she loves being entertained by us, she enjoys her solo time playing with her toys - her energy level is very high, but she is very adaptable. She's extremely people-loving. We placed her in doggie day care for half a day so she can be socialised, and are glad we did, because she enjoys playing with other dogs."

Breeder Karol Watson Todd, of KaroColin Cockapoos, Lincolnshire, England, asked a number of her puppy parents just what they thought of their Cockapoos. (All the dogs are under three years old). Here's what they have to say:

Keith and Diane: "Any potential owners of Cockapoos need to think very hard about why they want one. These are not dogs for just sitting at your feet all day long. They need plenty of exercise. Our Zippy *(pictured)* has up to two or three hours a day and she always wants more! She needs grooming every day so the coat doesn't get matted and she visits a groomer for a trim etc. once every six to eight weeks. They are wonderful companions and learn things very, very quickly. They idolise their owners, especially if they are treated correctly and are well looked after.

"Zippy is also becoming a wonderful agility dog and she loves every minute of it. They must be well-trained or else they will take as many liberties with you as they possibly can. They do tend to jump up at people, but that really is part of their nature; they just love giving and receiving affection.

"They are a wonderful breed of dog - loving, friendly, caring, busy and we would not be without our Zippy. We may have only had her for a year, but she has completely transformed our lives, and we are loving every single minute of her being around us. She is absolutely gorgeous, but then we are big softies!"

Mal and Fiona: "Harry is EPIC! He is very greedy too; he will eat almost anything. He loves to be fussed – surprise, surprise! He's shy of people he doesn't know, but he usually gets used to them. Harry *(pictured)* usually takes shoes, socks, underwear, teddies and more. He's a quick learner and has dog training, so he knows Sit, Lie Down, Dance, High Five, Wait, Stay, Stand, Heel, Let's Go and Get Becky, Feedies, Play, Fetch and OK.

"He's a very loyal and caring dog who gets very excited when he sees someone he knows. Harry loves to play and have a good run; he loves walks. Harry's a joy and has already got a girlfriend! He is growing up in Stafford and loves to go and have a run off the lead and always comes back ...well, nearly always!"

Judith and Patrick: "Daisy is beautiful. She has a lovely gentle nature and is very calm, although there is a feisty side to her, too. She loves water and getting wet and muddy, and adores jumping and climbing. In the woods we have seen her try to run up tree trunks! Daisy is going to the hairdressers next week. There is never a dull moment with Daisy, but we wouldn't have it any other way. She has a wonderful character; she gives love unconditionally and is always smiling and wagging her tail."

Lorraine and Geoff: "Our lovely girl is called Daisy Mae and she is as mad as a box of frogs, but we love her to bits! She has changed our lovely quiet lives into utter turmoil and put years on us. Only today we walked into the lounge and Daisy has pulled the Xmas tree over and had lights wrapped around her.

"Daisy Mae loves to be fussed and has to follow the same daily walk routine in the hope of seeing all the people who love to fuss her. People think she is so pretty and Daisy Mae usually rolls on her back, legs in air so she can be tickled. We have just had an eight-week-old kitten and, right from the beginning, Daisy Mae and Tuppence spend lots of time together - mostly racing up and down and stealing each other toys and sleeping together on the bed. She is so good and gentle with Tuppence. We love her to bits she brightens our lives. She loves her toys and when she's out in the fields love to chase balls, she runs and tumbles but she does like to roll in fox poo, we think because she loves a bath."

Alexia and Lindsay: Millie *(pictured)* is an absolute joy. She can be manic, playful, cuddly and a couch potato, depending on what's going on. Her biggest disappointment in life is that our three cats don't want to play with her. She loves running across the fields, springing up and down in the scrub, following her nose or chasing birds or leaves, often jumping like a Springer.

"She usually comes when called or whistled and has picked up every command I've taught her very quickly, but won't always DO them. She was one of the smallest of the litter and is now 10.45kg. She loves having a shower after a walk, and constantly wags her tail. She loves people, dogs and life - a very happy, smiling, bundle of excitement and joy."

Amanda: "Barney is such a lovely little dog; great with our two girls and known by everyone in our village. He loves cuddles and generally following me around all day. Millie looks as if she gets as dirty as Barney *(pictured),* who has at least one bath a week. I would highly recommend

Cockapoos, especially if you have children, as they are extremely loving, gentle and trustworthy. They do thrive on company and love affection. Barney loves playing with his ball and swimming."

Liz: "Alfie lives in Telford with Liz, Andy, Hannah (7) and Sam (5). Alfie is amazing - generally very chilled and, dare I say, a little bit lazy! He has his mad moments - generally with Sam (who has severe learning difficulties). Alfie has been fantastic with the children and is such a good addition to our family. He does like rolling in stinky stuff, though!"

Jo and Paul: "Jasper is a lovely dog who loves cuddles and having his tummy tickled. He is great with our children and most people who meet him liken him to a teddy bear! He loves playing rough and tumble with his brother, Alfie, and getting up to plenty of mischief if he thinks no one is looking. Alfie and Jasper live around the corner from each other."

Sarah and Debra: "We love Duffy and he's brought so much joy, fun and exercise to our family life. We own a motorhome and love to travel at any opportunity, so this year Duffy has been to Spain (twice), France, Italy, Germany, Austria and Belgium. He's dug in the sand, swum in the Med, been on a bus, a tram, a boat, the underground, a ski slope, a mountain stream...... in fact we've just calculated that he's travelled 8,500 miles since January! I think he's a walking ad for a pet passport!"

Jane and Jeremy: "We are the proud owners of Dylan, who had a huge appetite from Day One. What can we say about Dylan - lively, loyal (well, to Jeremy anyway), loving, adorable, wonderful with children and now thinks when passing anyone in the street that they are there to see him and give cuddles. I've lost count of the number of people that stop us and want to know what breed he his and cuddle him. Oh yes, and he still has a huge appetite!"

Debra: "Teddy is absolutely gorgeous and so much fun to have around. She's gentle and playful and incredibly easy-going, taking just about everything in her stride. (She's not keen on men in hats, but then I guess we've all got our little quirks!) She loves playing with other dogs and takes every opportunity to try to when we're out on a walk - most are happy to play with her.

"Teddy *(pictured)* was very good at puppy training - she's great at recall, unless there's a bird flying around to distract her. And she loves shoes, probably her favourite thing in the world to chew. She also loves being in the mud."

Jo: "Luna is the ultimate family dog for us and so I've realised all my photos tend to be of her rolling about on the floor with the kids! I love to walk, however, and so the other thing I love about her is her gusto and great enthusiasm to walk too. I let her off the lead from the word go and her recall now is amazing - she's busy chasing a pheasant through the undergrowth, but the moment she hears her whistle, she's back. She gives her absolute attention and loves training."

Sarah: "Cockapoos are excellent family dogs; my nine-year-old daughter and Lola are the best of friends. They are such an intelligent breed and pick up most commands easily unless distracted - Lola loves barking at other dogs and chasing cats! I think it's really important to meet the puppy's parents as we all did. Lola's friendly temperament is often commented on. Lola loves lots of exercise and running with other dogs, and enjoys new experiences, like her first visit to the beach this year. She just went off kibble and is now on a raw diet - Natural Instinct - which she is thriving on. She has the sweetest temperament and everyone loves her!"

Christine: "We are utterly delighted with our little girl. Amber has a beautiful nature and is very gentle and affectionate with everyone - even the smallest of children. She is also very clever and picks up commands very easily. But it's more than that; she is so eager to please that she seems to know what is required without you training her. Seriously, we are quite amazed at times.

"One thing that we have discovered is how much exercise Amber needs. We give her at least two hours a day on two or three walks, and she seems to have a never-ending supply of energy. Not a problem for us as we love walking, but anyone unable or unprepared for this commitment should probably think twice before parenting a Cockapoo!"

And finally, we asked owners and breeders to sum up Cockapoos in three or four words:

- Wonderful, loving, carefree, loyal
- Highly intelligent, playful, cute
- Affectionate, clever, fun, energetic
- Playful, loyal, funny, intelligent
- Affectionate, protective, intuitive
- Cute, smart, fun, tractable
- Loving, fun, happy, bouncy
- Friendly, loyal, intelligent, perfect!
- Loyal, loving, intelligent, playful
- Friendly, family-orientated, characters, stunning
- Loving, affectionate, playful, a true family member and the best dog you will ever own.... (OK, so it's not three or four words, but you get the picture!)

Now you've met the Cockapoo, read on to find the right puppy and then learn how to take good care of the newest member of your family for the rest of his or her life.

2. Before You Get Your Puppy

If you haven't got your puppy yet, then read this chapter before you commit to anything; it will help you find a happy, healthy puppy.

Once you have decided that the Cockapoo is your ideal dog, the best way to select a puppy is with your HEAD - and not with your heart! There are thousands of Cockapoo puppies out there, but only a few first-rate breeders. Unfortunately, due to the high price of puppies, the Cockapoo is one "designer crossbreed" that has attracted some people whose main aim is to make money.

With their big appealing eyes, silky soft fur and endearing personalities, there are few more appealing things on this Earth than a litter of Cockapoo puppies. If you go to view a litter, the pups are sure to melt your heart and it is extremely difficult — if not downright impossible - to walk away without choosing one.

As you know, the Cockapoo is a crossbreed created from the Cocker Spaniel and usually the Miniature or Toy Poodle. As with most breeds, the Poodle and Cocker Spaniel can have some genetic health issues, so your number one priority should be to buy a puppy free from inherited diseases.

 If you haven't yet chosen your pup and take only one sentence from this entire book, it is this: **FIND AN ETHICAL BREEDER WITH HEALTH-TESTED PARENTS**

- of the puppy, not the breeder! One who knows Cockapoos inside out and who does not breed lots of different types of dogs. After all, apart from getting married or having a baby, getting a puppy is one of the most important, demanding, expensive and life-enriching decisions you will ever make.

Just like babies, Cockapoo puppies will love you unconditionally - but there is a price to pay. In return for their loyalty and devotion, you have to fulfil your part of the bargain. In the beginning, you have to be prepared to devote much of your day to your new puppy. You have to feed her several times a day and housetrain virtually every hour, you have to give her your attention and start to gently introduce the rules of the house as well as take care of health and welfare. You also have to be prepared to part with hard cash for regular healthcare and pet insurance.

If you are unable to devote the time and money to a new arrival, if you have a very young family, a stressful life or are out at work all day, then now might not be the right time to consider getting a puppy. Cockapoos are highly affectionate people-loving dogs that thrive on being close to their owners. If left alone too long, these "Velcro" dogs can become unhappy, bored and even destructive. This is a natural reaction and is not the dog's fault; she is simply responding to the environment, which is failing to meet her needs.

Pick a healthy pup and he or she should live for 10 to 15 years if you're lucky - so getting a Cockapoo is certainly a long-term commitment. Before taking the plunge, ask yourself some questions:

Have I Got Enough Time?

In the first days after leaving her mother and littermates, your puppy will feel very lonely and probably even a little afraid. You and your family have to spend time with your new arrival to make her feel safe and sound. Ideally, for the first few days you will be around all of the time to help her settle and to start bonding. If you work, book a couple of weeks off if you can - although this is impossible for some of our American readers who get shorter vacations than their European counterparts, but don't just get a puppy and leave her all alone in the house a couple of days later.

Housetraining (potty training) starts the moment your pup arrives home. Then, after the first few days and once he's feeling more settled, start to introduce short sessions of a few minutes of behaviour training to teach your new pup the rules of the house. Cockapoo puppies want to please you and, while they are often gentle souls as adults, they are often very lively as puppies. This energy can become mischievous if not channelled - so training should start early to discourage puppy biting and jumping up.

FACT 〉 *Like Poodles, some Cockapoos can have sensitive natures and may be affected by all kinds of things: loud noises, shouting, arguments, unhappiness, other animals or new situations, to name but a few things.*

You'll also have to make time to slowly start the socialisation process by taking her out of the home to see buses, noisy traffic, other animals, kids, etc. - but make sure you CARRY her until the vaccinations have taken effect. Start socialising as soon as possible; that critical window for socialisation is all too short. The more positive experiences she is introduced to at this early stage, the better, and good breeders will already have started the process.

Once she has had the all-clear following vaccinations, get into the habit of taking her for a short walk every day — more as she gets older. While the garden or yard is fine, new surroundings stimulate interest and help to stop puppies becoming bored and developing unwanted behaviour issues. She also gets used to different experiences away from the home.

Make time right from the beginning to get your pup used to being handled, gently brushed, ears checked, and having her teeth touched and later cleaned.

We, and good breeders, recommend that you have your pup checked out by a vet within a couple of days of arriving home - but don't put your puppy on the clinic floor where she can pick up germs from other dogs. Factor in time to visit the vet's surgery for annual check-ups as well as vaccinations, although most now last several years — check with your vet.

How Long Can I Leave My Puppy?

This is a question we get asked all of the time and one that causes much debate among new and prospective owners. All dogs are pack animals; their natural state is to be with others. So being alone is not normal for them - although many have to get used to it. The Cockapoo has not been bred to be a guard dog; he or she most definitely wants to be around you.

Another issue is the toilet; Cockapoo puppies have tiny bladders. Forget the emotional side of it, how would you like to be left for eight hours without being able to visit the bathroom? So how many hours can you leave a dog alone?

 *In the UK, canine rescue organisations will not allow anybody to adopt if they are intending to leave the dog alone for more than four or five hours a day.*

Dogs left at home alone a lot get bored and, in the case of Cockapoos, i.e. a breed that thrives on companionship, they can become depressed. Of course, it depends on the character and temperament of your dog, but a lonely Cockapoo may display signs of unhappiness by barking, chewing, digging, urinating, soiling, bad behaviour, or just being plain sad and disengaged.

In terms of housetraining, a general rule of thumb is that a puppy can last without going to the toilet for **one hour or so for every month of age.** So, provided your puppy has learned the basics, a three-month-old puppy should be able to last for three hours or a little longer without needing the toilet. Of course, it doesn't work like this – until housetraining kicks in, young puppies just pee at will!

A puppy or fully-grown dog must never be left shut in a crate all day. It's fine to leave a dog in a crate if he or she is happy there, but the door should not be closed for more than a couple of hours during the day. It's fine to close the crate door at night until your puppy is housetrained. A crate is a place where a dog should feel safe, not a prison.

Family and Children

Cockapoos are great dogs for first-time owners and are known for being really good with children. You may find puppyhood a challenge as baby Cockapoos can be extremely lively! But survive that and adult Cockapoos are worth the effort and very rewarding. Of course, that comes with the usual caveat – you have to socialise your Cockapoo AND the kids! Your children will naturally be delighted about your new arrival, but remember that Cockapoo puppies are fragile, so avoid leaving babies or toddlers and dogs alone together – no matter how well they get along.

Due to their small bones, Cockapoos bred from Toy Poodles may not be the best choice for a family with lively pre-school or young children. Small kids lack co-ordination and may inadvertently poke a puppy in the eye, tread on her and break a bone or pull a joint out of place. Cockapoos from Miniature Poodles tend to be sturdier and more robust – with increased exercise needs.

Often puppies regard children as playmates - just like a child regards a puppy as a playmate; young pups and children are playful, both easily getting over-excited. A puppy may chase, jump and nip a small child – although it can be the other way around; a gentle pup may need protecting from the children! Lively behaviour is not aggression; it is normal play for puppies. See **Chapter 10. Training a Cockapoo** on how to deal with puppy biting.

Train your pup to be gentle with your children and your children to be gentle with your puppy.

Your dog's early experiences with children should all be positive. If not, a dog may become nervous or mistrustful - and what you want around children is most definitely a relaxed dog that does not feel threatened by a child's presence.

Teach your children respect for their dog, which is a living creature with her own needs, not a toy. Cockapoos are extremely loyal; they may even become protective and watch over your children. Take things steady in the beginning and your Cockapoo will undoubtedly form a deep, lifelong bond that your children will remember throughout their lives.

 Discourage the kids from picking up your gorgeous new puppy at every opportunity. Constantly picking up a Cockapoo puppy can lead to the dog becoming less independent and more needy.

Make sure puppy gets enough time to sleep – **which is most of the time in the beginning** - so don't let children (or adults!) constantly pester him. Sleep is very important to puppies, just as it is for babies. Also, allow your Cockapoo to eat at his or her own pace uninterrupted; letting youngsters play with the dog while eating is a no-no as it may promote gulping of food or food aggression.

One reason that some dogs end up in rescue centres is that owners are unable to cope with the demands of small children AND a dog. On the other hand, it is also a fantastic opportunity for you to educate your little darlings (both human and canine) on how to get along with each other and set the pattern for wonderful lasting friendships.

Single People

Many single adults own dogs, but if you live alone, be aware that getting a puppy will require a lot of dedication on your part. There will be nobody to share the responsibility, so taking on a dog requires a huge commitment and a lot of your time if the dog is to have a decent life.

If you are out of the house all day as well, it is not really fair to get a puppy, or even an adult dog – and a Cockapoo is definitely not a good choice as this hybrid thrives on interaction with humans. However, if you work from home or are at home for much of the day and can spend considerable time with the pup, then a Cockapoo will most definitely become your closest friend.

Older People

If you are older or have elderly relatives living with you, Cockapoos can be a good choice and great company. We would recommend getting one from show stock, rather than a Cockapoo from working stock, which would require more exercise. Puppies generally require a lot of energy and patience from any owner, so if you are older and/or less mobile, an older Cockapoo may be a better option.

Dogs can, however, be a great tonic for fit, older people. In his mid-80s my father still walked his dog for an hour to 90 minutes every day - a morning and an afternoon walk and then a short one last thing at night – even in the rain or snow. He grumbled occasionally, but it was good for him and it was good for the dog - helping to keep them both fit and socialised! They got fresh air, exercise and the chance to communicate with other dogs and their humans. My father's dog passed away, but at 89 he still walks with a friend's dog every day.

You're never alone when you've got a dog. Many older people get a canine companion after losing a loved one (a husband, wife or previous much-loved dog). A pet gives them something to care for and love, as well as a constant companion.

Bear in mind that dog ownership is not cheap, so budget for annual pet insurance, veterinary fees, a quality pet food, etc. The RSPCA in the UK has estimated that owning a dog costs an average of around £1,300 ($1,700) a year!

Other Pets

However friendly your puppy is, if you already have other pets in your household, they may not be too happy at the new arrival. Cockapoos generally get on well with other animals, but it might not be a good idea to leave your hamster or pet rabbit running loose; many young puppies have play and/or prey instincts – although if introduced slowly, they may well become best friends!

Both the Cocker and Poodle have hunting backgrounds, so it is no surprise that some Cockapoos do have quite a strong hunting instinct outdoors, when they love to chase cats, birds and other small creatures - but once back indoors they often get along perfectly happily with other small animals sharing their home.

Cockapoo puppies are naturally curious and playful and will sniff and investigate other pets. They may even chase them in the beginning. Depending on how lively your pup is, you may have to separate them to start off with, or put a playful Cockapoo into a pen or crate initially to allow a cat to investigate without being mauled by a hyperactive pup who thinks the cat is a great playmate.

This will also prevent your puppy from being injured. If the two animals are free and the cat lashes out, your pup's eyes could get scratched. A timid Cockapoo might need protection from a bold cat - or vice versa. A bold cat and a timid Cockapoo will probably settle down together quickest!

If things seem to be going well with no aggression, then let them loose together after one or two supervised sessions. Take the process slowly; if your cat is stressed or frightened, she may decide to leave. Our feline friends are notorious for abandoning home because the board and lodgings are better down the road...

More than One Dog

Well-socialised Cockapoos have no problem sharing their home with other dogs. Introduce your puppy to other dogs and animals in a positive, non-frightening manner that will give him or her confidence. Supervised sessions help everyone to get along and for the other dog or dogs to accept your new pup. If you can, introduce them for the first time outdoors on neutral ground, rather than in the house or in an area that one dog regards as her own. You don't want the established dog to feel she has to protect her territory, nor the puppy to feel she is in an enclosed space and can't get away.

Everything should hopefully run smoothly. The Cockapoo's popularity is due in no small part to the lack of aggression, affectionate nature, gentle temperament and ability to get on with children and other dogs.

If you are thinking about getting more than one pup, you may wish to consider waiting until your first Cockapoo is a few months old or an adult before getting a second, especially if you are a first-time owner. This enables you to give your full attention to one dog, get housetraining out of the way and your new puppy can learn some training from the older dog. On the other hand, some owners prefer to get the messy part over and done with in one go and get two together.

If you are thinking of getting two puppies at the same time, you should be prepared to devote a lot of time and energy to each dog for the first few weeks and months. Owning two dogs can be twice as nice - it's also double the food and vet's bills. Here is some cautionary advice from UK rescue organisation The Doodle Trust:

"Think about why you are considering another dog. If, for example, you have a dog that suffers from separation anxiety, then rather than solving the problem, your second dog may learn from your first and you then have two dogs with the problem instead of one. The same applies if you have an unruly adolescent; cure the problem first and only introduce a second dog when your first is balanced.

"A second dog will mean double vet's fees, insurance and food. You may also need a larger car, and holidays will be more problematic. Sit down with a calculator and work out the expected expense – you may be surprised. Two dogs will need training, both separately and together. If the dogs do not receive enough individual attention, they may form a strong bond with each other at the expense of their bond with you.

"If you are tempted to buy two puppies from the same litter - DON'T! Your chances of creating a good bond with the puppies are very low and behaviour problems with siblings are very common. If you have a very active dog, would a quieter one be best to balance her high energy or would you enjoy the challenge of keeping two high energy dogs? You will also need to think of any problems that may occur from keeping dogs of different sizes and ages.

"If you decide to purchase a puppy, you will need to think very carefully about the amount of time and energy that will be involved in caring for two dogs with very different needs. A young puppy will need to have her exercise restricted until she has finished growing and will also need individual time for training. If you decide to keep a dog and female together, then you will obviously need to address the neutering issue."

At the end of the day, the decision is, of course, entirely yours. You might want to consider getting another Cockapoo, Cavapoo or Poodle cross. Many owners report that their Doodles and Poos have an affinity with other Doodles and Poos - perhaps they have inherited the intuition of the Poodle.

Gender

You have to decide whether you want a male or a female puppy. In terms of gender, much depends on the temperament of the individual dog - the differences WITHIN the sexes are greater than the differences BETWEEN the sexes. One difference, however, is that females have heat cycles and, if she is intact, you will have to restrict your normal exercise routine when she comes into heat (every six months or so) to stop unwanted attention from other dogs.

Another is that some Cockapoos can be territorial and it is not uncommon for some males to "mark" their territory by urinating indoors. If your dog is to remain intact – i.e. not neutered or spayed - think carefully about which gender would be most suitable. Latest scientific studies show that it may be beneficial to wait until a dog has finished growing – or at least until one year old – before neutering. Dogs that mark usually start doing so during puberty, at six to 12 months of age.

If you already have dogs or are thinking of getting more than one, you have to consider gender. You cannot expect an unneutered male to live in a relaxed manner with an unspayed female on heat. Similarly, two uncastrated males may not always get along; there may simply be too much testosterone and competition. If an existing dog is neutered or spayed and you plan to have your second dog neutered or spayed, then gender should not be an issue.

NOTE: Some breeders will specify that your pup has to be spayed or neutered within a certain timeframe to prevent indiscriminate breeding.

Your main points of reference in terms of size, physical appearance and temperament are the puppy's parents. Even if the father is not present, you should always see the mother and watch how she interacts with the puppies – are they really hers? Discuss with your breeder which puppy would best suit you.

Colour

There are many colours of Cockapoos; some of the most common ones are:

- 🐾 **Apricot** – can be light, medium or dark
- 🐾 **Red** – deeper than apricot, but caused by the same gene
- 🐾 **Gold**
- 🐾 **Brown or Chocolate**
- 🐾 **White**
- 🐾 **Cream or Champagne**
- 🐾 **Black**
- 🐾 **Phantom**
- 🐾 **Roan or Merle** (mottled)
- 🐾 **Buff, Sable,**
- 🐾 **Tan**
- 🐾 **Silver**
- 🐾 **Brindle** - brown or buff with dark streaks
- 🐾 **Tri-Colour**

Some of these colours can be *Abstract,* with small white markings usually on the dog's chest, chin, paws, tail tip or neck, or *Parti,* patches of colour on a background of at least 50% white. A *Tuxedo* is a white splash on the chest, while a *Dilute* is a faded version of the original colour.

 Some of these combinations, such as brindle or phantom, are not natural to either the Cocker Spaniel or the Poodle, so another breed has been introduced somewhere along the line. If you have set your heart on a favourite colour, remember to check that all the health boxes have been ticked as well.

Puppy Stages

It is important to understand how a puppy develops into a fully-grown dog to help you become a good owner. **The first few months and weeks of a puppy's life will have an effect on her behaviour and character for life.** This Puppy Schedule outlines the early stages:

Birth to seven weeks	A puppy needs sleep, food and warmth. She needs her mother for security and discipline and littermates for learning and socialisation. The puppy learns to function within a pack and learns the pack order of dominance. She begins to become aware of her environment. During this period, puppies should be left with their mother.

Eight to 12 weeks	At the age of eight weeks, the brain is fully developed and she **now needs socialising with the outside world**. She needs to change from being part of a canine pack to being part of a human pack. This period is a fear period for the puppy, avoid causing her fright and pain.
13 to 16 weeks	Training and formal obedience should begin. **This is a critical period for socialising with other humans, places and situations.** This period will pass easily if you remember that this is a puppy's change to adolescence. Be firm and fair. Her flight instinct may be prominent. Avoid being too strict or too soft with her during this time and praise her good behaviour.
Four to eight months	Another fear period for a puppy is between seven to eight months of age. It passes quickly, but be cautious of fright or pain that may leave the puppy traumatised. The puppy reaches sexual maturity and dominant traits are established. Your Cockapoo should now understand the following commands: 'sit,' 'down,' 'come' and 'stay.'

Plan Ahead

Choosing the right breeder is one of the most important decisions you will make. Like humans, your puppy will be a product of his or her parents and will inherit many of their characteristics. Natural temperament and how healthy your puppy will be now and throughout her life will depend to some extent on the genes of her parents. Character is formed by a combination of temperament (or **nature**) and **nurture** - and how you treat your dog influences his or her character.

Responsible breeders health test their dogs; they check the health records and temperament of the parents and only breed from suitable stock. Sound Cockapoo puppies are not cheap – health screening, socialisation and first-rate care come at a cost.

Expect to pay more than $1,500 in the US and over £1,000 in the UK for a pup from health-tested parents. See **Chapter 11. Cockapoo Health** for more info on what certificates to ask to see.

 BE PATIENT. Start looking months or even a year before your planned arrival. There is usually a waiting list for Cockapoo pups from health-tested parents and good breeders, so once you know you can afford a well-bred Cockapoo, put your name down on a list.

Phone or email your selected breeders to find out about future litters and potential dates, but don't commit until you've asked lots of questions. Good breeders will also ask a lot of questions about yourself, your household and living conditions and how you will take care of their much-loved puppy.

A healthy Cockapoo will be your irreplaceable companion for the next decade or more, so why buy one from a pet shop or general advertisement? Would you buy an old car or a house with potential structural problems just because it looked pretty in a website photo or was cheap? The answer is probably no, because you know you'd have stress and expense at some point in the future.

Visit the breeder personally at least once. However, with the vast distances sometimes involved, this is not always possible in the USA. In this case, speak at length on the phone to the breeder and ask lots of questions. Ethical breeders, like the ones involved in this book, will be happy to answer all your questions - and will have lots for you too. They will provide photos and perhaps even videos and emails of your chosen pup's progress if you can't visit.

In the USA, some may also arrange escorted "Nanny Transport" to safely deliver the pup to your home, or an agreed meeting place. If you are satisfied with the answers to your questions, and have checked the Puppy Contract and Health Guarantee on offer, then go ahead and put your name down on the waiting list.

The age at which a puppy leaves a breeder varies, but Cockapoos should be at least eight weeks old. Puppies need to be given the time to physically develop and learn the rules of the pack from their mothers and litter mates.

In some US states it is illegal to sell a puppy younger than eight weeks. These Cockapoo puppies, *pictured,* are six weeks old.

FACT ❯ *Small breeds tend to mature later than larger breeds and, for this reason, some breeders like to hold on to the puppies for a little longer, particularly those breeding from Toy Poodles.*

Buyer Beware

Good breeders do not sell their dogs on general purpose websites, on Gumtree, eBay, Craig's List or Freeads, in car parks or somebody else's house. Puppies in pet shops often come from puppy mills. If you live in the UK and are looking online at dogs on Pets4Homes, follow their guidelines carefully, check the health screening and see the pup with her mother.

There is a difference between *a hobby breeder* and a *backyard or backstreet breeder*. Both may breed just one or two litters a year and keep the puppies in their homes, but that's where the similarity ends.

In the UK, hobby breeders often don't have a website and you will probably find out about them via word of mouth. Good hobby breeders are usually breed enthusiasts or experts; sometimes they show their pedigree dogs. They carry out health tests and lavish care and love on their dogs. While it is often a good sign in the UK, the term *hobby breeder* can have negative implications in the USA. All breeders, including hobby breeders, need to have in-depth knowledge of Cockapoos and potential health issues affecting Cocker Spaniels and Poodles.

Backyard breeders generally have less knowledge about a breed, pay little attention to the health and welfare of their dogs and are doing it primarily for extra cash.

 Our advice is the same: check the health certificates of the parents and the health and welfare of the dogs and puppies. Ask lots of questions - are the breeders very knowledgeable and passionate about their dogs and the Cockapoo?

Increasingly, the way most new owners are finding their puppies is by an online search. Many breeders have their own websites, and it's worth taking time to learn how to spot the good ones from the bad ones. Here are four reasons for buying from a good breeder:

1. **HEALTH:** Some new owners make the mistake of thinking that because they are buying a crossbreed dog, he or she will automatically be healthier than a purebred. However, genetic diseases can be passed on to crossbreed puppies too. Cockers and Poodles have potentially

inheritable health issues. Screening breeding stock and NOT breeding from those that fail the health tests is the best way of preventing genetic disorders from being passed on.

2. **SOCIALISATION:** Scientists and dog experts now realise that the critical socialisation period for dogs is up to the age of four months. An unstimulated puppy is likely to be less well-adjusted and more likely to have fear or behaviour issues as an adult. Good breeders start this process, they don't just leave the puppies in a shed or barn for eight weeks. Ideally, Cockapoo puppies should be bred in the home, not in outbuildings.

3. **TEMPERAMENT:** Good breeders select their breeding stock based not only on sound structure and health, but also on temperament. They will not breed from an aggressive or overly timid dog.

4. **PEACE OF MIND:** Most good breeders give a genetic health guarantee with their puppy of anything from a year to two or three years. Some even give a lifetime genetic guarantee. Many also agree to take the dog back at any time in its life if things don't work out - although you may find it too hard to part with your beloved dog by then.

 If a pup is advertised at a price that seems too good to be true; then it is! You can bet that the parents are not superb examples, they haven't been fully health screened - and often the breeder has not started the all-important socialisation and housetraining processes.

Spotting Bad Breeders

Getting a puppy is such an emotional decision - and one that will hopefully have a wonderfully positive impact on you and your family's life for over a decade. Because Cockapoo puppies command such high prices, sadly there are some unscrupulous people breeding puppies.

Here is some advice to try and help you avoid the pitfalls of getting a puppy from a puppy mill, a puppy broker (somebody who makes money from buying and selling puppies) or even an importer.

If you suspect that this is the case, walk away. You can't buy a Rolls Royce or a Lamborghini for a couple of thousand pounds or dollars - you'd immediately suspect that the 'bargain' on offer wasn't the real thing. No matter how lovely it looked, you'd be right - and the same applies to Cockapoos.

Here are some signs to look out for:

- Avoid websites where there are no pictures of the owners, home or environment
- If the website shows lots of photos of cute puppies with little information about the family, breeding dogs, health tests and environment, click the **X** button
- Don't buy a website puppy with a shopping cart symbol next to her picture
- See the puppy with his or her mother face-to-face. If this is not possible due to distances, speak at length on the phone with the breeder and ask questions
- Good breeders are happy to provide lots of information and at least one reference before you commit
- If the breeder is reluctant to answer your questions, look elsewhere
- Pressure selling: on the phone, the breeder doesn't ask you many questions and then says: "There are only X many puppies left and I have several other buyers interested." Walk away

- At the breeder's, ask to see where the puppy is living. If the breeding dogs are not housed in the family home, as is sometimes the case in the USA, they should be in suitable, clean buildings, not too hot or cold, with access to grass and time spent with humans

- Ask to see the other puppies from the litter

- The mother is not with the puppies, but brought in to meet you

- You hear: *"You can't see the parent dogs because......"* ALWAYS ask to see the parents and, as a minimum, see the mother and how she looks and behaves with the pups. If the pups are really hers, she will interact with them.

- If the breeder says that the dam and sire are Kennel Club or AKC registered, ask to see the registration papers

- Photographs of so-called 'champion' ancestors do not guarantee the health of the puppy

- The puppies look small for their stated age

- The person you are buying the puppy from did not breed the dog themselves. Deal with the breeder, not an intermediary

- The place you meet the puppy seller is a car park, somebody else's house or place other than the puppies' home

- The seller tells you that the puppy comes from top, caring breeders from your or another country. Good breeders don't sell their puppies through brokers

- Price – if you are offered a very cheap Cockapoo, he or she almost certainly comes from dubious stock. Anyone selling their puppies at a knock-down price has cut corners and it's often health screening

- Ask to see photos of the puppy from birth to present day

- If you get a rescue Cockapoo, make sure it is from a recognised rescue group and not a ***"puppy flipper"*** who may be posing as a do-gooder, but is in fact getting dogs (including stolen ones) from unscrupulous sources

- NEVER buy a puppy because you feel sorry for it; you are condemning other dogs to a life of misery

- If you have any doubt, go with your gut instinct and WALK AWAY - even if this means losing your deposit. It will be worth it in the long run

One UK Poodle-cross breeder adds this about websites: "Avoid websites that want money straight away to go on their waiting list. Feedback or reviews may not be genuine, so always ask if you can be put in contact with a few of them and ask lots of questions to see if the info adds up. My reviewers are always open for contact.

"If there are a lot of different breeds on the website, then you know they are breeding on a big scale, which means there is no attention to detail or one-to-one rearing. This is why puppies often develop behavioural problems that are hard to reverse – and then you may need to get a professional behaviourist involved. Your gut instinct is a good one to follow if something is just not right or adding up when looking through any website."

....

Advice from the Experts

The British Cockapoo Society says: "So after a lot of thought you have decided to get a Cockapoo puppy and are starting on your search. It is an exciting time and all you want to do is go out and bring home the little bundle of fun. It is important though to stop for a minute and think, because this is a really important decision you are making and you need to do it properly.

"Your puppy will grow into a pooch that could be with you and your family for ten years or more so you want to make sure you choose the right one, and that it has had a good, healthy start in life. Don't just go with the first breeder you find - you need one with a good reputation and who breeds healthy Cockapoo pups. Unfortunately, not all breeders are ethical or good, so take a bit of time and do your research.

"Starting off on your search can seem a bit daunting - it is a big responsibility after all, but there are some simple things to do to start you off. Talking to other Cockapoo owners is a great way of finding out information and views, not only about the dogs, but where they come from and whether a particular breeder offered a good service. We have an active Facebook chat page where members chat, exchange stories and ask for advice: www.facebook.com/britishcockapoosociety

"Some Cockapoo forums and clubs organise members' walks - ask if you can go along and meet them even if you don't have a dog yet. There is nothing better than seeing a load of Cockapoos running and playing together! Check out the British Cockapoo Society Events page for details of our walks: www.britishcockapoosociety.com

"Search online for Cockapoo breeders' websites but don't take them at face value. The glitzy, smart looking page may not be all it seems, so read what they have to say, but keep an open mind. Look at pet advertising sites like Breeders Online www.breedersonline.co.uk for breeders in your area and to see if they have pups available.

"Don't be fooled by a flashy website and just decide to go with that person - unfortunately there are some unscrupulous people out there and care has to be taken. Have a word with other owners, your local vet, do a search online and join forums and clubs and ask on there too. You can never have too much information.

"Decide if you want to go with a large scale, commercial breeder (breeding more than five litters a year and licensed with the local council) a hobby breeder who breeds less than five litters a year or a person who just breeds a litter now and then, often from their own pet."

In the UK, The Cockapoo Club of GB (CCGB) has lots of excellent advice for people searching for a Cockapoo puppy. They also have a list of **CCGB Approved Cockapoo Breeders** who have agreed to abide by their Code of Ethics, which strongly promotes animal welfare and breeding from only the best and healthiest dogs: www.cockapooclubgb.co.uk/ccgb-approved-breeders.html This is the paperwork that the CCGB says new owners can expect to receive from approved breeders:

- 🐾 Vet record of first vaccination
- 🐾 CCGB Puppy Care and Training leaflet
- 🐾 Worming and flea treatments details
- 🐾 Microchip paperwork
- 🐾 Health testing on parent(s)
- 🐾 Pedigree Certificates from both parents (only applies to F1 puppies)

ACC Breeder Code of Ethics

In the USA a good place to start your search for a breeder is at the American Cockapoo Club (ACC) www.americancockapooclub.com who also has a list of breeders who have all agreed to abide by the ACC's Code of Ethics. This states:

We encourage spay and neutering of all Cockapoos not being used in a breeding program and that are not of breeding quality. It is important that only Cockapoos that show breed standard be used in breeding programs.

General:

1. Members of the American Cockapoo Club have an obligation to protect the interest of the breed by conducting themselves with integrity in all manner of business relating to the American Cockapoo Club.

2. Members are expected to observe the highest standards of sportsmanship.

3. Members breeding litters or who allow the use of their stud dog to the same end, shall direct their efforts toward producing Cockapoos of exceptional quality, temperament and condition.

4. Members shall not engage in false or misleading advertising or misrepresentation of the breed, nor shall they malign their competition by making false or misleading statements regarding their competitors' dogs, breeding practice or person.

5. Inappropriate words or photos are not allowed on the American Cockapoo Club website. The American Cockapoo Club reserves the right to, immediately and without notice, remove any and all material posted on this website if it is deemed inappropriate by the owners of the American Cockapoo Club. A violation of this policy may result in immediate termination of membership.

Breeders shall:

6. Be familiar with the breed standards for their breeding dogs and strive to breed only those dogs which conform to each breed standard.

7. Be familiar with the Terms of Membership of the American Cockapoo Club and abide by these rules.

8. Use for breeding only those dogs which they believe to be healthy and free from serious congenital and hereditary defects.

9. Produce puppies only when they have the time and facilities to provide adequate attention to physical and emotional development.

10. Retain or house only the number of dogs for which they have adequate facilities.

11. Not knowingly breed a dog that has become affected with or has produced any serious inherited defects.

12. Keep clear records of dogs bred, dates of breedings and whelpings, and number of puppies in each litter.

13. Maintain the best possible standards of health for the animals and care of their kennels. This includes, but is not limited to, keeping all dogs in sanitary conditions, housing appropriate for the climate, adequately sized runs, proper nutrition and veterinary care.

14. Ensure that puppies are never shipped or delivered in dirty, matted condition.

15. Not sell puppies to pet shops, either outright or on consignment, or supply puppies for auctions, raffles or other such enterprises.

16. Take responsibility for any and all Cockapoos that they have bred for the life of that Cockapoo in order to take the burden off rescue groups. Provide written, fully executed guarantee, health records, and American Cockapoo Club registration material to the puppy buyer before or during the delivery of the puppy.

17. Breeders must provide American Cockapoo Registration Numbers of sire and dam on the written guarantee.

18. Remember that a Code of Ethics is more than a set of rules; it is a commitment to a high standard of practice in owning and breeding your dogs.

Of course, there are no cast iron guarantees that your puppy will be healthy and have a good temperament, but choosing a breeder who conforms to a code of ethics is a very good place to start.

If you've never bought a puppy before, how do you avoid buying one from a 'backstreet breeder' or puppy mill? These are people who just breed puppies for profit and sell them to the first person who turns up with the cash. Unhappily, this can end in heartbreak for a family months or years later when their puppy develops health or temperament problems due to poor breeding.

Price is a good guide; a cheap puppy usually means that corners have been cut somewhere along the line. If a puppy is advertised at a couple of hundred pounds or dollars or so, then you can bet your last penny that the dam and sire are not superb examples of their breed and they haven't been fully health tested, that the puppies are not being fed premium quality food or even kept in the house with the family where the breeder should start to socialise and housetrain them.

Bad breeders do not have two horns coming out of their head! Most will be perfectly pleasant when you phone or visit. After all, they want to make the sale – it's only later when problems develop. Use this chapter to learn how to spot the signs.

Puppy Mills and Farms

Unscrupulous breeders have sprung up to cash in on the high price of "designer crossbreed" dogs and unfortunately, the Cockapoo attracts more than its fair share of breeders whose main aim is to make money. That's not to say there aren't some excellent Cockapoo breeders out there; there are. You just have to - as the ancient saying goes - separate the wheat from the chaff!

While new owners might think they have bagged "a bargain," this more often than not turns out to be false economy and emotionally disastrous when the puppy develops health problems due to poor breeding, or behavioural problems due to poor temperament or lack of socialisation.

The UK's Kennel Club has issued a warning of a puppy welfare crisis, with some truly sickening statistics. As many as one in four puppies bought in the UK may come from puppy farms - and the situation is no better in North America. The KC Press release stated: "As the popularity of online pups continues to soar:

> 🐾 **Almost one in five pups bought (unseen) on websites or social media die within six months**

> 🐾 One in three buys online, in pet stores and via newspaper adverts - outlets often used by puppy farmers – this is an increase from one in five in the previous year

> 🐾 The problem is likely to grow as the younger generation favour mail order pups, and breeders of fashionable breeds flout responsible steps."

The Kennel Club added: "We are sleepwalking into a dog welfare and consumer crisis as new research shows that more and more people are buying their pups online or through pet shops, outlets often used by cruel puppy farmers, and are paying the price with their pups requiring long-term veterinary treatment or dying before six months old. The increasing popularity of online pups is a particular concern. Of those who source their puppies online, half are going on to buy "mail order pups" directly over the internet."

The KC research found that:

> 🐾 One third of people who bought their puppy online, over social media or in pet shops failed to experience "overall good health"

> 🐾 Some 12% of puppies bought online or on social media end up with serious health problems that require expensive on-going veterinary treatment from a young age

Caroline Kisko, Kennel Club Secretary, said: "More and more people are buying puppies from sources such as the internet, which are often used by puppy farmers. Whilst there is nothing wrong with initially finding a puppy online, it is essential to then see the breeder and ensure that they are doing all of the right things.

"This research clearly shows that too many people are failing to do this, and the consequences can be seen in the shocking number of puppies that are becoming sick or dying. We have an extremely serious consumer protection and puppy welfare crisis on our hands."

The research revealed that the problem was likely to get worse as mail order pups bought over the internet are the second most common way for the younger generation of 18 to 24-year-olds to buy a puppy (31%). Marc Abraham, TV vet and founder of Pup Aid, said: "Sadly, if the *"buy it now"* culture persists, then this horrific situation will only get worse. There is nothing wrong with sourcing a puppy online, but people need to be aware of what they should then expect from the breeder.

"For example, you should not buy a car without getting its service history and seeing it at its registered address, so you certainly shouldn't buy a puppy without the correct paperwork and health certificates and without seeing where it was bred. However, too many people are opting to buy directly from third parties such as the internet, pet shops, or from puppy dealers, where you cannot possibly know how or where the puppy was raised.

"Not only are people buying sickly puppies, but many people are being scammed into paying money for puppies that don't exist, as the research showed that 7% of those who buy online were scammed in this way." The Kennel Club has a lot of info on the dos and don'ts of buying a puppy at www.thekennelclub.org.uk/paw Now you know what to avoid, what should you look out for? Read on to find out:

Top 10 Signs of a Good Breeder

1. His or her breeding dogs are health tested with certificates to prove it.

2. The area where the puppies are kept is clean and the puppies look clean.

3. Their Cockapoos appear happy and healthy. The pups have clean eyes, ears, nose and bum (butt) with no discharge. They are alert, excited to meet new people and don't shy away from visitors.

4. **You see the puppy interact with the mother and other puppies.** The breeder encourages you to spend time with the puppy's parents - or at least the mother - when you visit. He or she is happy for you to visit more than once. If a female dog is brought in to a waiting room, how do you know she is the puppy's real mother?

5. Good breeders are very familiar with Cockapoos, although some may also have one other breed - many more breeds is a warning sign.

6. They feed their adults and puppies high quality dog food and give you some to take home and guidance on feeding and caring for your puppy. They will also be available for advice afterwards.

7. They provide you with a written Puppy Contract, Health Guarantee and Puppy Pack or Going Home Bag with items to help the pup's transition. They will show you records of the puppy's visits to the vet, vaccinations, worming medication, etc. and explain what other vaccinations your puppy will need.

8. They don't always have pups available, but keep a list of interested people for the next available litter. They don't over-breed, but do limit the number of litters from their dams.

9. They will, if asked, provide references from other people who have bought their puppies; call at least one.

10. And finally ... good Cockapoo breeders want to know their beloved pups are going to good homes and will ask YOU a lot of questions about your suitability as owners.

When visiting puppies, take your time to have a good look around and go inside and outside. Are the breeders happy to show you around everywhere or a bit secretive? You will probably know if it's right or not when you see the surroundings. Walk away promptly if you have any doubts. It's a massive decision, you want to make sure that the puppy you choose will be healthy and happy. If you think it could be a puppy mill, report it to the relevant authorities.

Take your puppy to a vet to have a thorough check-up within 48 hours of purchase. If your vet is not happy with the health of the dog, no matter how painful it may be, return the pup to the breeder. Keeping an unhealthy puppy causes more distress and expense.

Puppy Contracts

Most good breeders provide their puppy parents with an official Puppy Contract. This protects both buyer and seller by providing information on the puppy until he or she leaves the breeder. You should also have a health guarantee for a specified time period. A Puppy Contract will answer such questions as whether the puppy:

- Is covered by breeder's insurance and can be returned if there is a health issue within a certain period of time
- Was born by Caesarean section
- Has been micro-chipped and/or vaccinated and details of worming treatments
- Has been partially or wholly toilet trained
- Has been socialised and where he or she was kept
- And what health issues the pup and parents have been screened for
- What the puppy is currently being fed and if any food is being supplied
- Details of the dam and sire

It's not easy for caring breeders to part with their puppies after they have lovingly bred and raised them, and so many supply extensive care notes for new owners, which may include details such as:

- The puppy's daily routine
- Feeding schedule
- Vet and vaccination schedule
- General puppy care
- Toilet training
- Socialisation

In the UK, The Royal Society for the Prevention of Cruelty to Animals (RSPCA) has a downloadable puppy contract *(pictured)* endorsed by vets and animal welfare organisations; you should be looking for something similar from a breeder. You can type *"RSPCA Puppy Contract"* into Google or read it in full at: https://puppycontract.rspca.org.uk/home

The AKC (American Kennel Club) has this article on Puppy Contracts: www.akc.org/expert-advice/dog-breeding/preparing-a-contract-for-puppy-buyers

Choosing a Healthy Cockapoo

Once you've selected your breeder and a litter is available, you then have to decide WHICH puppy to pick, unless the breeder has already earmarked a pup for you after asking lots of questions. Here are some health signs relating to young puppies

1. Your chosen puppy should have a well-fed appearance. She should not, however, have a distended abdomen (pot belly) as this can be a sign of worms - or other illnesses. The ideal puppy should not be too thin either; you should not be able to see her ribs.

2. Her nose should be cool, damp and clean with no discharge.

3. The pup's eyes should be bright and clear with no discharge or tear stain. Steer clear of a puppy that blinks a lot, this could be the sign of a problem.

4. The pup's ears should be clean with no sign of discharge, soreness or redness and no unpleasant smell.

5. Check the puppy's rear end to make sure it is clean and there are no signs of diarrhoea.

6. The pup's coat should look clean, feel soft, not matted - and puppies should smell good! The coat should have no signs of ticks or fleas. Red or irritated skin or bald spots could be a sign of infestation or a skin condition. Also, check between the toes of the paws for signs of redness or swelling.

7. The puppy should be alert, *like this American Cockapoo pictured,* and curious about you and her surroundings, not timid.

8. Gums should be clean and pink.

9. Choose a puppy that moves freely without any sign of injury or lameness. It should be a fluid movement, not jerky or stiff, which could be a sign of joint problems.

10. When the puppy is distracted, clap or make a noise behind her - not so loud as to frighten her - to make sure she is not deaf.

11. Finally, ask to see veterinary records to confirm your puppy has been wormed and had her first injections.

If you are unlucky enough to have a health problem with your pup within the first few months, a reputable breeder will allow you to return the pup. Ask what health guarantee the breeder provides.

Also, if you get the Cockapoo puppy home and things don't work out for whatever reason, some breeders will also take the puppy back — either within a limited time frame or for the whole life of the puppy - although if it is more than one year later, you cannot expect the breeder to financially reimburse you.

Picking the Right Temperament

You've picked a Cockapoo because you love the look of them and are attracted to their many good points: their friendly nature, low-shedding, manageable size, eagerness to please, cheekiness, loyalty, close bond with humans, trainability and ability to get on well with children and other animals.

Presumably, you're planning to spend a lot of time with your new dog, as Cockapoos love being with humans, and they also have daily exercise needs.

While different Cockapoos may share many characteristics and temperament traits, each puppy also has her own individual character, just like humans.

Visit the breeder to see how your chosen pup interacts and get an idea of her character in comparison to the littermates. Some puppies will run up to greet you, pull at your shoelaces and playfully bite your fingers. Others will be more content to stay in the den sleeping. Watch their behaviour and energy levels.

Are you an active person who enjoys lots of daily exercise or would a less energetic crossbreed be more suitable? One thing that surprises some new owners about their Cockapoos is the amount of energy they have - adult Cockapoos with working Cocker Spaniel ancestry can run all day - which is great for an active outdoorsy family, but not ideal if you are juggling a lot of commitments and can only spare the dog 30 minutes a day.

FACT ⟩ *A submissive dog will by nature be more passive, less energetic and also possibly easier to train. A dominant dog will usually be more energetic and livelier. He or she may also be more stubborn and need a firmer hand and more patience when training, or socialising with other dogs.*

If you already have a dominant dog at home, you have to be careful about introducing a new dog into the household; two dominant dogs may not live comfortably together.

THERE IS NO GOOD OR BAD, it's a question of which type of character will best suit you and your lifestyle.

Here are a couple of quick tests to try and gauge your puppy's temperament; they should be carried out in familiar surroundings so the puppy is relaxed. It should be pointed out that there is some controversy over temperament testing, as a dog's personality is formed by a combination of factors, which include inherited temperament, socialisation, training and environment (or how you treat your dog):

🐾 You (or the breeder) put the pup on her back on your lap and gently rests your hand on the pup's chest, or

🐾 You put your hands under the pup's tummy and gently lift the pup off the floor for a few seconds, keeping the pup horizontal

A puppy that struggles to get free is less patient than one that makes little effort to get away. A placid, patient dog is likely to fare better in a home with young children than an impatient one.

Here are some other useful signs -

🐾 Watch how she interacts with other puppies in the litter. Does she try and dominate them, does she walk away from them or is she happy to play with her littermates? This may give you an idea of how easy it will be to socialise her with other dogs

🐾 After contact, does the pup want to follow you or walk away from you? Not following may mean she has a more independent nature

🐾 If you throw something for the puppy, is she happy to retrieve it for you or does she ignore it? This may measure willingness to work with humans

🐾 If you drop a bunch of keys behind the puppy, does she act normally or does she flinch and jump away? The latter may be an indication of a timid or nervous disposition. Not reacting could also be a sign of deafness

Decide which temperament would fit in with you and your family and the rest is up to you. Whatever hereditary temperament your Cockapoo has, it is true to say that dogs that have constant positive interactions with people and other animals during the first few months of life will be happier and more stable.

In contrast, a puppy plucked from its family too early and/or isolated for long periods will be less happy, which may lead to behaviour issues later in life.

Puppies are like children. Being properly raised contributes to their confidence, sociability, stability and intellectual development. The bottom line is that a pup raised in a warm, loving environment with people is likely to be more tolerant and accepting, and less likely to develop behaviour problems.

To sum up: a good course of action would be something like this:

1. Decide to get a Cockapoo.
2. Do your research.
3. Find a good breeder whose dogs are health tested.
4. Register your interest - and WAIT until a puppy becomes available.
5. Decide on a male or female.
6. Pick one with a suitable temperament to fit in with your family.
7. Enjoy 10 to 15 years with a beautiful, healthy Cockapoo.

Some people pick a puppy based on how the dog looks. If coat colour, for example, is very important to you, make sure the other boxes are ticked as well.

3. Bringing Puppy Home

Getting a new puppy is so exciting. You can't wait to bring the little bundle of joy home. Before that happens, you probably dream of all the things you are going to do together; going for hikes in the countryside, playing games, snuggling down by the fire, setting off on adventures, or maybe taking part in canine competitions or shows.

Your pup has, of course, no idea of your big plans, and the reality when she arrives can be a bit of a shock for some owners!

Puppies are wilful little critters with minds of their own and sharp teeth. They leak at both ends, chew anything in sight, constantly demand your attention, nip the kids or anything else to hand, often cry or whine for the first few days and don't pay a blind bit of notice to your commands... There is a lot of work ahead before the two of you develop that unique bond!

Your pup has to learn what is required before she can start to meet some of your expectations - and you have to learn what your pup needs from you.

....

Once your new arrival lands in your home, your time won't be your own, but you can get off to a good start by preparing things before the big day. Here's a list of things to think about getting beforehand - your breeder may supply some of these:

Puppy Checklist

- ✓ A large dog bed or basket
- ✓ Bedding – a Vetbed or Vetfleece would be a good choice, you can buy one online
- ✓ A towel or piece of cloth that has been rubbed on the puppy's mother to put in the bed
- ✓ A puppy gate or pen to initially contain the pup in one area of the house
- ✓ A crate if you decide to use one
- ✓ A collar with identification tag and lead (leash)
- ✓ Food and water bowls, preferably stainless steel
- ✓ Puppy food – find out what the breeder is feeding and stick with that to start with
- ✓ Puppy treats, healthy ones like carrots or apple are best, no rawhide
- ✓ Newspapers, and a bell if you decide to use one, for potty training
- ✓ Poop bags
- ✓ Toys and chews suitable for puppies
- ✓ A puppy coat if you live in a cool climate
- ✓ Old towels for cleaning and drying your puppy and partially covering the crate

AND PLENTY OF TIME!

Later on, you'll also need brushes, flea and worming products and maybe a travel crate. Many good breeders provide Puppy Packs to take home; they contain some or all of the following items:

- ✓ Registration certificate
- ✓ Pedigree certificate
- ✓ Buyer's Contract
- ✓ Information pack with details of vet's visits, vaccinations and wormings, parents' health certificates, diet, breed clubs, etc.
- ✓ Puppy food
- ✓ ID tag/microchip info
- ✓ Blanket that smells of the mother and litter
- ✓ Soft toy that your puppy has grown up with, possibly a chew toy as well
- ✓ Four or five weeks' free insurance

Puppy Proofing Your Home

Puppies are small bundles of instinct and energy when they are awake, with little common sense and even less self-control. Young Cockapoos love to play and have a great sense of fun. They may have bursts of energy before they run out of steam and spend much of the rest of the day sleeping. As one breeder says: *"They have two speeds – ON and OFF!"*

Cockapoos have an incredible sense of smell and puppies love to investigate with their nose and mouth. Check your garden or yard, make sure there are no poisonous or low plants with sharp leaves or thorns that could cause eye injuries. There are literally dozens of plants harmful to a puppy if ingested, including azalea, daffodil bulbs, lily, foxglove, hyacinth, hydrangea, lupin, rhododendron, sweet pea, tulip and yew.

The Kennel Club has a list of some of the most common ones, type *"Kennel Club poisonous plants"* into Google or visit: http://bit.ly/1nCv1qJ The ASPCA has an extensive list for the USA at: http://bit.ly/19xkhoG or Google *"ASPCA poisonous plants."*

Fence off any sharp plants, such as roses, that can injure a dog's eyes. If you have a garden or yard that you intend letting your puppy roam in, make sure that every little gap has been plugged. You'd be amazed at the tiny holes puppies can escape through - and your new arrival won't have any road sense.

Avoid leaving your puppy unattended in the garden or yard if you live near a road, as dognapping is on the increase, partly due to the high cost and resale value of dogs. In the UK, some 2,000 dogs are now being stolen each year. The figures are much higher for the US where the AKC reports that dog thefts are on the rise and warns owners against leaving their dog unattended – including tying them up outside a store.

While most people would not attempt to run off with an adult Cockapoo, they may try with a cute little puppy.

Inside the house, puppies are little chew machines and puppy-proofing your home involves moving anything sharp, breakable or chewable - including your shoes. Lift electrical cords, mobile phones and chargers, remote controls, etc. out of reach and block off any off-limits areas of the house, such as upstairs or your bedroom, with a child gate or barrier, especially as she may be shadowing you for the first few days. Just as with babies, it's up to you to keep them safe and set the boundaries – both physically, in terms of where they can wander, and also in terms of behaviour – but gently and one step at a time.

Create an area where puppy is allowed to go, perhaps one or two rooms, preferably with a hard floor that is easy to clean, and keep the rest of the house off-limits, at least until housetraining (potty training) is complete. The designated area should be near a door to the garden or yard for housetraining. Restricting the area also helps the puppy settle in. She probably had a den and an area to run around in at the breeders. Suddenly having the freedom of the whole house can be quite daunting - not to mention messy!

You can buy a barrier specifically made for dogs or use a baby gate, which may be cheaper. Although designed for infants, they work perfectly well with dogs; you might find a second-hand one on eBay. Choose one with narrow vertical gaps or mesh, and check that your puppy can't get her head stuck between the bars, or put a covering or mesh over the bottom of the gate initially. You can also make your own barrier, but bear in mind that cardboard and other soft materials will get chewed.

Gates can be used to keep the puppy enclosed in a single room or specific area or put at the bottom of the stairs. The gaps between the bars of some safety gates and pens are sometimes too big to keep very small puppies contained. One alternative is Dreambaby Retractable Gate, which has mesh instead of bars. It can be bought at Argos in the UK and Amazon in the USA.

A puppy's bones are soft, and studies have shown that if pups are allowed to climb or descend stairs regularly, or jump on and off furniture, they can develop joint problems later in life.

 Don't underestimate your puppy! Young Cockapoos can be lively and determined; they can jump and climb, so choose a barrier higher than you think necessary.

The puppy's designated area or room should not be too hot, cold or damp and it must be free from draughts. Little puppies can be sensitive to temperature fluctuations and don't do well in very hot or very cold conditions. If you live in a hot climate, your new pup may need air conditioning in the summertime.

Just as you need a home, so your puppy needs a den. This den is a haven where your pup feels safe, particularly in the beginning after the traumatic experience of leaving her mother and littermates. Young puppies sleep for 18 hours or longer each day at the beginning; this is normal. You have a couple of options with the den; you can get a dog bed or basket, or you can use a crate, which can also speed up potty training. **See Chapter 5. Crate Training and Housetraining** for getting your Cockapoo used to - and even to enjoy - being in a crate.

It may surprise some American readers to learn that common practice in the UK is to initially contain the puppy in the kitchen or utility room, and later to allow the dog to roam around the house at will. Some owners do not allow their dogs upstairs, but many do.

Most puppies' natural instinct is not to soil the area where they sleep. Put plenty of newspapers down in the area next to the den and your pup should choose to go to the toilet here if you are not quick enough to get outside. Of course, she may also decide to trash the designated area by chewing the blankets and shredding the newspaper – patience is the key!

Some owners prefer to create a safe penned area for their pup, rather than a crate, while others use both a pen and a crate. You can make your own barriers or buy a manufactured playpen. Playpens come in two types - mesh or fabric, **both pictured.** A fabric pen is easy to put up and take down, but can be chewed so may not last long. A metal mesh pen can be expanded and will last longer, but is not quite as easy to put up or take down.

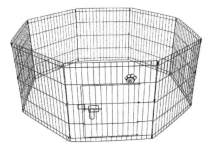

One breeder said: "A play pen can be used in much the same way as a crate and has an advantage of being very versatile in separating eating, sleeping and - in the early days - toileting. They are ideal for the busy Mum or Dad who has other things on their mind and can't possibly watch the puppy, children and try and tidy the house or prepare dinner. Again, it is peace of mind for the owner, knowing the pup is safe and not chewing anything it shouldn't."

The time any young children spend with the puppy should be limited to a few short sessions a day. Plenty of sleep is **essential** for the normal development of a young dog. You wouldn't wake a baby every hour or so to play, and the same goes for puppies. Wait a day or two before inviting friends round to see your gorgeous little puppy. However excited you are, your new arrival needs a few days to get over the stress of leaving mother and siblings and to start bonding with you.

For puppies to grow into well-adjusted dogs, they have to feel comfortable and relaxed in their new surroundings and need a great deal of sleep. They are leaving the warmth and protection of their mother and littermates and, while confident, well-socialised puppies may settle in right away, other puppies may feel sad and a little afraid. Make the transition as gentle and unalarming as possible.

 This early period is a very important time for you both - how you react and interact with each other during these first few days and weeks will help to shape your relationship and your dog's character for the rest of his or her life.

Chew Treats and Toys

There are some things you can't move out of puppy's way, like kitchen cupboards, doors, sofas, fixtures and fittings, so try not to leave your pup unattended for any length of time where she can chew something that is hard to replace. Like babies, puppies like to explore the world with their mouths, so chew toys are a must. Avoid giving old socks, shoes or slippers, or your pup will naturally come to think of your footwear as fair game!

A safe alternative to real bones or plastic chew bones are natural reindeer antler chew toys **(pictured),** which have the added advantage of calcium. Natural chews preferred by some breeders include ears, dried rabbit pelt and tripe sticks – all excellent for teething puppies - once you have got over the smell and gross factor!

Other choices include the fairly indestructible Kong toy, which you can put treats (frozen or fresh) or smear peanut butter inside to keep your dog occupied while you are out. All of these are widely available online, if not in your local pet store.

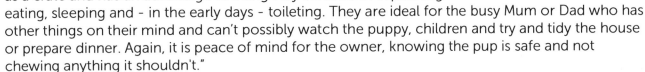

Rawhide chews are not recommended as they can get stuck in a dog's throat or stomach, but bully sticks (pictured) are a good alternative.

Made from a bull's penis(!) they can be a good distraction from chewing furniture, etc. and help to promote healthy teeth and gums. Bully sticks are highly digestible, break down easily in the stomach and are generally considered safe for all dogs. They are made from 100% beef, normally contain no additives or preservatives, come in different sizes and dogs love 'em. NOTE: Puppies should be supervised while eating bully sticks or any other treats.

Dental sticks are good for cleaning your dog's teeth, but many contain preservatives and don't last very long with a determined chewer. One that does last is the Nylabone Dura Chew Wishbone, made of a type of plastic infused with flavours appealing to dogs. Get the right size and throw it away if it starts to splinter after a few weeks. Or use a natural alternative, such as antlers or bully sticks.

Another long-lasting treat option is the Lickimat *(pictured),* which you smear with a favourite food. This inexpensive mat, available online, will keep your Cockapoo occupied for quite some time.

As far as toys go, the Zogoflex Hurley and the Goughnut are both strong and float, so good for swimmers – and you'll get your money back on both if your Cockapoo destroys them! For safety, the Goughnut has a green exterior and red interior, so you can tell if your dog has penetrated the surface - as long as the green is showing, you can let your dog "goughnuts." A natural hemp or cotton tug rope is another option, as the cotton rope acts like dental floss and helps with teeth cleaning. It is versatile and can be used for fetch games as well as chewing.

Puppies' stomachs are sensitive - so be careful what goes in. Even non-poisonous garden plants can cause intestinal blockages and/or vomiting. Like babies, pups can quickly dehydrate if they are vomiting or have diarrhoea. If either continues for a couple of days, seek medical advice.

What the Breeders Say

We asked a number of Cockapoo breeders what essential advice they would give to new owners and this is what they said, starting with Julie Shearman, of Crystalwood Cockapoos, Devon, UK: "We vet new owners carefully and tactfully turn away anyone we deem to be an unsuitable owner. However, we stress that bringing a puppy home is like having a toddler in the home! Gardens need to be secure and free from poisonous plants and hazards, as does the house with cleaning products, fires, electrical cords, stairs etc.

"Homes with children are reminded that pups are walking dustbins and any small toys will be in a pup's mouth and swallowed. Keeping puppy in a **safe zone** with a puppy pen, large crate or the use of baby gates is ideal. Make sure everyone in the household is clear of the puppy's "house rules" - is the pup allowed on furniture, in bedrooms etc? - or the pup will end up very confused. Equally, everyone in the household should use the same commands for toilet training; come and so on."

Karol Watson Todd, KaroColin Cockapoos, Lincolnshire, UK: "I give my new owners several pages of notes the week before they take their puppy home to read through and ask questions about. I'm very wary of collars being worn in a crate. It's a big issue as collars need to be worn, but I've seen dogs stuck by their collar in a crate and, worse still, two puppies playing and getting hooked onto their collars. Fancy iron dog beds are also an issue for a collar to get hung onto. New owners also need to be aware of any foods and plants poisonous to dogs."

Pat Pollington, Polycinders Cockapoos, Devon, UK: "When bringing a puppy home, remember they are just like babies. They will be very scared when they first enter your home. Dogs go by sense of smell and your home will have a completely different smell to what they are used to. Also, they have just travelled in a car, so they are also going to be very stressed. They may have upset tummies for a few days and this means that they are at higher risk of picking up any bug. Keep the first night calm for the puppy. Although the children will be very excited by the new member of the family, the puppy is going to be very unsure about what's going on.

"You need to do your research into things that are poisonous to dogs. There are a lot of plants and different foods that are very harmful to dogs, especially puppies, so make sure that you and your children know this before the puppy enters the house. Things such as Lego are very dangerous because puppies love to chew and the last thing you want is the puppy being harmed from chewing something like this. Make sure all electric wires are well hidden and, if you have an office room, block it off from the puppy with a stair gate, because there will be lots of dangerous electric wires in that room."

Rebecca Mae Goins, Moonshine Cockapoos, Indiana, USA, said: "My advice to new puppy parents is to stick to your breeder's schedule for feeding and training and do not overwhelm your new puppy with a house full of visitors. Before you bring your little one home, go through your house and puppy-proof your home: cabinet locks, puppy gates, etc.

"Make sure you are not using toxic cleaners or air fresheners, and you do not have any toxic plants inside or out. Do not take your puppy into public or for walks outside of the safety of your yard until you have completed the puppy shots. Use common sense and watch your new little one close. And most of all, enjoy the new little life you have chosen to join your family!"

Jackie Stafford, of Dj's Cockapoos, Texas: "The biggest danger to a new puppy is the children of the new puppy owners! It is essential that children are taught good puppy skills and safety. Pups are inquisitive and should be watched closely. Swimming pools are another danger to Cockapoo pups as they love water, but are unable to climb to safety if they fall in."

Jeanne Davis, Wind Horse Offering, Maryland, added: "Don't isolate your puppy, spend time with him. Be consistent with your training so that he knows exactly what to expect from you."

Jessica Sampson, Legacy Cockapoos, Ontario, Canada: "Puppy-proof your home; make sure you pick up and secure any loose wires and small toys. Check your fence perimeter for any spots your puppy could potentially escape through and secure them. Secure stairs with a safety gate until your puppy can competently manage them on his or her own. Make sure to get puppy-safe chew toys for the teething stage. Sign up for a puppy obedience class and be consistent; this is the key to successful training."

Pictured is Jessica's standard F2 Cockapoo, Nessa, who was born snow white, but whose wavy fleece coat is now dark apricot.

The First Few Days

Before you collect your puppy, let the breeder know what time you will arrive and ask her not to feed the pup for a couple of hours beforehand - unless you have a very long journey, in which case the puppy will need to eat something. She will be less likely to be car sick and should be hungry when she lands in her new home. The same applies to an adult dog moving to a new home.

When you arrive, ask for an old towel or toy that has been with the pup's mother — you can leave one on an earlier visit to collect with the pup. Or take one with you and rub the mother with it to collect her scent and put this with the puppy for the first few days. It will help her to settle in. In the US, some puppies are flown to their new homes; but you should still get a Puppy Pack that includes something with the mother's scent and a toy.

Get copies of any health certificates relating to the parents - again, good breeders have a Contract of Sale or Puppy Contract that outlines everyone's rights and responsibilities — see **Chapter 2. Before You Get Your Puppy** for details. It should also state that you can return the puppy if there are health issues within a certain time frame — although if you have picked your puppy carefully, it should not come to this. The breeder will also give you details of worming and any vaccinations, as well as an information sheet.

Find out exactly what the breeder is feeding and how much; dog's digestive systems cannot cope with sudden changes in diet - unless the breeder has deliberately been feeding several different foods to her puppies, in which case they will be used to different foods. In the beginning, stick to whatever the pup is used to; good breeders send some food home with the puppy.

The Journey Home

Bringing a new puppy home in a car can be a traumatic experience. Your puppy will be sad at leaving her mother, brothers and sisters and a familiar environment. Everything will be strange and frightening and she may whimper and whine - or even bark - on the way home.

If you can, take somebody with you on that first journey — some breeders insist on having somebody there to hold and cuddle the pup to make the journey less traumatic. Under no circumstances have the puppy on your lap while driving. It is simply too dangerous - a Cockapoo puppy is extremely cute, often wriggly and far too distracting.

Have an old towel between your travel companion and the pup as she may quite possibly pee - the puppy, not the passenger! *Photo courtesy of Jeanne Davis.*

If you have to travel any distance, take a crate — either a purpose-made travel crate or a wire crate that she will use at home. Travel crates can be soft canvas or hard plastic. A plastic one should have holes in the sides to allow air flow. Cover the bottom of the crate with a waterproof material and then put a comfortable blanket on top. You can put newspapers in half of the crate if the pup is partly housetrained.

If you have a journey of more than a couple of hours, take water to give the puppy en route. She may need the toilet, but don't let her outside on to the ground as she is not yet fully vaccinated.

Arriving Home

As soon as you arrive home, let your puppy into the garden or yard and when she "performs," praise her for her efforts. These first few days are critical in getting your puppy to feel safe and confident in her new surroundings. Spend time with the latest addition to your family, talk to her often in a reassuring manner. Introduce her to her den and toys, slowly allow her to explore and show her around the house — once you have puppy-proofed it.

Cockapoo puppies are extremely curious - and amusing, you might be surprised at their reactions to everyday objects. Puppies explore by sniffing and mouthing, so don't scold for chewing. Instead, put objects you don't want chewed out of reach and replace them with chew toys. Some puppies can be more "mouthy" than others; if yours is like this, make sure she has safe toys to chew.

Almost all Cockapoo owners say that theirs get on well with other animals. However, it is important to introduce them to each other in the right conditions. Do it slowly and in supervised sessions on neutral territory or outdoors where there is space so neither feels threatened - preferably once the pup has got used to her new surroundings, not as soon as you walk through the door. Gentleness and patience are the keys to these first few days, so don't over-face your pup.

Have a special, gentle puppy voice and use her new name frequently - and in a pleasant, encouraging manner. Never use her name to scold or she will associate it with bad things. The sound of her name should always make her want to pay attention to you as something good is going to happen - praise, food, playtime, and so on.

Resist the urge to pick your puppy up – no matter how irresistible she is! Let her explore on her own legs, encouraging a little independence - this is important for Cockapoos. It is so tempting to pick them up and cuddle them all the time, but this will only encourage them to become "clingy."

Pictured chilling out is nine-week-old Chummy, bred by Julie Shearman, of Crystalwood Cockapoos, Devon, UK.

One of the most important things at this stage is to ensure that your puppy has enough sleep – **which is nearly all of the time** - no matter how much you want to play with her, cuddle her or watch her antics when awake. If you haven't decided what to call your new puppy yet, "Shadow" might be a good suggestion, as she will follow you everywhere!

Many puppies do this, but Cockapoos have been bred for companionship, not working, hunting or herding like some other breeds, and they do like to stick particularly close to their owners – both as puppies and adults. Our website receives many emails from worried new owners. Here are some of the most common concerns:

- ❧ My puppy won't stop crying or whining
- ❧ My puppy is shivering
- ❧ My puppy won't eat
- ❧ My puppy is very timid
- ❧ My puppy follows me everywhere, she won't let me out of her sight
- ❧ My puppy sleeps all the time, is this normal?

These behaviours are quite common at the beginning. They are just a young pup's reaction to leaving her mother and littermates and entering into a strange new world. It is normal for puppies to sleep most of the time, just like babies. It is also normal for some puppies to whine a lot during the first couple of days. A few puppies might not whine at all. If they are confident and have been well-socialised and partly housetrained by the breeder, settling in will be much easier.

Make your new pup as comfortable as possible, ensuring she has a warm (but not too hot), quiet den away from draughts, where she is not pestered by children or other pets. Handle her gently, while giving her plenty of time to sleep. Some breeders recommend keeping the pup in a crate near your bed for the first couple of nights, so she knows she is not alone. If she makes sad little whimpering noises or barks, talk softly and gently stroke her. Resist the urge to pick her up and cuddle her every time or she will learn that crying always gives her the reward of your attention.

A puppy will think of you as her new mother and it is quite normal for them to want to follow you everywhere, but after a few days start to leave your pup for short periods of a few minutes, gradually building up the time. A puppy unused to being left alone at all can grow up to have separation anxiety - see **Chapter 7. Cockapoo Behaviour** for more information.

If your routine means you are normally out of the house for a few hours during the day, get your puppy on a Friday or Saturday so she has at least a couple of days to adjust to her new surroundings. A far better idea is to book time off work to help your puppy to settle in, if you can, or if you don't work, leave your diary free for the first couple of weeks.

Helping a new pup to settle in is virtually a full-time job. This can be a frightening time for some puppies. Is your puppy shivering with cold or is it nerves? Avoid placing your pup under stress by making too many demands. Don't allow the kids to pester the pup and, until they have learned how to handle a dog, don't allow them to pick her up unsupervised, as they could inadvertently damage her delicate little body.

If your pup won't eat, spend time gently coaxing. If she leaves her food, take it away and try it later. Don't leave it down all of the time or she may get used to turning her nose up at it. Some baby Cockapoos would rather play than eat, so for the first few days you may have to hand-feed kibble or sit with them so they think they are eating with a sibling.

If your puppy is crying, it is probably for one of the following reasons:

- 🐾 She is lonely
- 🐾 She is hungry
- 🐾 She wants attention from you
- 🐾 She needs to go to the toilet

If it is none of these, then physically check her over to make sure she hasn't picked up an injury. Try not to fuss too much! If she whimpers, reassure her with a quiet word. If she cries loudly and tries to get out of her allotted area, she probably needs to go to the toilet. Even if it is the middle of the night, get up and take her outside. Praise her if she goes to the toilet.

The strongest bonding period for a puppy is between eight and 12 weeks of age. The most important factors in bonding with your puppy are TIME and PATIENCE, even when she makes a mess in the house or chews something. Spend time with your pup and you will have a loyal friend for life. Cockapoos are very focused on their humans and that emotional attachment may grow to become one of the most important aspects of your life – and certainly hers.

Where Should the Puppy Sleep?

Where do you want your new puppy to sleep? In the beginning, you cannot simply allow a pup to wander freely around the house – at least not initially. Ideally, she will be in a contained area, such as a pen or crate, at night. While it is not acceptable to shut a dog in a cage all day, you can keep your puppy in a crate at night until housetrained. Even then, some adult dogs still prefer to sleep in a crate.

You also have to consider whether you want the pup to permanently sleep in your bedroom or elsewhere. If it's the bedroom, do not allow her to jump on and off beds and/or couches or race up and down stairs until she has stopped growing, as this can cause joint damage.

 Some breeders recommend putting the puppy in a crate (or similar) next to your bed for the first two or three nights before moving her to the permanent sleeping place. Knowing you are close and being able to smell you will help overcome initial fears.

She may still cry when you move her further away or out of your bedroom, but that should soon stop - you just have to block your ears for a couple of nights! She will have had those few days to get used to her new surroundings and feeling safe with you.

Eight or nine-week-old puppies can't go through the night without needing to pee (and sometimes poo); their bladders simply aren't up to it. To speed up housetraining, consider getting up half way through the night from Day One for the first week or so to let your pup outside for a pee. Just pick her up, take her outside with the minimum of fuss, praise the pee and put her back into the crate. After that, set your alarm for an early morning wake-up call.

NOTE: *While I and many breeders recommend getting up in the night in the beginning, a few breeders are against it, as they don't believe it speeds up housetraining. Ask your own breeder's advice on this one.*

We don't recommend letting your new pup sleep on the bed. She will not be housetrained and also a puppy needs to learn her place in the household and have her own safe place. It's up to you whether you decide to let her on the bed when she's older.

If you do allow your dog to sleep in the bedroom but not on the bed, be aware that it is not unusual for some Cockapoos - like many other types of dog – to snuffle, snore, fart and - if not in a crate - pad around the bedroom in the middle of the night and come up to the bed to check you are still there! None of this is conducive to a good night's sleep.

While it is not good to leave a dog alone all day, it is also not healthy to spend 24 hours a day together. Cockapoos can become very clingy and while this is very flattering for you, it actually means that the dog is more nervous and less sure of herself when you are not there. She becomes too reliant on you and this increases the chances of separation anxiety when you do have to leave her.

A Cockapoo puppy that is used to being on her own every night is less likely to develop attachment issues, so consider this when deciding where she should sleep. If you decide you definitely DO want your pup to sleep in the bedroom from Day One, put her in a crate or pen with newspapers, a soft blanket to cover part of the crate initially – and set your alarm clock!

Top Tips For Working Cockapoo Owners

We don't recommend getting a Cockapoo if you are out at work all day, as Cockapoos are companion dogs that thrive on interaction with humans. But if you're determined to get one when you're out for extended periods, here are some tips:

1. If you can afford it, leave her at doggie day care where she can socialise with other dogs. If you can't, come home during your lunch break or employ a dog walker (or neighbour) to take her out for a walk in the middle of the day.

2. Do you know anybody you could leave your dog with during the day? Consider leaving your dog with a reliable friend, relative or neighbour who would welcome the companionship of a dog without the full responsibility of ownership.

3. Take her for a walk before you go to work – even if this means getting up at the crack of dawn – and spend time with her as soon as you get home. Exercise generates serotonin in the brain and has a calming effect. A dog that has been exercised will be less anxious and more ready for a good nap.
Photo: An American Cockapoo puppy.

4. Leave her in a place where she feels comfortable. If you use a crate, leave the door open and restrict access to other areas of the house. If possible, leave her in a room with a view of the outside world, which is more interesting than staring at four blank walls.

5. Make sure that it does not get too hot during the day and there are no cold draughts.

6. Leave toys available to play with to prevent destructive chewing. Stuff a Kong toy with treats or peanut butter to keep her occupied or buy a Lickimat.

7. **Make sure she has access to water at all times.** Dogs cannot cool down by sweating; they do not have many sweat glands (which is why they pant, but this is much less efficient than perspiring) and can die without sufficient water.

8. Consider getting a companion for your Cockapoo, bearing in mind that this will involve even more of your time and twice the expense.

9. Consider leaving a radio or TV on very softly in the background. The "white noise" can have a soothing effect on some pets. If you do this, select your channel carefully – try and avoid one with lots of bangs and crashes or heavy metal music!

10. Stick to the same routine before you leave your dog home alone. This will help her to feel secure. Before you go to work, get into a daily habit of getting yourself ready, then feeding and exercising your Cockapoo. Dogs love routine. But don't make a huge fuss of her when you leave as this can also stress the dog; just leave the house calmly.

Similarly, when you come home, your Cockapoo may feel starved of attention and be pleased to see you. Greet her normally, but try not to go overboard by making too much of a fuss as soon as you walk through the door. Give a pat and a stroke then take off your coat and do a few other things before turning your attention back to your dog. Lavishing too much attention on your Cockapoo the second you walk through the door may encourage needy behaviour or separation anxiety.

Vaccinations and Worming

It is a good idea to have your Cockapoo checked out by a vet soon after picking her up. In fact, some Puppy Contracts stipulate that the dog should be examined by a vet once she has settled in and within a few days. This is to everyone's benefit and, all being well, you are safe in the knowledge that your puppy is healthy, at least at the time of purchase. Keep your pup on your lap away from other dogs in the waiting room as she will not yet be fully protected against canine diseases.

Vaccinations

All puppies need immunisation and currently the most common way of doing this is by vaccination. An unimmunised puppy is at risk every time she meets other dogs as she has no protection against potentially fatal diseases – and it is unlikely a pet insurer will cover an unvaccinated dog.

It should be stressed that vaccinations are generally quite safe and side effects are uncommon. If your Cockapoo is unlucky enough to be one of the **very few** that suffer an adverse reaction, here are some signs to look out for; a pup may exhibit one or more of these:

MILD REACTION - Sleepiness, irritability and not wanting to be touched. Sore or a small lump at the place where she was injected. Nasal discharge or sneezing. Puffy face and ears.

SEVERE REACTION - Anaphylactic shock. A sudden and quick reaction, usually before leaving the vet's, which causes breathing difficulties. Vomiting, diarrhoea, staggering and seizures.

A severe reaction is rare. There is a far greater risk of your Cockapoo either being ill and/or spreading disease if she does not have the injections.

The usual schedule is for the pup to have the first vaccination at eight or nine weeks of age, usually before leaving the breeder. This gives protection from a number of diseases in one shot.

In the UK these are Distemper, Canine Parvovirus (Parvo), Infectious Canine Hepatitis (Adenovirus) and Leptospirosis. Most vets also recommend vaccinating against Kennel Cough (Bordetella). In the US this is known as DHPP. Puppies in the US also need vaccinating separately against Rabies. There are optional vaccinations for Coronavirus and - depending on where you live and if your dog is regularly around woods or forests - Lyme Disease.

A puppy requires a second vaccination two to four weeks later. She is clear to mix with other animals two weeks after the second vaccinations.

- 🐾 Boosters for Distemper, Parvo and Canine Hepatitis are every three years
- 🐾 Boosters for Leptospirosis are every year

Leptospirosis is a bacterial infection that attacks the body's nervous system and organs. It is spread through infected rat pee and contaminated water, so dogs are at risk if they swim in or drink from stagnant water or canals. Outbreaks can often happen after flooding.

Diseases such as Parvo and Kennel Cough are highly contagious and you should not let your new arrival mix with other dogs - unless they are your own and have already been vaccinated - until two weeks after her last vaccination, otherwise she will not be fully immunised. Parvovirus can also be transmitted by fox faeces.

The vaccination schedule for the USA is different, depending on which area you live in and what diseases are present. Full details can be found by typing *"AKC puppy shots"* into Google, which will take you to this page: www.akc.org/content/health/articles/puppy-shots-complete-guide

You shouldn't take your new puppy to places where unvaccinated dogs might have been, like the local park. This does not mean that your puppy should be isolated - far from it. This is an important time for socialisation. It is OK for the puppy to mix with other dogs that you 100% know are up-to-date with their vaccinations and annual boosters. Perhaps invite a friend's dog round to play in your yard/garden to begin the socialisation process.

Once your puppy is fully immunised, you have a window of a few weeks when it's the best time to introduce her to as many new experiences as possible - dogs, people, traffic, noises, other animals, etc. This critical period before the age of four and a half to five months is when she is at her most receptive to socialisation. It is important that all of the experiences are **positive** at this stage of life; don't frighten or over-face your little puppy. Socialisation should not stop after a few months, but should continue for the rest of your dog's life.

The vet should give you a record card or send you a reminder when a booster is due, but it's also a good idea to keep a note of the date in your diary. Tests have shown that the Parvovirus vaccination gives most animals at least seven years of immunity, while the Distemper jab provides immunity for at least five to seven years. In the US, many vets now recommend that you take your dog for a titer test once she has had her initial puppy vaccinations and one-year booster.

Titres (Titers in the USA)

Some breeders and owners feel strongly that constantly vaccinating our dogs is having a detrimental effect on our pets' health. Many vaccinations are now effective for several years, yet some vets still recommend annual "boosters."

One alternative is titres. The thinking behind them is to avoid a dog having to have unnecessary repeat vaccinations for certain diseases as she already has enough antibodies present. Known as a VacciCheck in the UK, they are still relatively new here; they are more widespread in the USA.

Not everybody agrees with titres. One English vet we spoke to commented that a titre is only good for the day on which it is carried out, and that antibody levels may naturally drop off shortly afterwards, possibly leaving the animal at risk. He added that the dog would still need vaccinating against Leptospirosis. His claim is strongly refuted by advocates of titre testing.

To "titre" is to take a blood sample from a dog (or cat) to determine whether she has enough antibodies to guarantee immunity against a particular disease, usually Parvovirus, Distemper and Adenovirus (Canine Hepatitis). If so, then an annual injection is not needed. Titering is not

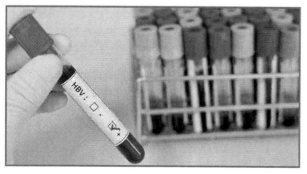

recommended for Leptospirosis, Bordetella or Lyme Disease, as these vaccines provide only short-term protection. Many US states also require proof of a Rabies vaccination.

The vet can test the blood at the clinic without sending off the sample, thereby keeping costs down for the owner. A titre for Parvovirus and Distemper currently costs around $100 or less in the US, and a titre test in the UK costs as little as £40.

Titre levels are given as ratios and show how many times blood can be diluted before no antibodies are detected. So, if blood can be diluted 1,000 times and still show antibodies, the ratio would be 1:1000, which is a strong titre, while a titre of 1:2 would be "weak." A *strong (high) titre* means that your dog has enough antibodies to fight off that specific disease and is immune from infection. A **weak titre** means that you and your vet should discuss revaccination - even then your dog might have some reserve forces known as "memory cells" that will provide antibodies when needed. (If you are going on holiday and taking your dog to kennels, check whether the kennel accepts titre records; many don't as yet).

One UK breeder said: "Most people don't realise that there are tests you can do to ensure that you don't over-vaccinate or over-worm your dog. It is well known that, although very rare, all vaccinations can have potential adverse reactions. These can range from mild problems such as cystitis to a severe autoimmune disease. There are also a lot of discussions going on as to whether the over-vaccination of dogs may be linked to the increased rates of cancers.

"When my puppies go to their new homes, I tell all my owners to follow their vet's advice about worming and vaccinating, as the last thing new owners require is to be at odds with their vets. However, a few owners do express concern about all the chemicals we are introducing into our puppies' lives and if they do, I explain how I try to give my dogs a chemical-free life, if possible, as adult dogs. All dogs must have their puppy vaccinations.

"Instead of giving my adult dogs their core vaccinations for Canine Distemper, Parvovirus and Adenovirus (Hepatitis) every three years, I just take my dogs down to the local vet and ask them to do something called a titre test, also known as a VacciCheck. They take a small amount of blood and send it to a lab and the lab checks for antibodies to the diseases. If they have antibodies to the diseases, there is no reason to give dogs a vaccination. If a puppy has its puppy vaccinations, it is now thought that the minimum duration of immunity is between seven and 15 years.

"However, you should note that there is a separate vaccination for Leptospirosis and Canine Parainfluenza, which is given annually. Leptospirosis is recommended by the BSAVA (British Small Animal Veterinary Association). Leptospirosis is more common in tropical areas of the world and not that common in England. In order to make a decision about whether to give this to your dog annually, you need to talk to your vet and do some research yourself so you can make an informed decision. It may be that Leptospirosis is a problem in your area.

"If you want to do some of your own research, then Ronald Schulz and Catherine O'Driscoll are some of the leading authorities on vaccinations and The Pet Welfare Alliance is also a good source of information. We vaccinate our children up to about the age of 16. However, we don't vaccinate adults every one to three years, as it is deemed that the vaccinations they receive in childhood will cover them for a lifetime. This is what is being steadily proved for dogs and we are so lucky that we can titre test our dogs so we don't have to leave it to chance."

Another breeder added: "A healthy Cockapoo is dependent on the owner feeding, maintaining, training and exercising the dog. Some factors in ill health are considered to be environmental and this is beyond the control of the breeder. However, I do not vaccinate my dogs beyond the age of four to five years, I now have them titre tested. Every dog I have titre tested aged five to 10 years has been immune to the diseases vaccinated against when younger. I believe many vets over-vaccinate. Also, many dogs are given too many flu and worming chemicals."

The (UK) Kennel Club now includes titre testing information into its Assured Breeder Pack, but has yet to include it under its general information on vaccines on its website. The AKC (American Kennel Club) discusses titering here: www.barkingbulletin.com/great-akc-wellness-plus-benefit or type **"titer test Embrace Pet Insurance"** into Google for more info.

Worming

All puppies need worming (technically, deworming). A good breeder will give the puppies their first dose of worming medication at around two weeks old, then probably again at five and eight weeks before they leave the litter – or even more often. Get the details and inform your vet exactly what treatment, if any, your pup has already had.

The main worms affecting puppies are roundworm and tapeworm. In certain areas of the US, the dreaded heartworm can also pose a risk. If you live in an affected area, discuss the right time to start heartworm medication when you visit your vet for puppy vaccinations – it's usually from a few months old. The pill should be given every month when there is no heavy frost (frost kills mosquitos that carry the disease); giving it all year round gives the best protection. The heartworm pill is by prescription only and deworms the dog monthly for heartworm, round, hook, and whip worm. Roundworm can be transmitted from a puppy to humans – often children - and can in severe cases cause blindness, or miscarriage in women, so it's important to keep up to date with worming.

 Worms in puppies are quite common, often picked up through their mother's milk. If you have children, get them into the habit of washing their hands after they have been in contact with the puppy – lack of hygiene is the reason why children are susceptible.

Most vets recommend worming a puppy once a month until she is six months old, and then around every two to three months. If your Cockapoo is regularly out and about running through woods and fields, it is important to stick to a regular worming schedule, as she is more likely to pick up worms than one which spends less time in the Great Outdoors.

 Fleas can pass on tapeworms to dogs, but a puppy would not normally be treated unless it is known for certain she has fleas - and then only with caution. You need to know the weight of your puppy and then speak to your vet about the safest treatment to get rid of the parasites. It is not usually worth buying a cheap worming or flea treatment from a supermarket, as they are usually far less effective than more expensive vet-recommended preparations, such as Drontal. **NOTE:** Buy age-appropriate worming treatments.

Several people living in the US have contacted our website claiming the parasite treatment **Trifexis** has caused health issues in their dogs. http://www.max-the-schnauzer.com/trifexis-side-effects-in-schnauzers.html US Cockapoo breeder Rebecca Goins says: "I have lost two dogs to Spinosad poisoning, which is the active ingredient in Trifexis and Comfortis. There are reports of death, seizures, liver and kidney failure, and many other serious health issues." Rebecca recommends the Seresto eight-month collar, and Heartgard for heartworm.

Breeders must worm their puppies as they are all born with worms picked up from the mother's milk. However, there are ways to reduce worming treatments for adult dogs. Following anecdotal reports of some dogs experiencing side effects with chemical wormers, more owners are looking to use natural wormers on their dogs. If you go down this route, check exactly which worms your chosen herbal preparation deals with – it may not be all of them.

A method of reducing worming medication by testing your dog's stools is becoming more popular. You send a small sample of your dog's poo(p) off in an envelope every two to three months. If the result is positive, your dog needs worming, but if negative, no treatment is necessary. In the UK this is done by veterinary labs like Wormcount www.wormcount.com and similar options are available in the USA – there is even a *"fecal worm test"* available at just over $20 from Amazon.com.

4. Cockapoos for People with Allergies

Allergies are on the increase. Amazingly, 50 million Americans are allergy sufferers, according to the Asthma and Allergy Foundation of America. They affect as many as 30% of adults and 40% of children according to the American College of Allergy, Asthma, and Immunology. Of these, some 10 million people are pet allergy sufferers.

In fact, allergic disease, including asthma, is the fifth leading chronic disease in the U.S. in people of all ages and the third most common chronic disease in children aged under 18.

In the UK, pets are the second most common cause of allergy in the home, with 40% of asthmatic children reacting to dogs. According to Allergy UK, each year the number of people affected increases by 5% and half of all sufferers are children. The UK is one of the top three countries in the world for the most allergies, with 50% of youngsters having one or more allergy within the first 18 years of life (Journal of Clinical & Experimental Allergy).

It's a common misconception that people are allergic to animal hair, but that's not true. What they are actually allergic to are proteins - or allergens. These are secreted by the animal's oil glands and then shed with the *dander,* which is dead skin cells (like dandruff).

They are also found in dog saliva and urine, and if you are allergic to either, it is unlikely you will ever to be able to successfully share your home with a dog, even a hypoallergenic breed.

This is what Allergy UK has to say: "**Dog and cat allergen is found in the animals' saliva, sweat and urine. Animals frequently groom themselves, so the allergens coat the hair and skin cells (dander) which, when shed, spread throughout the home or other buildings. Once the saliva dries, it becomes airborne very easily.**

"These allergens can be very persistent in the environment, with detectable levels found in homes where no pets have lived for many years, and dog allergen can be found in schools, having been brought there on the clothing and shoes of pupils and teachers. Cat allergen in particular is very 'sticky' in this way.

"In dogs, routine and proper grooming, preferably outdoors, has been shown to greatly decrease shedding of hair and may decrease skin irritation and secondary bacterial infection. Grooming, preferably by someone other than the sensitive individual, should therefore be an important part of a management strategy for dog-allergic patients."

FACT ❯ *There is no such thing as a non-shedding dog; all dogs shed some hair. "Hypoallergenic" means "having a decreased tendency" to provoke an allergic reaction. This does not mean that an individual dog won't provoke a reaction in somebody.*

Without the human and the dog spending time together, it is impossible to say that a specific allergy sufferer will NOT have a reaction to a specific puppy. Every dog is different; every person's allergy is different. This is why some breeders won't let their dogs go to allergy sufferers; they simply don't want to see their beloved pup out of a home if the sneezing starts.

It IS possible for many pet allergy sufferers to enjoy life with a dog without spending all of their time sneezing, wheezing, itching or breaking out in rashes. Millions of people are proving the case. Any dog can cause an allergic reaction, although you stand a far higher chance of having no reaction to a low-shedding, hypoallergenic dog.

Cockapoo Coats and Allergies

Cockapoos make excellent family pets; they are handsome, have cheerful temperaments, get along well with people and other animals and you've heard they are non-shedding and *"hypoallergenic."*

The Poodle, with its unique tightly-curled wool coat, is regarded as a minimal shedder and a hypoallergenic breed. This is one of the main reasons why Poodle hybrids like the Cockapoo have become so popular. There is plenty of anecdotal evidence that individual Cockapoos with wool or wavy coats shed little to no hair and do not trigger a reaction in many allergy sufferers.

Some Cockapoos have coats similar to the Cocker Spaniel, which does shed hair.

There is no breed that will never cause an allergic reaction in someone. This is particularly true with crossbreeds like the Cockapoo, as there are even more variables than with a purebred dog – even puppies in the same litter often look different, are different sizes and have different coat types.

The Cockapoo can have several different types of coat:

- 🐾 **Loose, wavy coat,** this is the most popular and is also low shedding
- 🐾 **Tight, curly coat,** with tight curls like the Poodle; this is low-shedding and more common in backcross (b) Cockapoos
- 🐾 **Straighter coat, slightly wavy,** this has more of the Spaniel's coat properties

You may be surprised to know that all of the dogs below are Cockapoos. Note the differences in size, appearance, age and coat type. Most prospective owners want puppies with **loose, wavy** low-shedding coats and Teddy bear looks, *(like the dogs pictured far left and second from right).*

FACT ❯ *There has been a recent breakthrough in genetics. A test has been developed to determine coat type and some Doodle breeders at the cutting edge, particularly in the US, are testing their breeding dogs with the aim of consistently producing hypoallergenic puppies.*

Scientists have identified a particular allele, or gene variant, called MC5R that affects the degree of shedding in various breeds. (It's never quite that simple, as the degree of shedding is actually regulated by a combination of genes!)

However, further research has found a link between the shedding allele, named the SD locus, and the *Furnishings* or *Improper Coat* allele, F locus. (*"Furnishings"* are longer eyebrows and moustache). Dogs that inherit two copies of the *Improper Coat* allele - described as *F/F* - have the lowest level of shedding. Those that inherit two copies of the SD locus, **SD/SD,** shed most.

Although there are no guarantees, when good Cockapoo breeders select their breeding stock, coat is an important factor – whether through scientific tests or by knowing the characteristics of their breeding stock. In the future, more breeders will use the **Improper Coat** genetic test as it is relatively easy and inexpensive and takes much of the guesswork out. This will undoubtedly have an influence on how our Cockapoos look in the future.

Choosing a Puppy

Selecting an experienced breeder is essential. She knows her dogs and is, in all likelihood, breeding for a low-shedding coat. The more experience breeders have, the more likelihood they have of knowing which dogs will produce low shedding puppies.

If you have allergies and decide you can't live without a dog, put in extra time to make sure you pick the right puppy and make adjustments to your home as well to increase your chances of successfully living together. Allergies are all about tolerance loads - and a dog could tip you over the edge if your body is already battling triggers from other fronts.

Allergy sufferers should be aware that they may be fine with a Cockapoo puppy because tiny puppies often don't shed. But the coat changes in adolescence and this could trigger a reaction later on. It would be distressing if you were suddenly allergic to your one-year-old Cockapoo who has become a dearly-loved member of your family. If you have any doubts at all about a puppy - even a tiny reaction – please don't get him.

For those people with severe allergies, the only scientific way to discover what triggers them is to undergo a series of medical tests and immunisation therapy. Remember:

NO DOG IS TOTALLY NON-SHEDDING. NO DOG IS TOTALLY HYPOALLERGENIC

Two further points to consider are that people's pet allergies vary greatly. Sufferers may react differently to different dogs within a breed or crossbreed, or even litter. A person may be fine with one puppy, yet have a reaction to his brother or sister. In broad terms, all dogs - even so-called 'hairless' dogs - have hair, dander, saliva and urine. Therefore all dogs *can* cause allergic reactions, but not all dogs do.

If a dog is shedding minimal amounts of hair, then the dander remains trapped within the coat. Hypoallergenic dogs shed very little - you might find the *occasional* dog hair or small fur ball around the house - which is why they have to be clipped.

If you have friends or neighbours with a Cockapoo, spend some time inside their house with their dog, stroke the dog, touch your face with the same hand, allow the dog to lick you - do you have a reaction? Did you have a reaction the following day? Rub the dog with a cloth, take it home and rub your face with it the following day. Any reaction? Look on Facebook for Poo or Doodle get-togethers in your area, ask if you can go along and meet some Cockapoos.

Once you have chosen your breeder, ask if you can visit the litter – this shouldn't be a problem in the UK. Once there, handle the dog, rub your hands on your face and lick your hands after you have touched the dog in order to absorb as much potential allergen as you can on your short visit. Take an old towel or piece of cloth and rub the puppy with it. Take this home with you and handle it to see if you get a delayed reaction - which can occur up to 48 hours later. You should also do this if you are buying a puppy or dog online. Once you've visited the dog and taken a cloth or towel home, wait at least 48 hours to see if you have a reaction before committing to buy. An honest seller will not have a problem with this; they will want to see their puppy settled in a suitable home.

If, as may be the case in the US, you cannot visit the breeder personally, ask if she will send a towel or cloth with the dog's saliva and hair on - just as Labradoodle creator Wally Conron did decades ago before sending the first hypoallergenic Doodle puppy all the way from Australia to Miami, Florida.

Check with the breeder to see if you can return the pup within a certain time period were you to have a reaction back at home. However, you cannot expect the breeder to take the dog back if the allergies only occur once the dog has reached adulthood.

Top 12 Tips for Reducing Pet Allergens

Here's an interesting fact: **Everyone with pet allergies can tolerate a certain number of allergens** (things they are allergic to). If that person is just below his or her tolerance, any additional allergen will push him or her over the edge, thus triggering a reaction.

So, if you reduce the general allergen load in the home, you'll be much more successful when you bring your dog home. Here are some tips for doing just that:

1. Get a HEPA air cleaner in the bedroom and/or main living room. HEPA stands for High Efficiency Particle Air - a type of air filter that removes 99.97% of all particles.

2. Use a HEPA vacuum cleaner. Neither the HEPA air nor vacuum cleaner is cheap, but if you suffer allergies and really want to share your life and home with a dog, they are worth considering. Both will dramatically improve the quality of the air you breathe in your home. Regardless of what vacuum you use, clean and dust your home regularly.

3. Carpets and curtains trap allergens and dust, so consider having hard floor coverings and blinds in the rooms where you spend most time.

4. **Keep the dog out of your bedroom**. We spend around a third of our lives here and keeping animals out can greatly reduce allergic reactions.

5. Wash your hands with an antibacterial soap after handling the dog and before eating – and make sure your children do the same. Avoid contact with other dogs and always wash your hands after you have handled any dog, including your own.

6. Get a non-allergic member of your family to brush your dog regularly - always outdoors - and regularly clean the bedding. Avoid using normal washing powder, as it may trigger a reaction in dogs with sensitive skin.

7. Do not allow your dog on the couch, bed or any other furniture. Have clean seat covers or blankets that are washed regularly if your Cockapoo travels in the car.

8. Keep your dog's skin healthy by regularly feeding a good multivitamin and a fatty acid supplement, such as Omega 3 fish oil.

9. You can try *"allergy control solutions"* that alter animal allergens to make them less reactive. They can be sprayed on carpets and soft furnishings, and can be added to water when washing fabrics or clothing.

10. Wipe your dog's underbelly and paws with a damp cloth - or hose him down - after walks, particularly in spring and summer when there are more allergens around.

11. Consider using a dander-reducing treatment such as Allerpet *(pictured),* which helps to cleanse the dog's hair of dander, saliva and sebaceous gland secretions. There are also products to reduce allergens from carpets, curtains and furniture.

12. If your allergies are chronic, seek medical help to determine the nature of them and discuss immunotherapy or medication. There are medical advances being made in the treatment of allergies and a range of tablets, sprays and injections are currently available.

Experts aren't sure whether bathing your dog has any effect on allergy symptoms. Some studies have shown that baths reduce the amount of airborne dander, while others haven't found a difference. We wouldn't recommend bathing your dog more than once a month unless she has a skin problem, as this could cause dry skin, which would then be shed. What is clear is that a dirty dog is more likely to cause allergies.

Of course, the only sure-fire way to GUARANTEE no allergic reaction is not to have a dog.... but that's not what you want to hear!

It wasn't what we wanted to hear either when we decided to get another dog over 13 years ago, knowing that one of our family members had allergies. We followed the advice given in this chapter before we got our dog and can honestly say that we never had a problem. It pays to do your homework.

5. Crate and Housetraining

Used correctly, crates can be a very useful tool for speeding up housetraining (potty training). They also give you and your puppy short breaks from each other and keep the dog safe at night or when you are not there. Many breeders, trainers, behaviourists, and people who show, compete or train working dogs use them.

Getting Your Dog Used to a Crate

The first thing to remember is that a crate should only be used in a humane manner. It's important to spend time getting your puppy or adult dog used to a crate so he comes to regard it as his own safe little haven, and not a punishment cell or prison.

Crates may not be suitable for every dog. Cockapoos are not like hamsters or pet mice that can adapt to life in a cage; they are "Velcro" dogs that like sticking close to you. Being caged for long periods is a miserable existence for any dog, but particularly the Cockapoo, who is reliant on human contact for happiness.

A crate should never be used as a means of confinement because you are out of the house all day. A couple of other points with crates:

1.   Always remove your dog's collar before leaving him inside when you are not there. Sadly, dogs have been known to die after their collars got caught and they panicked.

2.   If the door is closed, your puppy must have access to water while inside. Non-spill water bowls are available from pet shops and online, as are bowls to attach to the bars.

If you do decide to use a crate - perhaps to put your dog in for short periods while you leave the house, or at night, especially in the beginning - the best place for it is in the corner of a room away from cold draughts or too much heat. And because Cockapoos like to be near their family, which is you and any other dogs, avoid putting the crate in a utility room or garage away from everybody else or your Poo will feel lonely and isolated.

Dogs can't sweat like humans and many Cockapoos shed only very lightly, so they can overheat. When you buy a crate, get a wire one that is robust and allows air to pass through, not a plastic one that may get very hot.

Covering the crate with an old blanket is a good way of creating a den for your new puppy, especially at night. Only cover on three sides - leave the front uncovered - and leave a gap of a few inches at the bottom to allow the air to flow.

The crate should be large enough to allow your dog to stretch out flat on his side without being cramped, and he should be able to turn around easily and to sit up without hitting his head on the top. Cockapoos from Miniature Poodles are medium-sized dogs, so a 30" to 36" crate is the right size for a fully-grown Cockapoo. Personally, I would go for the 36" to give the dog plenty of room. Smaller Cockapoos from Toy Poodles will probably do well in a 30" crate, and if you have a large Cockapoo from a Standard Poodle, you could be looking at a 42" crate.

If you only intend buying one, get the right size for an adult and divide it until your puppy grows into the full-sized crate. You can buy adjustable crate dividers **(pictured)**, make them yourself, or put a box inside - preferably wood as cardboard will get chewed. Blocking part of it off while will help him to feel safe and secure, which he won't do in a very big crate.

You have a number of options when it comes to deciding where to put it. Consider leaving it in the kitchen or another room (preferably one with an easy-to-clean floor) where there are people during the day. If you have noisy children, you have to strike the balance between putting the crate somewhere where the pup won't feel isolated, yet can get some peace and quiet from the kids.

You could bring it into your bedroom for the first couple of nights until the puppy settles. Some breeders advise putting the crate right next to the bed for the first night or two – even raised up next to the bed, so the puppy doesn't feel alone, and some owners keen to give the puppy a good start even sleep next to the crate on the floor for a night!

A couple of nights with broken sleep is worth it if it helps the young pup to settle in, as he will often then sleep through the night quicker. After that, you could put the crate in a nearby place where the dog can hear or smell you at night-time, such as the landing, or you could leave it in the same place, like the kitchen, 100% of the time.

It is only natural for any dog to whine in the beginning. He is not crying because he is in a cage. He would cry if he had the freedom of the room and was alone - he is crying because he is separated. However, with patience and the right training, he will get used to it and dogs often come to regard the crate as a favourite place. Some owners make the crate their dog's only bed, so he feels comfortable and safe in there. Not every owner wishes to use a crate, but used correctly they can:

- Create a canine den
- Be a useful housetraining tool
- Give you a bit of a break
- Limit access to the rest of the house until potty trained
- Be a place for the dog to nap or sleep
- Be a safe way to transport your dog in a car

If you use a crate right from Day One, initially cover half of it with a blanket to help your puppy regard it as a den – even during the day. He also needs bedding, and a chew is a good idea. A large crate may allow your dog to eliminate at one end and sleep at the other, but this may slow down housetraining.

Consider buying a purpose-made crate mat or a "Vet Bed" (widely available) to cover the bottom and then put bedding on top. Vet Beds are widely used by vets to make dogs feel warm, secure and cosy when receiving treatment, but they're just as good for using in the home. Made from double-strength polyester with high fibre density to

retain extra heat and allow air to permeate, they have drainage properties, so if your pup has an accident, he will stay dry.

They are also a good choice for older dogs as the added heat is soothing for aging muscles and joints. Bear in mind that most Cockapoo puppies are little chew machines so, at this stage, don't spend a lot of money on a fluffy floor covering for the crate, as it is likely to get destroyed.

Many breeders recommend **not** putting newspapers in one part of the crate, as this encourages the pup to soil there. If you bought your puppy from a good breeder, she will probably already have started the housetraining process, and eight to 12-week-old pups should be able to last a couple of hours without needing the toilet. Some people say that a pup can last one hour or so without needing to urinate for every month of age.

During the night, set your alarm clock to get up after four or five hours to let the pup out to do his or her business for the first week. You might hate it, but it will speed up housetraining.

For the very house-proud, crates aren't the most attractive objects to have in your home. There are, however, some chic alternatives now available for the style-conscious owner. We particularly like the 36" Fido Studio Dog Crate available in the UK from Omlet www.omlet.co.uk *pictured, courtesy of James Tuthill.*

Admittedly, it's not cheap, but not only does it look good, it also boasts "the world's first doggie wardrobe" (the closed section on the left) where you can store your dog's coats, toys, blankets, etc.

Once you've got your crate, you'll need to learn how to use it properly so that it becomes a safe, comfortable den for your dog. Many breeders will have already started the process but, if not, here's a tried-and-tested method of getting your dog firstly to accept a crate, and then to actually want to spend time in there. These are the first steps:

1. Drop a few tasty puppy treats around and then inside the crate.
2. Put your puppy's favourite bedding or toy in there.
3. Keep the door open.
4. Feed your puppy's meals inside the crate. Again, keep the door open.

Place a chew or treat INSIDE the crate and close the door while your puppy is OUTSIDE the crate. He will be desperate to get in there! Open the door, let him in and praise him for going in. Fasten a long-lasting chew inside the crate and leave the door open. Let your puppy go inside to spend some time eating the chew.

After a while, close the crate door and feed him some treats through the mesh. At first just do it for a few seconds at a time, then gradually increase the time. If you do it too fast, he may become distressed. Slowly build up the amount of time he is in the crate. For the first few days, stay in the room, then gradually leave for a short time, first one minute, then three, then 10, 30 and so on.

Next Steps

5. Put your dog in his crate at regular intervals during the day - maximum two hours.
6. Don't crate only when you are leaving the house. Place the dog in the crate while you are home as well. Use it as a 'safe' zone.

7. By using the crate both when you are home and while you are gone, your dog becomes comfortable there and not worried that you won't come back, or that you are leaving him alone. This helps to prevent separation anxiety later in life.

8. If you are leaving your dog unattended, give him a chew and remove his collar, tags and anything else that could become caught in an opening or between the bars.

9. Make it very clear to any children that the crate is NOT a playhouse for them, but a 'special room' for the dog.

10. Although the crate is your dog's haven and safe place, it must not be off-limits to humans. You should be able to reach inside at any time.

The next point is important:

11. Don't let your dog out of the crate when he is barking or whining, or he'll think that this is the key to opening the door. Wait until it has stopped for at least 10 or 20 seconds before letting him out.

 A couple of breeders recommend putting a Snuggle Puppy in the crate with the new puppy. The Snuggle Puppy (pictured) is a safe soft toy with a heartbeat.

One adds: "In their new home, the puppies have the heartbeat sound like they had from laying on mum. We've had really good feedback from families about the Snuggle Puppies."

A puppy should not be left in a crate for long periods except at night-time, and even then he has to get used to it first. Whether or not you decide to use a crate, the important thing to remember is that those first few days and weeks are a critical time for your puppy. Try and make him feel as safe and comfortable as you can. Bond with him, while at the same time gently and gradually giving him positive experiences with new places, humans and other animals.

Special travel crates are useful for the car, or for taking your dog to the vet's or a show. Choose one with holes or mesh in the side to allow free movement of air rather than a solid plastic one, in which a dog can soon overheat. Alternatively, you can buy a metal grille to keep your dog or dogs confined to the back on the car.

A crate is one way of transporting your Cockapoo in the car. Put the crate on the shady side of the interior and make sure it can't move around; put the seatbelt around it. If it's very sunny and the top of the crate is wire mesh, cover part of it so your dog has some shade and put the windows up and the air conditioning on. Don't leave your Cockapoo unattended in a vehicle for more than a few minutes, especially if it's hot as they can overheat very quickly - or be targeted by thieves.

Allowing your dog to roam freely inside the car is not a safe option, particularly if you - like me – are a bit of a "lead foot" on the brake and accelerator! Even though it looks cute, try to avoid letting your dog put his head out of the window, as wind pressure can cause ear infections or bits of dust, insects, etc. to fly into unprotected eyes; a dog can also slip or fly forward if you brake suddenly.

Cockapoo Breeders and Owners on Crates

Traditionally crates have been more popular in America than in the UK and the rest of Europe, but opinion is slowly changing and more owners are starting to use crates on both sides of the Atlantic. This is perhaps because people's perception of a crate is shifting from regarding it as a prison to thinking of it, if used correctly, as a safe haven as well as a useful tool to help with housetraining and transportation.

Without exception, the breeders we contacted believed that the crate should not be used as a means of imprisoning a dog for hours on end while you are away from the house. This is cruel for any dog, but particularly a Cockapoo, whose greatest desire is to be with his humans. This is what they said – and as you will read, there is a wide variation of opinions:

Julie, of Crystalwood Cockapoos, Devon, UK: "Yes, crates are a good idea if the right-sized crate is used. It should be large enough for dog to stand up and turn around freely. They are ideal for young pups. We sleep our dogs in crates overnight and if out shopping etc, but the maximum time we would leave a dog in a crate is three hours - and then after a good walk. Puppy pens are excellent, but some Cockapoo pups have proved to be very good climbers!"

Karol Watson Todd, KaroColin Cockapoos, Lincolnshire, UK: "Personally I prefer puppy pens, and then no more than a couple of hours, except for overnight. I suggest new owners look at second-hand puppy pens as this stage doesn't last long. I don't like crates or pens as a place of punishment. They should be a sanctuary for the puppy. I recommend feeding in the pen if using one. Crates and pens have become very popular, but they aren't a necessity."

Pat Pollington, of Polycinders Cockapoos, Devon: "We really suggest a crate for a puppy because every puppy needs a safe place where he or she can go when they get tired and need to get away

from the children, or when you are trying to cook with hot sauce pans at least you can put them into a crate so you know they are safe. Or when you go out for an hour you know they are not chewing on wires or doing something they shouldn't be because they are safe in their crate.

"No puppy should be left in a crate for longer than a couple of hours, except at night when they are sleeping. During the day they will not want to sleep for more than a couple of hours and then they will be desperate to play and go to the toilet. At night time it is dark so they like to sleep, so they can stay in their crate for longer." ***This attractive trio of four-week-old F1 English Cockapoos was bred by Pat and granddaughter Chloe.***

Jessica Sampson, Legacy Cockapoos, Ontario, Canada: "I believe crate training is very positive. It creates a safe and familiar environment for your puppy or adult dog. Crating your dog ensures a safe environment for him or her while you are unable to supervise them. It is also a useful tool in potty training as well. You should not leave your dog in a crate longer than three to four hours during the day. They may remain in their crate throughout the night."

Jackie Stafford, Dj's Cockapoo Babies, Texas, USA: "I do believe in crate training and I think that pups should not be left more than two hours at the age of 10 weeks, three hours at 11 weeks and four hours at 12 weeks. As an adult, a dog should not be crated more than eight hours overnight. When a dog is crated, you must ensure they have empty bowels and bladder prior to confinement."

Rebecca Goins, Moonshine Babies Cockapoos, Indiana, USA: "We crate train all our puppies; dogs are den animals and they see their crate as a safe spot that is all theirs. We usually cover the crate to make it dark, which helps to soothe them. We always tell our new puppy parents that if the puppy has to be left in a crate longer than four to five hours, then purchase a round pen and attach it to the crate, so the puppy has a place for food and water and a litter pan area.

Pictured is Rebecca's handsome F2b male, Phoenix Rising by the Light of the Red Moon.

Jeanne Davis, Wind Horse Offering, Maryland, USA: "We use a crate initially for housebreaking, then for time-out, and for the pet's own protection. Do not leave a puppy unattended in a crate; it isolates them and then they panic."

Ann Draghicchio, owner of two three-year-old Cockapoos, says: "We use a crate at night but our two are now out during the day as they are trustworthy. We would just continue to repeat *"Kennel up"* and put a treat in the kennel. Toby goes in only with a treat, but Winston does not even eat a treat if we put it in there. He just will go in the kennel with the command."

Stacy Robinson, owner of four-year-old Mabel, adds: "We used to use the crate early on when we were training her. We coaxed her with a yummy treat and after a time, she was quite happy to go on her own. This is the first time I have crate-trained a dog and didn't like the idea, but now see it is a great training tool and the dog loves her little house."

Tiff Atkinson says: "We use a crate only when we leave the house. We crate-trained Dolce when she was a puppy, so she actually likes her crate. Her introduction to her crate has always been positive, so she views it as her safe haven. Throughout the day she will go in there and sleep or hang out. She loves pulling all her blankets and toys out."

Arleen King says: "I advise everyone to crate train! We weren't consistent enough and had trouble - an extended training time because of that."

Housetraining

How easy are Cockapoos to housetrain (potty train)? Well, you won't be surprised to hear that... it varies! Some can be stubborn to learn, while others pick it up within days or a week or two.

Toy breeds have a reputation of being slower than some other larger breeds to potty train. This isn't because they are less intelligent, it's simply that their little bodies can take longer to mature. If your Cockapoo has some Toy Poodle ancestry, it might help to explain why he might be a bit slower to get the hang of it than you expected.

FACT 》 *The speed and success of housetraining depends to some degree on the individual dog and how much effort the breeder has already put in. However, the single most important factor is undoubtedly the owner.*

The more vigilant you are during the early days, the quicker your Cockapoo will be housetrained. It's as simple as that. How much time and effort are YOU prepared to put in at the beginning to speed up housetraining? Taking the advice in this chapter and being consistent with your routines and repetitions is the quickest way to get results. Clear your schedule for a week or so and make housetraining your No. 1 priority - it will be worth it.

Of course, if yours is a rescue Cockapoo, he may have picked up some bad habits before arriving at your home. In such cases, time and patience are needed to help the dog forget the old ways before he can begin to learn the new ones.

You have five big factors in your favour when it comes to toilet training a Cockapoo:

1. They want to please their owners.
2. They are biddable (willing to learn).
3. Most would do anything for praise or a treat.
4. Dogs do not naturally soil their beds.
5. The Cockapoo is a clean breed.

From about the age of three weeks, a pup will leave his sleeping area to go to the toilet. Most good breeders will have already started the housebreaking process, so when you pick up your puppy, all you have to do is ensure that you carry on the good work.

If you're starting from scratch when you bring your puppy home, your new arrival thinks that the whole house is his den and doesn't realise that this is not the place to eliminate. Therefore, you need to gently and persistently teach him that it is unacceptable to make a mess inside the home. Cockapoos, like all dogs, are creatures of routine - not only do they like the same things happening at the same times every day, but establishing a regular routine with your dog also helps to speed up obedience and toilet training.

Dogs are tactile creatures, so they pick a toilet area that feels good under their paws.

Many dogs like to go on grass - but this will do nothing to improve your lawn, so think carefully about what area to encourage your puppy to use. You may want to consider a small patch of crushed gravel in your garden – but don't let the puppy eat it - or a particular corner of the garden or yard away from any attractive plants.

Some breeders advise against using puppy pads at all, and certainly for weeks on end, as puppies like the softness of the pads. Long-term use may also encourage them to eliminate on other soft areas - such as carpets or bed. However, there are plenty of breeders and owners that do use puppy pads for a limited period, alongside regularly taking the puppy outside. They gradually reduce the area covered by the pads over a period of a couple of weeks, and a few dogs living in apartments permanently use puppy pads. Follow these tips to speed up housetraining:

1. **Constant supervision** is essential for the first week or two if you are to housetrain your puppy quickly. This is why it is important to book time off work when you bring him home, if you can. Make sure you are there to take him outside regularly. If nobody is there, he will learn to urinate or poo(p) inside the house.

2. **Take your pup outside at the following times:**
   - As soon as he wakes – every time
   - Shortly after each feed
   - After a drink
   - When he gets excited
   - After exercise or play
   - Last thing at night
   - Initially every hour - whether or not he looks like he wants to go

You may think that the above list is an exaggeration, but it isn't! Housetraining a pup is almost a full-time job in the beginning. If you are serious about toilet training your puppy quickly, then clear your diary for a week or two and keep your eyes firmly glued on your pup...learn to spot that expression or circling motion just before he makes a puddle - or worse – on your floor.

3. Take your pup to **the same place** every time, you may need to use a lead (leash) in the beginning - or tempt him there with a treat. Some say it is better to only pick him up and dump him there in an emergency, as it is better if he learns to take himself to the chosen toilet spot. Dogs naturally develop a preference for going in the same place or on the same surface. Take or lead him to the same patch every time so he learns this is his toilet area.

4. **No pressure – be patient.** You must allow your distracted little darling time to wander around and have a good sniff before performing his duties – but do not leave him, stay around a short distance away. Unfortunately, puppies are not known for their powers of concentration; it may take a while for him to select the perfect bathroom spot!

   Photo of this 8.5-week-old courtesy of Karol Watson-Todd.

5. **Housetraining is reward-based.** Give praise and/or a treat immediately after he has performed his duties in the chosen spot. Cockapoos like to please you and love praise, and reward-based training is the most successful method for quick results.

6. **Share the responsibility.** It doesn't have to be the same person who takes the dog outside all the time. In fact, it's easier if there are a couple of you, as this is a very time-demanding business. Just make sure you stick to the same principles, command and patch of ground.

7. **Stick to the same routine.** Dogs understand and like routine. Sticking to the same times for meals, short exercise sessions, playtime, sleeping and toilet breaks will help to not only housetrain him quicker, but also help him settle into his new home.

8. **Use the same word** or command when telling your puppy to go to the toilet – or while he is in the act. He will gradually associate this phrase or word with toileting and you will even be able to get him to eliminate on command after some weeks.

9. **Use your voice if you catch him in the act indoors.** A short sharp negative sound is best - NO! ACK! EH! It doesn't matter, as long as it is loud enough to make him stop. Then start running enthusiastically towards your door, calling him into the garden and the chosen place and patiently wait until he has finished what he started indoors. It is no good scolding your dog if you find a puddle or unwanted gift in the house but don't see him do it; he won't know why you are cross with him. Only use the negative sound if you actually catch him in the act.

10. **No punishment.** Accidents will happen at the beginning, do not punish your pup for them. He is a baby with a tiny bladder and bowels, and housetraining takes time - it is perfectly natural to have accidents early on. Remain calm and clean up the mess with a good strong-smelling cleaner to remove the odour, so he won't be tempted to use that spot again. Dogs have a very strong sense of smell; use a special spray from your vet or a hot solution of washing powder to completely eliminate the odour. Smacking or rubbing his nose in it can

have the opposite effect - he will become afraid to do his business in your presence and may start going secretly behind the couch or under the bed, rather than outside.

11. **Look for the signs.** These may be:

   a. Whining

   b. Sniffing the floor in a determined manner

   c. Circling and looking for a place to go

   d. Walking uncomfortably - particularly at the rear end!

Take him outside straight away, and try not to pick him up all the time. He has to learn to walk to the door himself when he needs to go outside.

12. **If you use puppy pads, only do so for a short time** or your puppy will get to like them.

13. **Use a crate at night-time** and, for the first few nights, set your alarm clock. An eight-week-old pup should be able to last a few hours if the breeder has already started the process. For the first few nights, consider getting up four or five hours after you go to bed to take the pup outside, gradually increasing the time by 15 minutes.

By the age of four or five months a Cockapoo pup should be able to last through (a short night) without needing the toilet – provided you let him out last thing at night and first thing in the morning. Before then, you will have a lot of early mornings!

If using a crate, remember that during the day the door should not be closed until your pup is happy with being inside. At night-time it is acceptable to close the door. Consider keeping the pup close to you for the first two or three nights. He needs to believe that the crate is a safe place and not a trap. If you don't want to use a crate, then use pet gates, section off an area inside one room or use a puppy pen to confine your pup at night.

Photo shows a Cockapoo puppy in a travel crate on the way to a vet check.

And finally, one British breeder added this piece of advice: "If you are getting a puppy, invest in a good dressing gown and an umbrella!"

Advice From Breeders and Owners

Good breeders provide new owners with information to take home that helps them to understand their puppy's needs. In her **Notes For Buyers** one breeder says: "Your puppy has already started to ask to go out when she needs the toilet; in any case you will need to take her outside regularly. Typically, this would be every time she wakes up as well as after meals.

"Watch for the signs: searching the ground and sniffing is a good indication she needs to pass water. Puppies have relatively small bladders. Always choose the same place in the garden; remain with the puppy until she has performed and then give her plenty of praise. Remember, accidents will happen. If you catch her in the act, simply take her outside and then praise her for her efforts. Never shout at or hit your puppy as this will cause confusion and is likely to make matters worse.

"During the times when puppy has no access to the garden, it is a good idea to place some newspaper on the floor. The newspaper could be moved nearer and nearer to the outside door until puppy realises to go to the door to ask to go out. Puppy training pads are also available from pet shops, although we find that puppies prefer to rip them up rather than to use them for their correct purpose!"

Rebecca Goins sends this schedule home with her Cockapoo puppies:

7:00 am:	Get up-Take Dog Outside-Feed Dog ½ Cup and ½ NuVet Wafer-Offer Water-Take Dog Outside-Play with Dog up to 15-30 mins-Put Dog in Crate
Noon:	Take Dog Outside-Offer Water-Play with dog up to 15-30 mins-Put Dog in Crate
5:30 pm:	Take Dog Outside-Feed Dog ½ Cup and ½ NuVet Wafer-Offer Water-Play with Dog for up to One Hour
7:00 pm:	Remove Water
Before Bed:	Take Dog Outside-Put Dog in Crate

Rebecca also has a list of possible scenarios and action to take:

- **Puppy peed when your back was turned** - Never let them out of their crate or living area unless you are prepared to watch their every move

- **Puppy peed or pooped in their crate** - Make sure their crate isn't too big for them; it should be just enough for her to stand up and turn around. Also make sure they are not left in their crate for too long – three to four hours maximum

- **Puppy pooped without warning** - Observe what she does immediately before she makes a deposit. That way, you'll be able to scoop the pup up and take her outside before an accident happens

- **Puppy pees on the same indoor spot daily** - Make sure you clean up completely, and don't give your puppy too much indoor freedom too soon

Here is the routine from another breeder: "We have a pretty strict routine for toilet training which is a little intensive, but not unreasonable. It definitely works. They learn that 10pm till 6am is sleep time, which any new home could do. This matters as obviously they learn through conditioning. So, with a sleep routine, they know how long it is until they next can pee and near 10pm they know it's nearly bedtime, so learn quickly to pee then.

"Then, during the day, it's a case of taking them out every two hours on the hours so 6am, 8am, 10am and so on... I find that every time they go out, they pee so therefore they would probably struggle waiting longer. It's also important that they don't have free reign to go outside whenever they feel like it (unsupervised) which is tempting in summer months, but it's absolutely vital to notice every time they pee and when they do one to let them know what they're doing. *"Go toilet"* is what we use. Then reward immediately. Eventually, you'll be able to ask them to *"Go toilet"* as they've formed the association.

"This doesn't mean they categorically can't go longer than two hours, but it's better to set them up to win rather than fail. We then don't have a specified age where the length of time is extended as that's definitely an individual basis, so when they stop going every time you take them out, the time can be very gradually increased."

Another breeder added: "Some breeders do not advocate putting newspaper in the crate for the puppy to toilet. I agree, as by doing this it makes it much harder to get the puppy fully toilet trained. The idea of getting up in the night to toilet the puppy may not suit everyone. What we do is to use a fairly spacious puppy pen at night for a young puppy and not a crate. We have a bed at one end and newspaper at the far end where the puppy can eliminate.

"We still have a crate for the puppy to go in during the day if he so wishes and we leave the door open. This then becomes his own little den. But at night he is put in the playpen. By the time the puppy is about four-and-a-half to five months old we find that they can usually go all night without toileting and so we then put them in a crate at night."

 Your breeder may use a particular phrase, such as "Go toilet!" "Pee pee!" or "Go potty!" Ask your breeder if she has started the housetraining process and what words she uses to encourage the pups to go.

Here are some Cockapoo owners' personal experiences, starting with Caroline Littlewood, of Yorkshire, who is the proud new owner of a red F1 Cockapoo puppy. Coco is just 15 weeks old and housetraining is taking a little longer than Caroline had hoped. She says: "I guess the housetraining requires a lot of time - and eyes in the back of your head. You sometimes feel it will never happen, then you get progress and it keeps you going!

"As soon as we are up, Coco goes out and usually has wee and then poo; she might not if it's raining, but is getting better at this. We take her out after sleeping or playing, and every 30-60 minutes depending what she is doing. Now she sometimes cries by the door. Accidents happen still, there's not really any reason, except that we are maybe missing the sniffing, or not quick enough if I've gone in another room, as she doesn't always cry. She is now getting better at going out for walks - she wasn't too keen at first - and will now wee and occasionally poo on her walk."

Stacy Robinson added: "We found that crate training worked well with Mabel. I watched her like a hawk, gave her many opportunities to go outside, lots of walks, praised her success and had lots of patience."

Ann Draghicchio says: "Toby and Winston were super easy to potty train. We had very few accidents, although once they were neutered, they had a few more accidents in protest to the surgery, I believe!

"Consistency is the key. Bell training was very helpful. I did make the mistake of letting them sniff around a lot outside and on a long leash to finally go. With any future dogs, I would put them on a six-foot leash and not let them "play" when they were going out to do their business. That way they won't get used to needing a large area to sniff before relieving themselves."

Tiff Atkinson had an easier time with Dolce, now aged four, *pictured:* "Our housetraining journey was easy because we were consistent and we reward, reward, reward. When we brought her home, my husband woke up every hour and took her outside. He would say "Dolce, tee tee!"

"Most times she would sit there and look at him. When she "tee teed" for the first time, we made a big deal out of it and she was rewarded. Every time after she was rewarded for every direction, command and so on. We talked to her non-stop in two to four-word sentences and she began to understand - and we read lots of Cockapoo books!"

Bell Training

Bell Training is a method that can work particularly well with Cockapoos. There are different types of bells, the simplest are inexpensive and widely available online. They consist of a series of adjustable bells that hang on a nylon strap from the door handle *(pictured, right)*. Another option is a small metal bell attached to a metal hanger that fixes low down on the wall next to the door with two screws *(pictured, below right).*

The technique is quite simple. As with all puppy training, do it in short bursts of five to 10 minutes or your easily-distracted little student will switch off!

1. Show your dog the bell, either on the floor, before it is fixed anywhere or by holding it up. Point to it and give the command *"Touch," "Ring,"* or whatever word you decide.

2. Every time he touches it with his nose, reward with praise.

3. When he rings the bell with his nose, give him a treat. You can rub on something tasty, like peanut butter, to make it more interesting.

4. Take the bell away between practice sessions.

5. Once he rings it every time you show him the bell, go on to the next step.

6. Take the bell to the door you use for housetraining. Place a treat just outside the door while he is watching. Then close the door, point to the bell and give the command.

7. When he rings the bell, open the door and let him get the treat outside.

8. When he rings the bell as soon as you place a treat outside, fix the bell to the door or wall.

9. The next time you think he needs the toilet, walk to the door, point to the bell and give the command. Give him a healthy treat if he rings it, let him out immediately and reward again with enthusiastic praise when he performs his duty.

 In between training sessions, ring the bell yourself EVERY time you open the door to let her outside.

Some Cockapoos can get carried away by their own success and will ring the bell any time they want your attention, fancy a wander outdoors or see a squirrel!

Make sure that you ring the bell every time he goes out through the door to potty, but DON'T ring the bell if he is going out to play. And if he starts playing or pottering about in the garden or yard, bring him in!

6. Feeding a Cockapoo

To keep your dog's biological machine in good working order, it's important to supply the right fuel, as the correct diet is an essential part of keeping your dog fit and healthy.

The topic of feeding can be something of a minefield; owners are bombarded with endless choices as well as countless adverts from dog food companies, all claiming that theirs is best. There is not one food that will give every single dog the healthiest coat and skin, the brightest eyes, the most energy, the best digestion, the least gas, the longest life and stop her from scratching or having skin problems.

Dogs are individuals, just like people, which means that you could feed a quality food to a group of dogs and find that most of them thrive on it, some do not do so well, while a few might get an upset stomach or even an allergic reaction. The question is: *"Which food is best for my Cockapoo?"*

If you have been given a recommended food from a breeder, rescue centre or previous owner, stick to this as long as your dog does well on it. If you do decide - for whatever reason - to change diet, then this must be done gradually. There are several things to be aware of when it comes to feeding:

1. Food is a big motivator for many dogs, making a powerful training tool. You can use feeding time to reinforce a simple command on a daily basis.

2. Greedy dogs have no self-control when it comes to food, so it is up to you to control your dog's intake. Dogs of all breeds, including Cockapoos, can have food sensitivities or allergies - more on this topic later.

3. Some dogs do not do well on diets with a high grain content. There is enough anecdotal evidence from owners to know that this is true of some Cockapoos.

4. One of the main reasons for flatulence (farting!) is the wrong diet.

5. There is evidence that some dogs thrive on home-cooked or raw diets, particularly if they have been having issues with manufactured foods, but you need the time and money to stick to them.

6. With processed dried foods (kibble), you often get what you pay for, so a more expensive food is usually – but not always - more likely to provide better nutrition in terms of minerals, nutrients and high quality meats. Cheap foods often contain a lot of grain; read the list of ingredients to find out. Dried foods have improved a lot over the last few years and some of the best are a good choice for a healthy, complete diet. Dried foods also contain the least fat and most preservatives. Foods such as Life's Abundance dry formulas do not contain any preservatives.

7. Sometimes elderly dogs just get bored with their diet and go off their food. This does not necessarily mean that they are ill, simply that they have lost interest and a new food should be gradually introduced.

One of our dogs had inhalant allergies. He was fed a quality dried food that the manufacturers claimed was *"hypoallergenic,"* i.e. less likely to cause allergies. Ours did well on it, but not all dogs thrive on dried food. We tried several other foods first; it is a question of owners finding the best food for their dog. If you got your dog from a good breeder, they should be able to advise you.

FACT ❯ *Beware foods described as "premium" or "natural" or both, many manufacturers blithely use these words, but there are no official guidelines as to what they mean. However, "Complete and balanced" IS a legal term and has to meet standards laid down by AAFCO (Association of American Feed Control Officials) in the USA.*

Always check the ingredients on any food sack, packet or tin to see what is listed first; this is the main ingredient and it should be meat or poultry, not grain. If you are in the USA, look for a dog food endorsed by AAFCO. In general, tinned foods are 60-70% water and often semi-moist foods contain a lot of artificial substances and sugar. Choosing the right food for your dog is important; it will influence health, coat, longevity and sometimes even temperament.

There are three stages of your dog's life to consider when feeding: *Puppy, Adult* and *Senior* (also called Veteran). Some manufacturers also produce a *Junior* feed for adolescent dogs. Each represents a different physical stage of life and you should choose the right food during each particular phase. This does not necessarily mean that you have to feed Puppy, then Junior, then Adult, then Senior food; some owners switch their young dogs to Adult formulas fairly soon. Ask your breeder or vet for advice on the right time to switch.

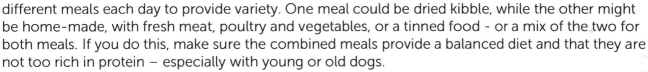

Most breeders and owners feed their Cockapoos twice a day; this helps to stop a hungry dog gulping food down in a mad feeding frenzy and also reduces the risk of Bloat although this is not a particular concern for Cockapoos. Some owners of fussy eaters, or older dogs who have gone off their food, give two different meals each day to provide variety. One meal could be dried kibble, while the other might be home-made, with fresh meat, poultry and vegetables, or a tinned food - or a mix of the two for both meals. If you do this, make sure the combined meals provide a balanced diet and that they are not too rich in protein – especially with young or old dogs.

Food allergies are a growing problem in the canine world generally. Sufferers may itch, lick or chew their paws and/or legs, rub their face or get *"hot spots."* They may also get frequent ear infections or redness and swelling on their face. Switching to a grain-free diet can help to alleviate the symptoms, as your dog's digestive system does not have to work as hard.

In the wild, a dog or wolf's staple diet would be meat with some vegetable matter from the stomach and intestines of the herbivores (plant-eating animals) that she ate – but no grains. Dogs do not efficiently digest corn or wheat - both of which are often staples of cheap commercial dog food. Grain-free diets provide carbohydrates through fruits and vegetables, so a dog still gets all the necessary nutrients.

NOTE: Although there is no conclusive scientific proof, there is emerging anecdotal evidence that the recent trend for grain-free diets has, in some cases, resulted in a Taurine (amino acid) deficiency, contributing to the enlarged heart disease DCM (Dilated Cardiomyopathy). One breeder said: "We only recommend no corn or wheat. Good grains are OK, but some gluten-free foods add bad starches, like potatoes or peas."

So, if you are looking at *grain-free* food for your dog, avoid those containing large quantities of various legumes (peas, chickpeas, lentils, etc.).

20 Tips For Feeding Your Cockapoo

1. If you choose a manufactured food, don't pick one where meat or poultry content is NOT the first item listed on the bag or tin. Foods with lots of cheap cereals or sugar are not the best choice.

2. Some Cockapoos suffer from sensitive skin, hot spots or allergies. A cheap food, often bulked up with grain, will only make this worse. If this is the case, choose a high quality – usually more expensive – food, or consider a raw or home-cooked diet. You'll probably save money in vets' bills in the long run and your dog will be happier.

3. Consider feeding your dog twice a day, rather than once. Smaller feeds are easier to digest and reduce flatulence (gas). Puppies need to be fed more often; discuss exactly how often with your breeder.

4. Establish a feeding regime and stick to it. Dogs like routine. If you are feeding twice a day, feed once in the morning and then again at tea-time. Stick to the same times of day. Do not give the last feed too late, or your dog's body will not have chance to process or burn off the food before sleeping. She will also need a walk or letting out in the garden or yard after her second feed to allow her to empty her bowels. Feeding at the same times each day helps your dog establish a toilet regime.

5. Some owners practise *"free feeding,"* which allows the dog to eat when she wants. However, if your Cockapoo is fussy, consider taking away any uneaten food between meals. (Even then some dogs can still refuse to eat). Put the food bowl down twice a day and take it up after 20 minutes – even if there is some left. If she is healthy and hungry, she'll look forward to her next meal and most soon stop leaving food. If a Cockapoo does not eat anything for a couple of days, it either means that she is unwell or you will have to try a different diet.

NOTE: The exception to this is with very young puppies – under three months – where the breeder might recommend free feeding so the dog can eat at will. Also, some fussy eaters do better with free feeding. Dishes must be washed daily and old uneaten food thrown away.

6. If your puppy is a fussy eater, don't be too quick to switch foods. Try removing the bowl between meals, so she is hungry when it's time for the next meal. Switching foods too quickly or tempting a young dog with treats can be a sure-fire way of encouraging fussy eating.

7. Some owners find that their dog eats better if the food is presented on a small plate.

8. If your dog is a fussy eater, try giving the teatime feed after a long walk when your dog is more likely to be hungry. (Wait until an hour after vigorous exercise).

9. Do not feed too many titbits (tidbits) and treats between meals. Extra weight will place extra strain on your Cockapoo's heart, other organs and joints, causing a detrimental effect on health and even lifespan. Unhealthy treats also throw a balanced diet out of the window. Avoid feeding your dog from the table or your plate, as this encourages attention-seeking behaviour, begging and drooling.

10. If you feed leftovers, feed them INSTEAD of a balanced meal, not as well as - unless you are feeding a raw diet. High quality commercial foods already provide all the nutrients, vitamins, minerals and calories that your dog needs. Feeding titbits or leftovers may be too rich for

your Cockapoo in addition to her regular diet and cause gas, scratching or other problems, such as obesity. You can feed your dog vegetables as a healthy low-calorie treat.

__Get your puppy used to eating raw carrots, pieces of apple, etc. as a treat and she will continue to enjoy them as an adult. If you wait until she's fully grown before introducing them, she may well turn her nose up.__

11. Never give your dog cooked bones, as these can splinter and cause choking or intestinal problems.

12. Avoid rawhide, as greedy dogs have a tendency to swallow without first nibbling it down into smaller pieces. Rawhide also contains glue and chemicals that are toxic in large quantities.

13. NEVER feed the following items to your dog: grapes, raisins, chocolate, onions, Macadamia nuts, any fruits with seeds or stones, tomatoes, avocados, rhubarb, tea, coffee or alcohol. All of these are poisonous to dogs.

14. If you switch to a new food, do the transition gradually. Unlike humans, dogs' digestive systems cannot handle sudden changes. Begin by gradually mixing some of the new food in with the old and increase the proportion so that after seven to eight days, all the food is the new one. The following ratios are recommended by Doctors Foster & Smith Inc: Days 1-3 add 25% of the new food, Days 4-6 add 50%, Days 7-9 add 75%, Day 10 feed 100% of the new food. By the way, if you stick to the identical brand, you can change flavours in one go.

    NOTE: The exception is when switching to a raw diet as raw and processed or cooked food are digested at different rates, and the stomach produces different acids for the digestion of each. Raw takes around four hours to digest, whereas kibble takes 12 hours. To switch to raw, give the last bowl of kibble then start feeding raw the following day.

15. If you have more than one dog, consider feeding them separately. Cockapoos normally get on well with other dogs, but feeding dogs together can sometimes lead to food aggression from one dog either protecting her own food or trying to eat the food designated for another.

16. Check your dog's faeces (aka stools, poo or poop!). If her diet is suitable, the food should be easily digested and produce dark brown, firm stools. If your dog produces soft or light stools, or has a lot of gas or diarrhoea, then the diet may not suit her, so consult your vet or breeder for advice.

17. Feed your dog in stainless steel or ceramic dishes. Plastic bowls don't last as long and can also trigger an allergic reaction around the muzzle in some sensitive dogs. Ceramic bowls are best for keeping water cold. Elevated bowls with narrow tops (**pictured,** available on Amazon, eBay, etc.) are good if your Cockapoo has long Spaniel-like ears, as they keep ears out of food and drink.

18. Keep your dog's weight in check. Obesity can lead to the development of serious health issues, such as heart disease, diabetes and high blood pressure. Although weight varies from

dog to dog, a good rule of thumb is that your Cockapoo's tummy should be higher than her rib cage. If her belly is level or hangs down below it, she is overweight.

19. Some owners feed vitamins and/or supplements to help keep their Cockapoos healthy, particularly if they have skin issues. Check with your breeder or vet as to which, if any, to feed. These may include fish oil for the coat, a probiotic to aid digestion, or glucosamine for joints.

20. And finally, always make sure that your dog has access to clean, fresh water. Change the water and clean the bowl regularly – it gets slimy!

Many breeders feed their adult dogs twice a day, others feed just once, and yet others feed some dogs once a day and some dogs twice a day. As one US breeder put it: "They are not all made from the same cookie cutter." Start your dog on twice-daily feeds from four to six months old and, if she seems to be thriving on this regime, stick to it.

....

Types of Dog Food

We are what we eat. The right food is a very important part of a healthy lifestyle for dogs as well as humans. Here are the main options explained:

Dry dog food - also called kibble, is a popular and relatively inexpensive way of providing a balanced diet – look for *"Complete and Balanced"* on the packet in the UK. However, kibble was created for the convenience of owners, not dogs, and it doesn't suit all dogs. Kibble comes in a variety of flavours and with differing ingredients to suit the different stages of a dog's life. Cheap foods are often false economy, particularly if your Cockapoo does not tolerate grain/cereal very well. You may also have to feed larger quantities to ensure she gets sufficient nutrients.

Canned food - another popular choice - tends to be more expensive than dried food and comes in a variety of flavours, but many owners don't like the mess. Dogs, however, love the taste. Canned food is often mixed with dry kibble, which often works well for a dog that has lost interest in dry food.

These days there are hundreds of options, some are very high quality and made from natural, organic ingredients and contain herbs and other beneficial ingredients. A part-opened tin can sometimes smell when you open the fridge door. As with dry food, read the label closely. Generally, you get what you pay for and the origins of cheap canned dog food are often somewhat dubious. Some dogs can suffer from diarrhoea or soft stools and/or gas with too much tinned or soft food.

Freeze-Dried (*pictured*) - This is made by a special process that freezes the food, then removes the moisture before vacuum packing. The product is sealed with an oxygen-absorbing substance to increase shelf life. It doesn't need a fridge and can be kept at room temperature for up to six months. Usually with a very high meat content and no grain, many freeze-dried meals contain high quality, natural, human-grade ingredients. So what's the catch? ....Price! If you can afford it, freeze-dried will not only give you a quality, natural food, but your dog will love it. Many raw feeders use freeze-dried and it's also handy for those travelling with their dogs.

Home-Cooked - Some owners want the ability to be in complete control of their dog's diet, know exactly what their dog is eating and to be sure that her nutritional needs are being met. Feeding your dog a home-cooked diet of meat and vegetables can be time-consuming and more expensive than kibble, and the difficult thing is sticking to it once you have started out with the best of intentions. But many owners think the extra effort is worth it. If you decide to go ahead, spend the time to become proficient and learn about canine nutrition to ensure your dog gets all the vital nutrients and right amount of calories. You can also buy ready-made frozen home-cooked food from companies such as Butternut Box.

We know of several cases of itchy dogs who are all now doing better having switched from a commercial, dried dog food to a home-cooked diet - usually involving chicken and vegetables, and possibly rice.

Semi-Moist - These are commercial dog foods shaped like pork chops, salamis, bacon *(pictured),* burgers or other meaty foods and they are the least nutritional of all dog foods. They are full of sugars, artificial flavourings and colourings to help make them visually appealing.

Cockapoos don't care two hoots what their food looks like, they only care how it smells and tastes; the shapes are designed to appeal to humans. While you may give your dog one as an occasional treat, they are not a diet in themselves and do NOT provide the nutrition your dog needs. Steer clear of them for regular feeding.

How Much Food?

This is another question I am often asked. The answer is ... there is no easy answer! The correct amount of food for a dog depends on a number of factors:

- Breed
- Gender
- Age
- Health
- Environment
- Number of dogs in the house
- Quality of the food
- Natural energy levels
- Amount of daily exercise
- Whether your dog is working, competing, performing a service or simply a pet

Some breeds have a higher metabolic rate than others, and energy levels vary tremendously from one dog to the next. Some individual Cockapoos — especially those from working English Cocker Spaniels - are very energetic, while others are more laid back. Generally:

- *Smaller dogs have faster metabolisms so require a higher amount of food per pound of body weight*
- *Female dogs that have been spayed can be more prone to putting on weight*
- *Growing puppies and young dogs need more food than old dogs with a slower lifestyle*

Every dog is different; you can have two Cockapoos with different body shapes, energy levels and capacity for exercise. The energetic dog will burn off more calories.

Maintaining a healthy body weight for dogs — and humans — is all about balancing what you take in with how much you burn off. If your dog is exercised two or three times a day and/or has regular play sessions with other dogs, she will need more calories than a couch potato Cockapoo. Certain health conditions such as heart disease, an underactive thyroid, diabetes and arthritis can all lead to dogs gaining weight, so their food has to be adjusted accordingly.

FACT ❭ *A dog kept in a cold environment will need more calories to keep warm than a dog in a warm climate, as they burn extra calories to keep themselves warm. And a dog kept on her own is more likely to be overweight than a dog kept with other dogs, as she receives all of the food-based attention.*

The daily recommended amount listed on cheap processed foods is usually on the high side, as much of the food is made up of cereals, which are not doing much except bulking up the weight of the food – and possibly triggering allergies. And the more your dog eats, the more they sell!

What the Breeders Feed

We asked a number of Cockapoo breeders what they fed their dogs, starting with Jeanne Davis, of Wind Horse Offering, Maryland, USA: "Feeding is slightly complex. For me there is no simple answer. I feed the moms a dry kibble that is no less than 28% protein and about two weeks before they whelp, I start feeding them a bit of canned food. Any dry or canned food that I feed HAS to be devoid of wheat, corn, soy, gluten (and of course any kind of sugars/corn syrup). These days there are many manufacturers who are catching up with that nutritional preference.

"To my thinking, the reason why so many dogs develop allergies is that many of the foods have been corn-based (supposedly to make the coat shiny), but dogs are not grain eaters, so it messes with their pH, and slowly they "get sick."

"I feed the moms a really good vitamin during gestation and throughout the time that they have their puppies. When the puppies are about a month old, they will start getting into mom's food. Since their teeth are only just coming through, 'eating' kibble doesn't really happen, but they do get a certain amount of the canned/wet food." *Photo courtesy of Jeanne.*

"I continue the puppies on the 28% kibble with some canned food; and send them home with a bag of what they have been eating and a small can of wet food. I tell the new puppy owners to put a dollop of wet food on the puppy's food for a while to keep him or her eating during the transition to their new home, but they need not stay on the canned food.

"At eight weeks, they are fully eating kibble anyway. I also suggest that if the puppy is fussy, to pour some (organic) chicken or beef broth over the kibble for a while to keep the puppy hydrated and eating. I also provide new owners with literature about, and a sample of, the vitamins (from NuVet) that the moms have been eating."

Jessica Sampson, Legacy Cockapoos, Ontario, Canada: "We feed a high-quality commercial diet - Dick Van Patten's Natural Balance. We love this food as it is made from high quality ingredients and has no fillers (corn, wheat, rice, etc.) and is packed full of vitamins and minerals. We have had great success with this food over the years. It is an all-stages diet, which means we feed the same food to all our dogs and puppies. We do not feed our puppies a food formulated specifically for puppies as our vet years ago advised us against it. The reasoning was that when you feed puppy food it causes puppies to grow too quickly and can give a higher rate of joint issues (hip dysplasia, luxating patella etc.). The bone and muscle development have trouble keeping up with each other which can lead to issues.

"When you feed an all-stages diet to puppies they grow at a slower rate, which allows their bone and muscle development to keep up with one another. They still reach the same finished size and weight as they would if they ate puppy food. They just get there slower, which is better for their development."

Linda Zarro, of Sugar and Spice Cockapoos, South Carolina, added: "We use Kirkland brand dog/puppy food from Costco. We used to give raw chicken legs and thighs to our dogs when we only had about six dogs, but we don't see any difference in their health, so give them the Costco food, which has a very high rating for dog foods. We also give our dogs and puppies (starting at six weeks of age) a nutritional supplement called NuVet Plus. This supplement helps to boost the immune system of dogs and puppies. It is full of herbs, vitamins and minerals to help keep them in the best of health. We believe that giving it to our dogs and puppies reduces the risk of many potential health issues."

In the UK, Karol Watson Todd, of KaroColin Cockapoos, Lincolnshire said: "I feed Royal Canin dried food and go right through all the stages, so HT42 (a special food formulated to meet the nutritional needs of breeding females) from first day of season to day 42 of pregnancy, then we go to starter food for mum and it's also the weaning food - I purée it down to gruel consistency. Then at eight weeks the puppies go on to Junior and mum goes onto the Cocker Maintenance Food.

"I like Royal Canin because it's a well-known food and an easy-to-buy brand for the new owners. The nutrition is good; I have tried all sorts of other foods and found them to be too rich and not enough quantity (like Eden). All my girls look fantastic after having a litter of puppies on the Royal Canin and I have never had a bitch that is thin or in poor condition after a litter. That speaks volumes as puppies take a lot out of the bitch, but she can only give it if she has it there to give. *Photo courtesy of Karol.*

"I also feed chicken, which I cook in the slow cooker, to all my dogs and add it to the dry food. The mums can get several breasts a day in addition to the huge amounts of Royal Canin. Further, I always have puppy formula in, and I give this to mum during the birthing process to keep her energy levels up, and I feed it slightly warm. It's called Nutrola: http://animal-health.co.uk/nutrolac.html. I like the formula for mums and puppies that have feeding problems and also as it is goat's milk-based. It is also very easy to mix up and I make up baby bottles and keep in fridge for 24 hours if I have a puppy that needs extra feeding. I use the sponge feeding method for any puppies that need supplementary feeding, as tubing a puppy will stop the sucking reflex and they will then miss out on an important part of their babyhood."

Another UK breeder who is a fan of Royal Canin is Pat Pollington, of Polycinders Cockapoos, Devon: "I feed my dogs on Royal Canin Adult. I feed my puppies on Royal Canin Mini Starter, they also have some Royal Canin Starter Mousse mixed in and I give them a bowl of Royal Canin Starter Milk to drink during weaning time. I feed my pregnant bitches a mixture of Royal Canin Mini Starter and Royal Canin Adult. A week before the end of their pregnancy, they have all Royal Canin Mini Starter and a bowl of Royal Canin Starter Milk.

"I feed Royal Canin because I feel it is a brilliant food. It keeps my dogs on tip top form. I don't need to feed them very much of it. I have tried lots of different food brands for both my dogs and puppies, but nothing compares to it. I have really fussy typical Poodles and the only food I can get them to eat is Royal Canin. All my puppies have a fantastic coat on them and they are always very healthy. The food you feed puppies is important because they need so many different things in their food to help them grow - and Royal Canin has it all. I never have a skinny bitch after pregnancy - they all hold their weight and, if anything, sometimes a bit too much weight."

Julie Shearman, of Crystalwood Cockapoos, Devon, added: "We fed Burns Natural dog and puppy food. It's made with natural quality ingredients and we find that both the pups and all our adult dogs thrive on it. A dry dog food gives the dogs something to crunch, which slows down their eating (Cockers are pigs!) and it is also good for teeth and gums."

Owner Arleen Stone King says: "I feed a grain-free diet because it was recommended by the breeder. For treats they get a three-calorie vegetable chip, since both of them are on the pudgy side."

Pictured is Arleen's F1, Daisy, who is having a "bad hair day," having just woken up from a nap!

Ann Draghicchio: "I use Purina Pro Plan, given it's good reputation. I did grain-free for a while, but with all the DCM (Dilated Cardiomyopathy) issues coming up, I switched and have not had any problems. I use Zuke's mini treats, along with some home-made peanut butter and pumpkin treats."

Stacy Robinson: "We feed Mabel a mixture of high quality dry (Taste of the Wild) and wet mixture. She is pretty particular about her food and requires privacy while eating. She loves her soft treats and performs tricks, so that I simply can't say no."

Tiff Atkinson: "We feed Dolce hydrolysed protein dog food. She has allergies, so this food helps a lot. She enjoy greenies in the morning after I brush her teeth. Monthly, she also enjoys chicken, carrots and other dog treats. Her treats are healthy and usually only contain one to three ingredients. She drinks spring water." Caroline Littlewood feeds 15-week-old Coco Royal Canin Puppy three times a day."

The Raw Diet

If there is one thing guaranteed to divide opinion, it is the raw diet! There is anecdotal evidence that some dogs thrive on a raw diet, particularly those with allergies or food intolerances - although scientific proof is lagging behind. However, I also know several breeders (of different breeds) who have tried feeding raw and say their dogs did badly on it, and some say their dogs actually dislike the taste.

Given that we had a dog with allergies for many years, I would say that had he been younger, I would have tried him on a home-cooked or raw diet — but that's just personal opinion. When we talk about a raw diet, we are referring to uncooked meat, poultry and vegetables. This may be fed in the natural state, which requires more work on the part of the owner, or bought pre-prepared, so all you have to do is open the packet.

Many Cockapoos thrive on a high quality dried commercial dog food or a mix of cooked/raw and kibble. **We are not suggesting that everybody rushes out and feeds their dog a raw diet!**

Due to various factors, including the time and expense involved, the raw diet is certainly not for every dog. Not all dogs do well on raw. We are simply providing the information for anyone considering feeding raw. This may include owners who are fans of a natural diet or who have a Cockapoo that has skin issues or is not doing well on a commercially-prepared kibble. In these circumstances, a raw diet is one of the options for owners to consider.

Claims made by fans of the raw diet include:

- **Reduced symptoms of - or less likelihood of - allergies, and less scratching**
- **Better skin and coats**
- **Easier weight management**
- **Improved digestion**
- **Less doggie odour and flatulence**
- **Higher energy levels**
- **Reduced risk of Bloat**
- **Helps fussy eaters**
- **Fresher breath and improved dental health**
- **Drier and less smelly stools, more like pellets**
- **Overall improvement in general health and less disease**
- **Most dogs love a raw diet**

Raw food emulates the way dogs ate before the existence of commercial kibble, which may contain artificial preservatives and excessive protein and fillers – causing a reaction in some dogs. Dry, canned and other styles of processed food were mainly created as a means of convenience - for the owner, not the dog!

However, nowadays, you also have the option of buying packets or boxes of balanced, ready-made raw meals for your dog. Made by companies such as such as Paleo Ridge or Naturaw, these meals can even be individually tailored to suit your dog. There is also the freeze-dried option if you don't fancy handling raw meats and poultry.

Some nutritionists believe that dogs fed raw whole foods tend to be healthier than those on other diets. They say there are inherent beneficial enzymes, vitamins, minerals and other qualities in meats, fruits, vegetables and grains in their natural forms that are denatured or destroyed when cooked. Many also believe dogs are less likely to have allergic reactions to the ingredients on this diet. Frozen food can be a valuable aid to the raw diet. The food is highly palatable and made from high quality ingredients. The downsides are that not all pet food stores stock it, it can be expensive and you have to remember to defrost it.

Critics of a raw diet say that the risks of nutritional imbalance, intestinal problems and food-borne illnesses caused by handling and feeding raw meat outweigh any benefits. Owners must pay strict attention to hygiene when preparing a raw diet.

A raw diet made at home from scratch may not be a good option if you have young children in the house, due to the risk of bacterial infection from the raw meat. The dog may also be more likely to ingest bacteria or parasites such as Salmonella, E. Coli and Ecchinococcus.

There are two main types of raw diet, one involves feeding raw, meaty bones and the other is known as the BARF diet *(Biologically Appropriate Raw Food* or *Bones and Raw Food),* created by Dr Ian Billinghurst.

Raw Meaty Bones

This diet is:

- Raw meaty bones or carcasses, if available, should form the bulk of the diet

- Table scraps both cooked and raw, such as vegetables, can be fed

- As with any diet, fresh water should be constantly available. **NOTE: Do NOT feed cooked bones, they can splinter**

Australian veterinarian Dr Tom Lonsdale is a leading proponent of the raw meaty bones diet. He believes the following foods are suitable:

- Chicken and turkey carcasses, after the meat has been removed for human consumption

- Poultry by-products, including heads, feet, necks and wings

- Whole fish and fish heads

- Sheep, calf, goat, and deer carcasses sawn into large pieces of meat and bone

- Other by-products, e.g. pigs' trotters, pigs' heads, sheep heads, brisket, tail and rib bones

- A certain amount of offal can be included in the diet, e.g. liver, lungs, trachea, hearts, tripe

He says that low-fat game animals, fish and poultry provide the best source of food for pet carnivores. If you feed meat from farm animals (cattle, sheep and pigs), avoid excessive fat and bones that are too large to be eaten.

Some of it will depend on what's available locally and how expensive it is. Start with your local butcher or farm shop. Bear in mind that dogs are more likely to break their teeth on large knuckle bones and bones sawn lengthwise, than meat and bone together. A dog takes some time to eat a raw bone and will push it around the floor, so the kitchen may not be the most suitable or hygienic place. Outside is one option, but what do you do when it's raining? Establishing the right quantity to feed your Cockapoo is a matter of trial and error and depends on your dog's activity levels, appetite and body condition. A very approximate guide is:

15%-20% of body weight per week, or 2%-3% a day

So, if your Cockapoo weighs 16lb (7.27kg), she will require 2.4lb-3.2lb (1kg-1.45kg) of carcasses or raw meaty bones weekly. **These figures are only a rough guide** for adult dogs. Pregnant or lactating females and growing puppies need more food.

Dr Lonsdale says: "Wherever possible, feed the meat and bone ration in one large piece requiring much ripping, tearing and gnawing. This makes for contented pets with clean teeth. Wild carnivores feed at irregular intervals, in a domestic setting regularity works best and accordingly I suggest that you feed adult dogs and cats once daily. If you live in a hot climate I recommend that you feed pets in the evening to avoid attracting flies.

"I suggest that on one or two days each week your dog may be fasted - just like animals in the wild. On occasions you may run out of natural food. Don't be tempted to buy artificial food, fast your dog and stock up with natural food the next day. Puppies...sick or underweight dogs should not be fasted (unless on veterinary advice)."

Table scraps and some fruit and vegetable peelings can also be fed, but should not make up more than one-third of the diet. Liquidising cooked and uncooked scraps in a food mixer can make them easier to digest.

Things to Avoid:

- Excessive meat off the bone - not balanced
- Excessive vegetables - not balanced
- Small pieces of bone - can be swallowed whole and get stuck
- Cooked bones, fruit stones (pips) and corn cobs - get stuck
- Mineral and vitamin additives - create imbalance
- Processed food - leads to dental and other diseases
- Excessive starchy food - associated with Bloat
- Onions, garlic, chocolate, grapes, raisins, sultanas, currants - toxic to pets
- Milk - associated with diarrhoea. Animals drink it whether thirsty or not and can get fat

Points of Concern

- Old dogs used to processed food may experience initial difficulty when changed on to a natural diet, and raw meaty bones are not suitable for dogs with dental or jaw problems, or gulpers. Discuss the change with your vet first
- The diet should be varied, any nutrients fed to excess can be harmful. Liver is an excellent foodstuff, but should not be fed more than once weekly, and other offal, e.g. ox stomachs, should not make up more than half of the diet
- Weight bearing bones shouldn't be given as they damage teeth. One breeder added: "My general rule is that if I can cut it with poultry shears, they can eat it; anything harder should be avoided
- Whole fish are an excellent source of food, but avoid feeding one species of fish constantly. Some species, e.g. carp, contain an enzyme that destroys thiamine (vitamin B1)
- If you have more than one dog, do not allow them to fight over the food, feed them separately if necessary
- Be prepared to monitor your dog while she eats the bones, especially in the beginning, and do not feed bones with sharp points
- Make sure that children do not disturb the dog when feeding or try to take the bone away
- Hygiene: Make sure the raw meaty bones are kept separate from human food and clean thoroughly any surface the uncooked meat or bones have touched. This is especially important if you have children. Feeding bowls are unnecessary, your dog will drag the bones across the floor, so feed them outside if you can, or on a floor that is easy to clean

- Puppies can and do eat diets of raw meaty bones, but you should consult the breeder or a vet before embarking on this diet with a young dog

You will need a regular supply of meaty bones - either locally or online - and you should buy in bulk to ensure a consistency of supply. For this you will need a large freezer. You can then parcel up the bones into daily portions. You can also feed frozen bones; some dogs will gnaw them straight away, others will wait for them to thaw.

More information is available from the website www.rawmeatybones.com and I strongly recommend discussing the matter with your breeder or vet before switching to raw meaty bones.

The BARF diet

An odd choice of name for a diet! This is a variation of the raw meaty bones diet created by Dr Ian Billinghurst, who owns the registered trademark "Barf Diet." A typical BARF diet is made up of 60%-75% of raw meaty bones (bones with about 50% meat, such as chicken neck, back and wings) and 25%-40% of fruit and vegetables, offal, meat, eggs or dairy foods. Bones must not be cooked or they can splinter inside the dog. There is a great deal of information on the BARF diet on the internet.

 Only start a raw diet if you have done your research and are sure you have the commitment and money to keep it going. There are numerous websites and canine forums with information on switching to a raw diet and everything it involves.

Food Allergies

Dog food allergies affect about one in 10 dogs. They are the third most common canine allergy for dogs after atopy (inhaled or contact allergies) and flea bite allergies. Food allergies affect males and females in equal measure as well as neutered and intact pets. They can start when your dog is five months or 12 years old - although the vast majority start when the dog is between two and six years old. It is not uncommon for dogs with food allergies to also have other types of allergies. Here are some common symptoms to look out for:

- Itchy skin (this is the most common). Your dog may lick or chew her paws or legs and rub her face with her paws or on the furniture, carpet, etc.

- Excessive scratching

- Ear infections *(pictured)*

- Hot patches of skin – *"hot spots"*

- Hair loss

- Redness and inflammation on the chin and face

- Recurring skin infections
- Increased bowel movements (maybe twice as often as usual)
- Skin infections that clear up with antibiotics but recur when the antibiotics run out

Allergies or Intolerance?

FACT *There's a difference between dog food allergies and dog food intolerance (sensitivity). Typical reactions to <u>allergies</u> are skin problems and/or itching. Typical reactions to <u>intolerance</u> are diarrhoea and/or vomiting.*

Dog food intolerance can be compared to people who get diarrhoea or an upset stomach from eating spicy food. Both can be cured by a change to a diet specifically suited to the individual, although a food allergy may be harder to get to the root cause of.

With dogs, certain ingredients are more likely to cause allergies than others. In order of the most common triggers across the canine world in general they are: **Beef, dairy products, chicken, wheat, eggs, corn, and soy (soya).** There is also increasing evidence that some dogs cannot tolerate the preservatives and other chemicals in dried dog food.

Unfortunately, these most common offenders are also the most common ingredients in dog foods! In the past, dogs were often put on a rice and lamb kibble diet, which were thought to be less likely to cause allergies. However, the reason was simply because they were not traditionally included in many dog food recipes - therefore fewer dogs had reactions to them.

It is also worth noting that a dog is allergic or sensitive to an **ingredient**, not to a particular brand of dog food, so it is very important to read the ingredients label on the sack or tin. If your Cockapoo has a reaction to beef, for example, she will react to any food containing beef, regardless of how expensive it is or how well it has been prepared.

Tip *Food intolerances frequently start when a dog is less than one year old. If your Cockapoo starts scratching, has diarrhoea, ear infections or other symptoms, don't think that because she has always had this food that the problem lies elsewhere. It may be that she has developed an intolerance to the food as her body matures.*

Symptoms of food allergies are well documented. Unfortunately, the problem is that these conditions may also be symptoms of other issues such as environmental or flea bite allergies, intestinal problems, mange, and yeast or bacterial infections. You can have a blood test on your dog for food allergies, but many veterinarians now believe that this is not accurate enough.

The only way to completely cure a food allergy or intolerance is total avoidance. This is not as easy as it sounds. First you have to be sure that your dog does have a food allergy, and then you have to discover which food is causing the reaction.

Blood tests are not thought to be reliable and, as far as I am aware, the only true way to determine exactly what your dog is allergic to, is to start a food trial. If you don't or can't do this for the whole 12 weeks, then you could try a more amateurish approach, which is eliminating ingredients from your dog's diet one at a time by switching diets – remember to do this over a period of a week.

A food trial is usually the option of last resort, due to the amount of time and attention that it requires. It is also called *"an exclusion diet"* and is the only truly accurate way of finding out if your dog has a food allergy and what is causing it. Before embarking on one, try switching dog food.

If you wish to stick with commercial dog food, try switching to a grain-free, hypoallergenic one – preferably with natural (not chemical) preservatives. Although usually more expensive, hypoallergenic dog food ingredients do not include common allergens such as wheat protein or soya, thereby minimising the risk of an allergic reaction. Many may have less common ingredients, such as venison, duck or types of fish.

Here are some things to look for in a high-quality food:

- Meat or poultry as the first ingredient
- Vegetables
- Natural herbs such as rosemary or parsley
- Oils such as rapeseed (canola) or salmon

Here's what to avoid if your dog is showing signs of a food intolerance:

- Corn, corn meal, corn gluten meal
- Meat or poultry by-products (as you don't know exactly what these are or how they have been handled)
- Artificial preservatives including BHA, BHT, Propyl Gallate, Ethoxyquin, Sodium Nitrite/Nitrate and TBHQBHA
- Artificial colours, sugars and sweeteners like corn syrup, sucrose and ammoniated glycyrrhizin
- Powdered cellulose
- Propylene glycol

If you can rule out all of these and you've tried switching diet without much success, then a food trial may be your only option.

Food Trials

Before you embark on one of these, you need to know that they are a real pain-in-the-you-know-what to monitor. **A food trial involves feeding one specific food for 12 weeks,** something the dog has never eaten before, such as rabbit and rice or venison and potato. The food should contain no added colouring, preservatives or flavourings.

FACT ❯ *Surprisingly, dogs are typically NOT allergic to foods they have never eaten before.*

There are a number of these commercial diets on the market, as well as specialised diets that have proteins and carbohydrates broken down into such small molecular sizes that they no longer trigger an allergic reaction. These are called *"limited antigen"* or *"hydrolysed protein"* diets. Home-made diets are another option as you can strictly control the ingredients. The difficult thing is that this must be the **only thing** the dog eats during the trial.

If you want to give a treat, use the recommended diet. (Tinned diets can be frozen in chunks or baked and then used as treats). If you have other dogs, either feed them all on the trial diet or feed the others in an entirely different location. If you have a cat, don't let the dog near the cat litter tray. And keep your dog out of the room when you are eating – not easy with a hungry Cav! But even small amounts of food dropped on the floor or licked off of a plate can ruin a food trial, meaning you'll have to start all over again.

Although beef is the food most likely to cause allergies in the general dog population, there are plenty of stories to suggest that the ingredient most likely to cause a problem in many dogs is grain – just visit any canine internet forum to see that this is true.

"Grain" is wheat or any other cultivated cereal crop. Some dogs also react to starch, which is found in grains and potatoes (also bread, pasta, rice, etc.).

Some breeds (especially the Bully breeds, e.g. Bulldogs, Boxers, Pugs, Bull Terriers and French Bulldogs) can be prone to a build-up of yeast in the digestive system. Foods that are high in grains and sugar can cause an increase in unhealthy bacteria and yeast in the stomach. This crowds out the good bacteria in the stomach and can cause toxins to occur that affect the immune system.

And when the immune system is not functioning properly, the itchiness related to food allergies can cause secondary bacterial and yeast infections, which, in Cockapoos, may show as ear infections, hot spots, reddish or dark brown tear stains or other skin disorders. Symptoms of a yeast infection also include:

- Itchiness
- Skin lesions or redness on the underside of the neck, the belly or paws
- A musty smell

Although drugs such as antihistamines and steroids will temporarily help, they do not address the root cause. Wheat products are also known to produce flatulence, while corn products and feed fillers may cause skin rashes or irritations.

Switching to a grain-free diet may help to get rid of yeast and bad bacteria in the digestive system. Introduce the new food over a week or so and be patient, it may take two to three months for symptoms to subside – but you will definitely know if it has worked after 12 weeks.

 Some owners of dogs with sensitive stomachs feed a probiotic supplement or daily spoonful of natural or live yoghurt, which contains healthy bacteria and helps to balance the dog's gut bacteria.

And plenty of owners whose Cockapoos have struggled with conventional kibble have switched to a home-cooked or raw diet with some success.

It is also worth noting that some of the symptoms of food allergies - particularly the scratching, licking, chewing and redness - can also be a sign of inhalant or contact (environmental) allergies, which are caused by a reaction to such triggers as pollen, grass or dust. Some dogs are also allergic to flea bites - see **Chapter 12. Skin and Allergies** for more details.

If you suspect your dog has a food allergy, the first call should be to the vet to discuss the best course of action. Many vets' clinics promote specific brands of dog food, which may or may not be the best for your dog, so don't buy anything without first checking every ingredient on the label.

Canine Bloat

Bloat is known by several different names: twisted stomach, gastric torsion or Gastric Dilatation-Volvulus (GDV). It occurs mainly in larger breeds, however, there have been cases of smaller dogs getting Bloat. It is one reason why owners often feed their dogs twice a day - particularly if they are greedy gulpers.

Tips to Avoid Bloat:

- Buy an elevated feeding bowl, which not only keeps your dogs ears out of the food, but many people believe helps to prevent bloat. If you have a gulper, consider buying a bowl with nobbles *(pictured)* – and moisten your dog's food

- Feed twice a day rather than once

- Avoid dog foods with high fats or use citric acid preservatives, also avoid tiny pieces of kibble

- Don't let your dog drink too much water just before, during or after eating. Remove the water bowl just before mealtimes, but return it soon after

- Stress can possibly be a trigger, with nervous (and aggressive) dogs being more susceptible. Maintain a peaceful environment for your dog, particularly around mealtimes

- IMPORTANT: Allow one hour either side of mealtimes before vigorous exercise

Bloat can kill a dog in less than one hour. If you suspect your Cockapoo has bloat, get him or her into the car and off to the vet immediately. Even with treatment, mortality rates range from 10% to 60%. With surgery, this drops to 15% to 33%.

Overweight Dogs

Any dog can become overweight given too much food, too many treats or not enough exercise. It is very hard to resist those beautiful, big brown pleading eyes when it comes to food.

It's much easier to regulate your dog's weight than to try and slim down a starving Cockapoo when she becomes overweight. Sadly, overweight and obese dogs are susceptible to a range of illnesses and even a shortened lifespan. According to James Howie, Veterinary Advisor to Lintbells, some of the main ones are:

Heart and lung problems – fatty deposits within the chest cavity and excessive circulating fat play important roles in the development of cardio-respiratory and cardiovascular disease.

Joint disease – excessive body weight may increase joint stress, which is a risk factor in joint degeneration (arthrosis), as is cruciate disease (knee ligament rupture). Joint disease tends to lead to a reduction in exercise that then increases the likelihood of weight gain that reduces exercise further. A vicious cycle is created. Overfeeding growing dogs can lead to various problems, including the worsening of hip dysplasia. Weight management may be the only measure required to control clinical signs in some cases.

Diabetes – resistance to insulin has been shown to occur in overweight dogs, leading to a greater risk of diabetes mellitus.

Tumours – obesity increases the risk of mammary tumours in female dogs.

Liver disease – fat degeneration may result in liver insufficiency.

Reduced lifespan - one of the most serious proven findings in obesity studies is that obesity in both humans and dogs reduces lifespan.

Exercise intolerance – this is also a common finding with overweight dogs, which can compound an obesity problem as fewer calories are burned off and are therefore stored, leading to further weight gain. Obesity also puts greater strain on the delicate respiratory system of Cockapoos, making breathing even more difficult for them.

Cockapoos become very attached to their humans, who regard them as members of the family. However, beware of ascribing too many human characteristics to your lovable Cockapoo. Scientists have shown that dogs regarded as "family members" (i.e. anthropomorphised) by owners are at greater risk of becoming overweight. This is because attention given to the dog often results in food being given as well.

The important thing to remember is that many of the problems associated with being overweight are reversible. Increasing exercise increases the calories burned, which in turn reduces weight.

 *If you do put your dog on a diet, the reduced amount of food will also mean reduced nutrients, so she may need a supplement during this time.*

Feeding Puppies

Start out on the right foot with your baby Cockapoo by getting him or her interested in food right from the beginning - as some can soon become fussy eaters. Puppyhood is a time of rapid growth and development, and puppies require different levels of nutrients to adult dogs.

Initially, pups get all their nutrients from their mother's milk and then they are gradually weaned from three or four weeks of age. Many owners prefer to continue with the puppy food provided and recommended by the breeder. If your pup is doing well on this, there is no reason to change. However, if you do change food, it should be done very gradually by mixing in a little more of the new food each day over a period of seven or so days.

If at any time your puppy starts being sick, has loose stools or is constipated, slow the rate at which you are switching her over. If she continues vomiting, seek veterinary advice quickly - within a day or two - as she may have a problem with the food you have chosen.

FACT ⟩ *Puppies quickly dehydrate if they are vomiting or have diarrhoea.*

Because of their special nutritional needs, only give your puppy a food that is approved either just for **Puppies** or **All Life Stages.** A feed recommended for **Adult** dogs only won't have enough protein, and the balance of calcium and other nutrients will not be right for a pup.

Puppy food is very high in calories and nutritional supplements, so you want to switch to a **Junior** or **Adult** food once she leaves puppyhood, which is at about six months old. Feeding puppy food too long can result in obesity and orthopaedic problems.

DON'T:

- 🐾 Feed scraps from the table. Your Cockapoo will get used to begging for food; this will also affect a carefully balanced diet
- 🐾 Feed food or uncooked meat that has gone off. Puppies have sensitive stomachs

DO:

- 🐾 Check the weight of your growing puppy to make sure she is within normal limits for her age. There are charts available on numerous websites, just type *"puppy weight chart"* into Google – you'll need to know the exact age and current weight of your puppy

 Take your puppy to the vet if she has diarrhoea or is vomiting for two days or more

 Remove her food after it has been down for 15 to 20 minutes. Food available 24/7 encourages fussy eaters

How Often?

Most puppies have small stomachs but big appetites, so feed them small amounts on a frequent basis. Establishing a regular feeding routine with your puppy is good, as this will also help to toilet train her. Get her used to regular mealtimes and then let her outside to do her business straight away when she has finished. Puppies have fast metabolisms, so the results may be pretty quick!

You need to be there for the feeds because you want her and her body on a set schedule. Smaller meals are easier for her to digest and energy levels don't peak and fall so much with frequent feeds. There is some variation between recommendations, but as a general rule of thumb:

 **Up to the age of three or four months, feed your puppy three or four times a day**

 **Then three times a day until she is four to six months old**

 **Twice a day until she is one year old**

 **Then once or twice a day for the rest of her life**

 Cockapoos are known for their affectionate natures. If your dog is not responding well to a particular family member, a useful tactic is to get that person to feed the dog every day. The way to a dog's heart is often through her stomach!

Feeding Seniors

Once your adolescent dog has switched to an adult diet she will remain on it for several years. However, as a dog ages, her body has different requirements to those of a young dog. This is the time to consider switching to a senior diet. Generally, a dog is considered to be older or senior when in the last third of normal life expectancy.

A Cockapoo's average lifespan is 10 to 15 years, which is quite a wide variation. There are many factors that contribute to a longer life, including genetics and veterinary care, but one of the most important factors is better nutrition. Look for signs of your dog slowing down or having joint problems. You can describe any changes to the vet at your dog's annual check-up, rather than having the expense of a separate consultation.

FACT ❯ *As a dog ages her metabolism slows, her joints stiffen, her energy levels decrease and she needs less exercise, just as with humans. An adult diet may be too rich and have too many calories, so it may be the time to move to a senior diet.*

Having said that, some dogs stay on a normal adult diet all of their lives – although the amount is usually decreased and supplements often added, e.g. for joints, coat or digestion.

Just like me, your Cockapoo will thicken around the waist as she gets older! Keep her weight in check even though it may be harder, as she will not be burning off as many calories - and some older dogs become more food-focussed with age.

Obesity only puts more strain on an elderly dog's body - especially joints and organs - and makes any health problems even worse. Getting an older dog to slim down can be very difficult. It is much better not to let your Cockapoo get too chunky than to put her on a diet.

But if she is overweight, put in the effort to shed the extra pounds. This is one of the single most important things you can do to increase your Cockapoo's quality AND length of life.

Diet and Supplements

Other changes in canines are again similar to those in older humans and as well as stiff joints or arthritis, they may move more slowly and sleep more. Hearing and vision may not be so sharp and organs don't all work as efficiently as they used to; teeth may have become worn down or decayed.

When this starts to happen, it is time to consider feeding your old friend a senior diet, which will take these changes into account. Specially formulated senior diets are lower in protein and calories but help to create a feeling of fullness.

FACT ▶ *Older dogs are more prone to constipation, so senior diets are often higher in fibre - at around 3% to 5%.*

Wheat bran can also be added to regular dog food to increase the amount of fibre - but do not try this if your Cockapoo has a low tolerance to grain. If your dog has poor kidney function, then a low phosphorus diet will help to lower the workload for the kidneys.

Ageing dogs may have additional needs, some of which can be catered for with supplements, e.g. **glucosamine and chondroitin**, which help joints. Two popular joint supplements in the UK are GWF Joint Aid for dogs, used by several breeders, and Lintbell's Yumove.

If your dog is not eating a complete balanced diet, then a vitamin/mineral supplement is recommended to prevent any deficiencies. Some owners also feed extra antioxidants to an older dog — ask your vet's advice on your next visit. Antioxidants are also found naturally in fruit and vegetables.

While some older dogs suffer from obesity, others have the opposite problem — they lose weight and are disinterested in food. If your old dog is getting thinner and not eating well, firstly get her checked out by the vet to rule out any possible diseases. If she gets the all-clear, your next challenge is to tempt her to eat.

Tip *Old dogs sometimes stop eating when they are having trouble with their teeth. If yours is fed on dry food, try smaller kibble or moistening the food with warm water or gravy.*

Max, an old dog of ours loved his twice-daily feeds until he got to the age of 10 when he lost interest in his hypoallergenic kibble. We tried switching flavours within the same brand, but that didn't work. After a short while we mixed his daily feeds with a little gravy and a spoonful of tinned dog food — Bingo! He started wolfing it down again.

At 12 he started getting some diarrhoea, so we switched again and for the last year of his life he was mainly on home-cooked chicken and rice with a little *Senior* kibble, which worked well.

Home-made diets of boiled rice, potatoes, vegetables and chicken or meat with the right vitamin and mineral supplements can also be good. See **Chapter 14. Caring for Seniors** for more information on looking after ageing Cockapoos.

....

Reading Dog Food Labels

A NASA scientist would have a hard job understanding some manufacturers' labels, so it's no easy task for us lowly dog owners. Here are some things to look out for on the manufacturers' labels:

- The ingredients are listed by weight and the top one should always be the main content, such as chicken or lamb. Don't pick one where grain is the first ingredient; it is a poor-quality feed. Some dogs can develop grain intolerances or allergies, and often it is specifically wheat they react to

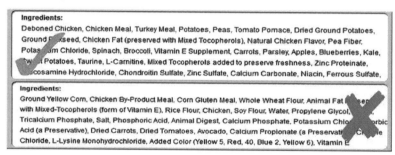

Ingredients:
Deboned Chicken, Chicken Meal, Turkey Meal, Potatoes, Peas, Tomato Pomace, Dried Ground Potatoes, Ground Flaxseed, Chicken Fat (preserved with Mixed Tocopherols), Natural Chicken Flavor, Pea Fiber, Potassium Chloride, Spinach, Broccoli, Vitamin E Supplement, Carrots, Parsley, Apples, Blueberries, Kale, Sweet Potatoes, Taurine, L-Carnitine, Mixed Tocopherols added to preserve freshness, Zinc Proteinate, Glucosamine Hydrochloride, Chondroitin Sulfate, Zinc Sulfate, Calcium Carbonate, Niacin, Ferrous Sulfate,

Ingredients:
Ground Yellow Corn, Chicken By-Product Meal, Corn Gluten Meal, Whole Wheat Flour, Animal Fat (preserved with Mixed-Tocopherols (form of Vitamin E), Rice Flour, Chicken, Soy Flour, Water, Propylene Glycol, Tricalcium Phosphate, Salt, Phosphoric Acid, Animal Digest, Calcium Phosphate, Potassium Chloride, Ascorbic Acid (a Preservative), Dried Carrots, Dried Tomatoes, Avocado, Calcium Propionate (a Preservative), Choline Chloride, L-Lysine Monohydrochloride, Added Color (Yellow 5, Red, 40, Blue 2, Yellow 6), Vitamin E

- High on the list should be meat/poultry or meat/poultry by-products, these are clean parts of slaughtered animals, not including meat. They include organs, blood and bone, but not hair, horns, teeth or hooves

- Chicken meal (dehydrated chicken) has more protein than fresh chicken, which is 80% water. The same goes for beef, fish and lamb. So, if any of these meals are number one on the ingredient list, the food should contain enough protein

- A certain amount of flavourings can make a food more appetising for your dog. Choose a food with a specific flavouring, like *"beef flavouring"* rather than a general *"meat flavouring,"* where the origins are not so clear

- **Guaranteed Analysis** – This guarantees that your dog's food contains the labelled percentages of crude protein, fat, fibre and moisture. Keep in mind that wet and dry dog foods use different standards. (It does not list the digestibility of protein and fat and this can vary widely depending on their sources). While the Guaranteed Analysis is a start in understanding the food quality, be wary about relying on it too much.

One pet food manufacturer made a mock product with a guaranteed analysis of 10% protein, 6.5% fat, 2.4% fibre, and 68% moisture (similar to what's on many canned pet food labels) – the ingredients were old leather boots, used motor oil, crushed coal and water!

GUARANTEED ANALYSIS	
Crude protein (min.)	28.00 %
Crude fat (min.)	12.00 %
Crude fiber (max.)	4.50 %
Moisture (max.)	11.00 %
Docosahexaenoic acid (DHA) (min.)	0.05 %
Calcium (min.)	1.20 %
Phosphorus (min.)	1.00 %
Omega-6 fatty acids* (min.)	2.20 %
Omega-3 fatty acids* (min.)	0.30 %
Glucosamine* (min.)	500 mg/kg
Chondroitin sulfate* (min.)	500 mg/kg

* Not recognized as an essential nutrient by the AAFCO Dog Food Nutrient Profiles.

- Find a food that fits your dog's age, breed and size. Talk to your breeder, vet or visit an online Cockapoo forum and ask other owners what they are feeding their dogs

- If your Cockapoo has a food allergy or intolerance to wheat, check whether the food is gluten free; all wheat contains gluten

- Natural is best. Food labelled *"natural"* means that the ingredients have not been chemically altered, according to the FDA in the USA. However, there are no such guidelines governing foods labelled *"holistic"* – so check the ingredients and how it has been prepared

- In the USA, dog food that meets minimum nutrition requirements has a label that confirms this. It states: *"[food name] is formulated to meet the nutritional levels established by the AAFCO Dog Food Nutrient Profiles for [life stage(s)]"*

Even better, look for a food that meets the minimum nutritional requirements *"as fed"* to real pets in an AAFCO-defined feeding trial, then you know the food really delivers the nutrients that it is *"formulated"* to. AAFCO feeding trials on real dogs are the gold standard. Brands that do costly feeding trials (including Nestlé and Hill's) indicate so on the package.

Tip *Look for the words "Complete and Balanced" on a commercial food. Dog food labelled "Supplemental" isn't complete and balanced. Check with your vet if in doubt.*

If it all still looks a bit baffling, you might find the following websites, mentioned earlier, very useful.

The first is www.dogfoodadvisor.com run by Mike Sagman. He has a medical background and analyses and rates hundreds of brands of dog food based on the listed ingredients and meat content. You might be surprised at some of his findings.

The second is www.allaboutdogfood.co.uk run by UK canine nutritionist David Jackson.

Photo by Sally Wynn.

As you have just read, no single food is right for every Cockapoo; you must decide on the best for yours. If you have a puppy, initially stick to the same food as the breeder. The best test of a food is how well your dog is doing on it.

If your Cockapoo is happy and healthy, interested in life, has enough energy, is not too fat and not too thin, doesn't scratch a lot and has healthy-looking stools, then...

Congratulations, you've got it right!

7. Cockapoo Behaviour

Just as with humans, a dog's personality is made up of a combination of temperament and character. While every Cockapoo is an individual, there are also certain shared character traits. Understanding your dog, what makes her tick and why she behaves like that will give you a greater understanding of - and ultimately a deeper bond with - your dog.

FACT Temperament is the nature — or inherited characteristics - a dog is born with; a predisposition to act or react in a certain way. Character varies from one dog to the next. It develops through the dog's life and is formed by a combination of temperament and environment - or NURTURE AND NATURE.

Getting your puppy from a good breeder is important. Their dogs must be physically healthy AND have good temperaments. This photo shows puppies exploring their brave new world, courtesy of CCGB-approved breeder Karol Watson Todd, of KaroColin Cockapoos, Lincolnshire, England.

Then, how you treat your dog will have a huge effect on her personality and behaviour. Starting off on the right foot with good routines is very important; so, treat your dog well and spend lots of time with her.

If you don't want your Cockapoo to be clingy, you must also get her used to being left for short periods and make time for socialisation and exercise. All dogs need different environments, scents and experiences to keep them stimulated, well-balanced and relaxed in new situations.

Despite being bred primarily as companion dogs, Cockapoos have ancestry from working dogs on both sides - the Cocker Spaniel and the Poodle, and this is often exhibited in their behaviour. Some — particularly those with working English Cocker Spaniel heritage - have high energy demands. Some also have a fairly strong prey drive (instinct to chase small birds and mammals), many love swimming and all enjoy running free off the lead (leash).

Tip When training your Cockapoo, set your dog set up for SUCCESS. Praise good behaviour, use positive methods and keep sessions short and fun.

At the same time, all dogs should understand the "No" (or similar) command. Just as with children, a canine has to learn boundaries to adapt successfully and to be content with her environment. Be consistent so your dog learns the guidelines quickly. All of these measures will help your dog grow into a happy, well-adjusted and well-behaved adult that is a delight to be with.

If you adopt a Cockapoo from a rescue centre, you may need a little extra patience. These eager-to-please people-loving dogs can arrive with some baggage. They have been abandoned by their previous owners for a variety of reasons and may still carry the scars of that trauma. They could be nervous and insecure, needy or aloof, and may not know how to behave in a house or interact with a loving owner. Your time and patience is needed to teach these poor animals to trust again and to become happy in their new forever homes.

....

Understanding Canine Emotions

As pet lovers, we are all too keen to ascribe human characteristics to our dogs; this is called *anthropomorphism* – "the attribution of human characteristics to anything other than a human being." Most of us dog lovers are guilty of that, as we come to regard our pets as members of the family - and Cockapoos certainly regard themselves as members of the family! An example of anthropomorphism might be that the owner of a male dog might not want to have him neutered because he will "miss sex," as a human might if he or she were no longer able to have sex. This is simply not true.

FACT ▶ *A male dog's impulse to mate is entirely governed by his hormones, not emotions. If he gets the scent of a female on heat, his hormones (which are just body chemicals) tell him he has to mate with her.*

He does not stop to consider how attractive she is or whether she is "the one" to produce his puppies. No, his reaction is entirely physical, he just wants to dive in there and get on with it!

It's the same with females. When they are on heat, a chemical impulse is triggered in their brain making them want to mate – with any male, they aren't at all fussy. So don't expect your little princess to be all coy when she is on heat, she is not waiting for Prince Charming to come along - the tramp down the road or any other scruffy pooch will do! It is entirely physical, not emotional.

Food is another example. A dog will not stop to count the calories of that lovely treat (you have to do that). No, she is driven by food and just thinks about getting the food or the treat. Most non-fussy eaters will eat far too much, given the opportunity.

Cockapoos are not only very attractive dogs, they are also extremely loving and eager to please you, not to mention quirky. If yours doesn't make you laugh from time to time, you must have had a humour by-pass! All of this adds up to one thing: a hugely engaging and affectionate family member that it's all too easy to reward - or spoil.

It's fine to treat your dog like a member of the family - as long as you keep in mind that she is a dog and not a human. Understand her mind, patiently train her to adjust to her place in the household and that there are household rules she needs to learn – like not jumping on the couch when soaking wet or covered in mud - and you will be rewarded with a companion who is second to none and fits in beautifully with your family and lifestyle.

Dr Stanley Coren is a psychologist well known for his work on canine psychology and behaviour. He and other researchers believe that in many ways a dog's emotional development is equivalent to that of a young child. Dr Coren says: "Researchers have now come to believe that the mind of a dog is roughly equivalent to that of a human who is two to two-and-a-half years old. This conclusion holds for most mental abilities as well as emotions.

"Thus, we can look to human research to see what we might expect of our dogs. Just like a two-year-old child, our dogs clearly have emotions, but many fewer kinds of emotions than found in adult humans. At birth, a human infant only has an emotion that we might call excitement. This indicates how excited he is, ranging from very calm up to a state of frenzy. Within the first weeks of life the excitement state comes to take on a varying positive or a negative flavour, so we can now detect the general emotions of contentment and distress.

"In the next couple of months, disgust, fear, and anger become detectable in the infant. Joy often does not appear until the infant is nearly six months of age and it is followed by the emergence of shyness or suspicion. True affection, the sort that it makes sense to use the label "love" for, does not fully emerge until nine or ten months of age."

So, our Cockapoos truly love us — but we knew that already!

Canine Emotions

According to Dr Coren, dogs can't feel shame, so if you are housetraining your puppy, don't expect her to be ashamed if she makes a mess in the house, she can't; she simply isn't capable of feeling shame. But she will not like it when you ignore her when she's behaving badly, and she will love it when you praise her for eliminating outdoors. She is simply responding to your reaction with her simplified range of emotions.

Dr Coren also believes that dogs cannot experience guilt, contempt or pride. I'm not a psychology expert, but I'm not sure I agree. Take a Cockapoo to a local dog show, obedience class or agility competition, watch her perform and maybe win a rosette and applause - is the dog's delight something akin to pride?

Pictured looking very pleased with herself after winning a rosette is Mabel, bred by Eileen Jackson, of Brimstone Cockapoos, Cambridgeshire, England.

Cockapoos can certainly experience joy. They love your attention and praise; is there a more joyful sight for you both than when your Cockapoo runs towards you, tail wagging like crazy, with those big, loving eyes that say you're the best person in the world?

If you want to see a happy dog, just watch Cockapoos running free, swimming or snuggling up on the sofa with you. And when they dash off and return with the ball, isn't there a hint of pride there? Cockapoos are the friendliest of dogs and can certainly show empathy - "the ability to understand and share the feelings of another." They can pick up people's moods and emotions, which probably comes from their Poodle heritage, as Poodles are known for being intuitive - although some Spaniels can also be sensitive. This sensitivity is one reason why they make excellent therapy dogs.

Here is a story from Arleen Stone King, of Wisconsin, USA, owner of F1 Cockapoos Murphy and Daisy: *"I'd describe Cockapoos as loving, protective, intuitive, and docile - unless they are trying to protect or defend. They are very good at warning or "telling us" something is wrong.*

"When Murphy was about a year old, we had a 13-year-old Border Collie, Molly. One night, Murphy (who usually slept thru the night without a sound) began barking incessantly. It was about 1 a.m., and we got up thinking he had to go out for a potty break.

"I found him standing and barking at the threshold to the bedroom where Molly usually slept; but I didn't see her on the bed. A movement under the desk caught my eye, and it was Molly having a seizure. Murphy had known something was wrong, and he was telling us in his

language. Molly didn't make it past that night, but we would never have found her until morning if Murphy hadn't alerted us. It still brings tears to my eyes when I revisit that moment."

One emotion that all dogs can experience is jealousy. It may display itself by possessive or aggressive behaviour over food, a toy or a person, for example.

An interesting article was published in the PLOS (Public Library of Science) Journal following an experiment into whether dogs get jealous. Building on research that shows that six-month old infants display jealousy, the scientists studied 36 dogs in their homes and videoed their actions when their owners displayed affection to a realistic-looking stuffed canine *(pictured)*.

Over 75% of the dogs were likely to push or touch the owner when they interacted with the decoy! The envious mutts were more than three times as likely to do this for interactions with the stuffed dog, compared to when their owners gave their attention to other objects, including a book. Around a third tried to get between the owner and the plush toy, while a quarter of the put-upon pooches snapped at the dummy dog!

The researchers think that the dogs believed that the stuffed dog was real. They cite the fact that 86% of the dogs sniffed the toy's rear end during and after the experiment!

Professor Christine Harris from University of California in San Diego said: "Our study suggests not only that dogs do engage in what appear to be jealous behaviours, but also that they were seeking to break up the connection between the owner and a seeming rival. We can't really speak of the dogs' subjective experiences, of course, but it looks as though they were motivated to protect an important social relationship.

"Many people have assumed that jealousy is a social construction of human beings - or that it's an emotion specifically tied to sexual and romantic relationships. Our results challenge these ideas, showing that animals besides ourselves display strong distress whenever a rival usurps a loved one's affection."

25 Typical Cockapoo Traits

Every dog is different, of course, but there are also shared traits. Here are some typical characteristics - some of them also apply to other breeds, but put them all together and you have a blueprint for the Cockapoo.

1. Cockapoos are bred as companions and should have a naturally sunny temperament.

2. They make excellent companions and family dogs and are patient with children, once trained – it is sometimes a gentle Cockapoo who needs protecting from the kids!

3. Cockapoo puppies can be very *"mouthy"* as their ancestors were bred to pick up and carry things in their mouths. Long lasting chews and toys, a sharp "ACK!" or "NO!" when puppy teeth meet human flesh or clothing, and withdrawing your attention are the best solutions.

4. They are friendly with everyone and love to be petted or made a fuss of. Unlike some breeds, Cockapoos often bond with the entire family, rather than just one person.

5. Because they are friendly with everyone, they do not make good guard dogs.

6. One thing which surprises many new owners is the amount of exercise some need. If your Cockapoo was bred from working English Cocker Spaniels, invest in a good pair of hiking boots - two or more hours of exercise a day is not unusual! Another factor affecting exercise needs is how much the dog gets used to when young.

7. Cockapoos have been described as "Velcro dogs"; most want to be with you 24/7 and they may follow you from room to room. Spend some time apart while the dog is young to avoid separation anxiety - which is stressful for both dog and owner.

8. They do not like being left alone for long. If you are away from the home a lot, consider another type of dog not so dependent on humans for happiness.

9. Some Cockapoos retain sporting instincts and enjoy chasing small mammals and birds when outdoors. However, most would not harm a small creature if they caught one.

10. Even if they chase things outdoors, most Cockapoos live happily with cats and other animals inside the house when introduced at a young age.

11. Again, due to their sporting heritage and the intelligence of the Poodle, Cockapoos are happiest with mental as well as physical challenges.

12. Provided you put the time in, they are *"biddable,"* i.e. easy to train. Both Spaniels and Poodles were originally bred to work alongside Man, and dogs who were unable or unwilling to do so were not used in breeding lines. Cockapoos love canine competitions, such as Fly Ball and Agility, where physical AND mental agility is required. This intelligence and eagerness to please are powerful training aids.

13. An under-exercised, under-stimulated Cockapoo will display poor behaviour, as any dog would.

14. Praise, praise and praise is the way to train a Cockapoo; they do not respond well to rough treatment or loud, harsh voices, which can lead to timidity or switching off.

15. The same goes for housetraining; a Cockapoo can get the hang of it in a few days, as long as you are extremely vigilant in the beginning.

16. Many - although not all - Cockapoos have an instinctive love of water, which comes from the Poodle side.

17. They usually have a highly developed sense of smell and love to run with their noses to the ground, like a Spaniel.

18. Cockapoos often love playing in the snow – although their feet may need gently "de-icing" afterwards.

19. All Cockapoos love running off the lead (leash), although many are adaptable when it comes to exercise. They can go hiking for hours or snuggle up on the sofa all day.

20. They are not aggressive dogs and generally get on well with other dogs, provided they have been properly socialised.

21. A few Cockapoos can be a little nervous around new people, dogs and situations. (Poodles can also be wary of strangers until they get to know them). Socialisation from an early age is the key. The more varied positive experiences a dog has when young, the more comfortable and relaxed she will be as an adult. Don't constantly pick your Cockapoo up unless there is a danger of injury; panicky owners trigger a fear response in their dogs.

22. Timid Cockapoos with a lot of Spaniel heritage can sometimes display submissive urination, especially if they are under-socialised, insecure or over-excited. Proper socialisation and plenty of exercise can help combat the issue.

23. They enjoy being the centre of attention.

24. They are sensitive dogs and can pick up on emotions.

25. Cockapoos will steal your heart. OK, so that's not very scientific - but ask anyone who owns one!

....

Cause and Effect

As you've read, properly socialised and trained, well-bred Cockapoos make superb canine companions. But any dog can develop behaviour problems given a certain set of circumstances.

Dr Jacqueline Boyd, Senior Lecturer in Animal Science at Nottingham Trent University, UK, says: *"Cockapoos are the result of crossing two very active and intelligent breeds. Both breeds have a drive to be active and carry things. They're also very social breeds, always wanting to be with people. If left alone for long periods of time, they can suffer from separation anxiety and boredom. But they're not intentionally destructive, and punishing them after the event will just create an anxious dog."*

Every Cockapoo is an individual with his or her own temperament and environment, both of which influence the way the dog interacts with the world. Poor behaviour can result from a number of factors, including:

🐾 Poor breeding

🐾 Boredom, due to lack of exercise or mental challenges

🐾 Lack of socialisation

🐾 Being badly treated

🐾 Being left alone too long

🐾 A change in living conditions

🐾 Anxiety or insecurity

🐾 Fear

🐾 Being spoiled

Bad behaviour may show itself in different ways:

🐾 Constantly demanding attention

🐾 Chewing or destructive behaviour

🐾 Jumping up

🐾 Excessive barking

🐾 Nipping or biting

- 🐾 Soiling or urinating inside the house
- 🐾 Aggression towards other dogs
- 🐾 Growling

....

10 Ways to Avoid Bad Behaviour

Different dogs have different reasons for exhibiting bad behaviour; there is no single cure for everything. The best chance of ensuring your dog is well-adjusted and well-behaved is to start out on the right foot by following these simple guidelines:

1. **Buy from a good breeder** who uses her expertise to match suitable breeding pairs, taking into account good temperament, health, appearance and being "fit for function."

2. **Start socialisation right away.** We now realise the vital role that early socialisation plays in developing a well-rounded adult dog. Lack of socialisation is one of the major causes of unwanted behaviour, timidity or aggression. It is essential to expose your puppy to other people, places, animals and experiences as soon as possible; it will go a long way towards helping her become a stable, happy and trustworthy companion.

FACT ❯ Dogs are social creatures that thrive on sniffing, seeing, hearing and even licking. While the foundation for good behaviour is laid down during the first few months, dogs behave better when socialisation and training continues throughout their life.

Cockapoos like to be involved and be the centre of attention and it is important they learn that they are not the centre of the universe! Socialisation helps them to learn their place in that universe and to become comfortable with it.

3. **Start training early** - you can't start too soon. Like babies, puppies have incredibly enquiring minds that absorb a lot of new information quickly. Start teaching your puppy to learn her own name as well as some simple commands a couple of days after bringing her home.

4. **Basic training should cover several areas:** housetraining, chew prevention, puppy biting, simple commands like "sit," "come," "here" or "stay" and familiarising her with a collar or harness and lead. Adopt a gentle approach and keep training sessions short. Start with five or 10 minutes a day and build up. Puppy classes or adult dog obedience classes are a great way to start, but follow up at home afterwards. Spend a few minutes each day reinforcing what you have both learned in class - owners need training as well as dogs!

5. **Reward your dog for good behaviour.** All behaviour training should be based on positive reinforcement. So, praise and reward your dog when she does something good. Cockapoos love to please their owners; this trait and their intelligence speeds up the training process. The main aim of training is to build a good understanding between you and your dog.

6. **Ignore bad behaviour,** no matter how hard this may be. If, for example, your dog is chewing her way through your shoes, the couch or toilet rolls or eating things she shouldn't, remove her from the situation and then ignore her. For some dogs even negative attention is some attention. Remove yourself from the room so she learns that you give attention when YOU want to give it, NOT when she demands it. The more time you spend praising and rewarding good behaviour, while ignoring bad behaviour, the more likely she is to respond. If your pup is a chewer – and nearly all are - make sure she has durable toys and chews.

7. **Take the time to learn what sort of temperament your dog has.** Is she by nature nervous or confident? What was she like as a puppy, did she rush forward or hang back? Does she fight to get upright when on her back or is she happy to lie there? Is she a couch potato or a ball of fire? Your puppy's temperament affects her behaviour and how she responds to the world. A timid Cockapoo will not respond well to a loud approach on your part, whereas an energetic, strong-willed one will require more patience, exercise and mental stimulation.

8. **Exercise and stimulation.** A lack of either is another major reason for dogs behaving badly. Regular daily exercise as well as indoor or outdoor games and toys are all ways of stopping your dog from becoming bored or frustrated.

9. **Learn to leave your dog.** Just as leaving your dog alone for too long can lead to problems, so can being with her all the time. Cockapoos are reliant on humans for their happiness, but also need to learn that being alone for short periods is fine too, and not a cause for anxiety. When a dog becomes over-reliant on you, she gets stressed when you leave; this is called *separation anxiety*. Start a few days after she arrives home by leaving her for a few minutes and gradually extend the time so that you can eventually leave her for up to four hours.

10. **Love your Cockapoo – but don't spoil her,** however difficult that might be. Resist the urge to pick her up all the time or to give too much attention or treats. Don't constantly respond to her demands for attention or allow her to behave as she wants inside the house.

Separation Anxiety

When a dog leaves the litter, her owners become her new family or pack, and separation anxiety is an exaggerated fear response to being separated. It's not just dogs that experience it, people do too. About 7% of adults and 4% of children suffer from it. Typical symptoms for humans are:

❧ Distress at being separated from a loved one

❧ Fear of being alone

FACT ❯❯ Some 10%-15% of dogs suffer from separation anxiety. It is on the increase and recognised as the most common form of stress in dogs. Cockapoos bred from Toy Poodles can be more susceptible than those bred from Miniature Poodles.

Tell-Tale Signs

Does your Cockapoo do any of the following?

❧ Get anxious or stressed when you're getting ready to leave the house?

❧ Howl, whine or bark when you leave?

- 🐾 Tear paper, or chew furniture or other objects?

- 🐾 Dig, chew, or scratch at the carpet, doors or windows trying to join you?

- 🐾 Soil or urinate inside the house, even though she is housetrained? (This **only** occurs when left alone)

- 🐾 Exhibit restlessness - such as licking her coat excessively, pacing or circling?

- 🐾 Greet you ecstatically when you come home – even if you've only been out to the garage?

- 🐾 Wait by the window or door until you return?

- 🐾 Dislike spending time alone in the garden or yard?

- 🐾 Refuses to eat or drink if you leave her?

- 🐾 Howl or whine when one person leaves - even though others are still in the room or car?

If so, she may suffer from separation anxiety. Fortunately, in many cases this can be cured.

 Cockapoos are known as *"shadow"* or *"Velcro"* dogs; they like to stick close. Following you around the house is not necessarily a sign of separation anxiety - unless she gets visibly distressed when you leave. However, if they even want to follow you into the toilet, this CAN be a sign that separation anxiety is developing.

Causes

Dogs are pack animals and being alone is not a natural state for them. A puppy will emotionally latch on to her new owner, who has taken the place of mother and siblings. Puppies should be patiently taught in a structured way to get used to short periods of isolation if they are to be comfortable with it. It is also important for them to have a den where they feel safe - this may be a crate or dog bed where they can sleep in peace and quiet.

One thing that surprises some first-time owners, is just how much love they feel for their Cockapoo - and this is reciprocated by the dog! Dogs are truly life-enhancing. In the beginning you are setting patterns for the future and it is all too easy to give a lovable Cockapoo pup a huge amount of attention and cuddles, pick them up a lot, and not leave them alone for any length of time.

As the dog reaches adolescence, this can lead to behaviour issues, as the dog thinks she has the upper hand or becomes anxious about you not being there – or both. It may lead to attention-seeking behaviour, excessive barking, fussiness with food or separation anxiety. There are several causes of separation anxiety:

- 🐾 Not being left alone for short periods when young

- 🐾 Being left for too long by owners who are out of the house for most of the day

- 🐾 Poor socialisation with other dogs and people, resulting in too much focus and dependence on the owner

- 🐾 Boredom - Cockapoos are intelligent and most need mental as well as physical exercise

- 🐾 Leaving a dog too long in a crate or confined space

- Being over-indulgent with your dog; giving her too much attention
- Making too much of a fuss when you leave and return to the house
- Mistreatment in the past; a dog from a rescue centre may have insecurities and feel anxious when left alone
- Wilful behaviour due to a lack of training

Separation anxiety can also develop in old dogs. As they age, their hearing, sense of smell and sight often deteriorates. When this happens, a dog can become more dependent on its owners and anxious when separated from them.

 It may be very flattering and cute that your dog wants to be with you all of the time, but insecurity and separation anxiety are distressing for the dog.

If your dog starts showing the first signs, help her become more self-reliant and confident; she will be happier and more relaxed. Every dog is different, but here are some techniques that have proved effective in helping some dogs with separation anxiety:

Tips to Combat Separation Anxiety

1. After the first few days, leave your new puppy or adult dog for short periods, starting with literally a minute or two and gradually lengthening the time you are out of sight.

2. Tire your dog out before leaving her. Take her for a walk or play a game and, if you can, leave her with a view of the outside world, e.g. in a room with a patio door or low window.

3. Keep arrivals and departures low key and don't make a big fuss. Don't say hello or goodbye – either in words or body language, and don't sneak in and out of the house either.

4. Leave your dog a *"security blanket,"* such as an old piece of clothing you have recently worn that still has your scent on it, or leave a radio on - not too loud - in the room with the dog. Avoid a heavy rock station! If it will be dark when you return, leave a lamp on a timer. One breeder leaves a TV on low, on the same channel, so her dogs become familiar with the same programmes. This also cuts out any background noise such as traffic, people and barking dogs.

5. Associate your departure with something good. As you leave, give a rubber toy, like a Kong filled with a tasty treat, or a frozen treat, or spread her favourite treat over a Lickimat. This may take her mind off your departure - some dogs may refuse to touch the treat until you return home! Give her the treat when you are at home as well, so she doesn't just associate it with being left.

6. If your dog is used to a crate, try crating her when you go out. Many dogs feel safe there, and being in a crate can also help to reduce destructiveness. Always take the collar off first.

Pretend to leave the house, but listen for a few minutes. NEVER leave a dog in a crate with the door closed all day; two or three hours are long enough during the day. **Warning:** if your dog starts to show major signs of distress, remove her from the crate immediately as she may injure herself.

7. Structure and routine can help to reduce anxiety in your dog. Carry out regular activities, such as feeding and exercising, at the same time every day. Dogs read body language very well; many Cockapoos are intuitive. They may start to fret when they think you are going to leave them. One technique is to mimic your departure routine when you have no intention of leaving. So, put your coat on, grab your car keys, go out of the door and return a few seconds later. Do this randomly and regularly and it may help to reduce your dog's stress levels when you do it for real.

Looking relaxed in her chocolate box is eight-week-old Hermione, bred by Julie Shearman, of Crystalwood Cockapoos, Devon.

8. Some dogs show anxiety in new places; get her better socialised and used to different environments, dogs and people.

9. However lovable your Cockapoo is, if she is showing early signs of anxiety when separating from you, do not shower her with attention all the time when you are there. She will become overly dependent on you.

10. If you have to leave the house for a few hours at a time, ask a neighbour or friend to call in - or drop the dog off with them.

11. Getting another dog to keep the first one company can help, but only if you have the time and money for two or more dogs. Can you afford double the vet and food bills?

Sit-Stay-Down

Another technique for helping to reduce separation anxiety is to practise the common *"Sit-Stay"* or *"Down-Stay"* exercises using positive reinforcement. The goal is to be able to move briefly out of your dog's sight while she is in the *Stay* position.

Through this your dog learns that she can remain calmly and happily in one place while you go about your normal daily life. You have to progress slowly with this. Get your dog to sit and stay and then walk away from her for five seconds, then 10, 20, a minute and so on. Reward your dog with a treat or toy every time she stays calm.

Then move out of sight or out of the room for a few seconds, return and give her the treat if she is calm, gradually lengthen the time you are out of sight. If you're watching TV with your Cockapoo snuggled up at your side and you get up for a snack, say "stay" and leave the room. When you come back, give her a treat or praise her quietly. It is a good idea to practise these techniques after exercise or when your dog is a little sleepy (but not exhausted), as she is likely to be more relaxed.

FACT Canine separation anxiety is NOT the result of disobedience or lack of training. It's a psychological condition; your dog feels anxious and insecure.

NEVER punish your dog for showing signs of separation anxiety – even if she has chewed your best shoes. This will only make her worse.

NEVER leave your dog unattended in a crate for long periods or if she is frantic to get out, it can cause physical or mental harm. If you're thinking of leaving an animal all day in a crate while you are out of the house, get a rabbit or a hamster - not a dog.

....

Excessive Barking

Cockapoos are not known for barking a lot, but like any dog, they can get into the habit of barking too much if you don't put a stop to it. Dogs, especially youngsters and adolescents, sometimes behave in ways you might not want them to, until they learn that this type of unwanted behaviour doesn't earn them any rewards. Dogs from the Toy Group, such as the Toy Poodle, can become yappy if their barking isn't checked.

Some puppies start off by being noisy from the outset, while others hardly bark at all until they reach adolescence or adulthood. Some may be triggered by other, noisier dogs in the household.

On our website we hear from owners worried that their young dogs are not barking enough. However, we get far more posts from owners whose dogs are barking too much!

We had one dog that hardly barked at all until he was two years old. We needn't have worried, by the time he got to five or six years old, he loved the sound of his own voice! We have been in contact with several Cockapoo owners in a similar position; their dog hardly barked when young and now barks too much. If that's the case, then try **the Speak and Shush** technique outlined later in this chapter.

Some Cockapoos will bark if someone comes to the door – and then welcome them like best friends - while others remain quiet.

There can be a number of reasons a dog barks too much, A dog may be:

- 🐾 Anxious or Fearful
- 🐾 Lonely
- 🐾 Bored
- 🐾 Attention-Seeking
- 🐾 Possessive
- 🐾 Over-Protective/Territorial
- 🐾 Copying Other Dogs

FACT *Excessive, habitual barking often develops during adolescence or early adulthood (before the age of two years), as your dog becomes more confident.*

If your barking dog is an adolescent, she is probably still teething, so get a good selection of hardy toys and healthy chew treats to keep her occupied and gnawing - give her these when she is *quiet*, not when she is barking.

Your behaviour can also encourage excessive barking. If your dog barks non-stop for several seconds or minutes and then you give her a treat to quieten her, she associates barking with getting a nice treat.

A better way to deal with it is to say in a firm voice: *"Quiet"* after she has made a few barks. When she stops, praise her and she will get the idea that what you want her to do is stop. The trick is to stop the bad behaviour straight away before it becomes ingrained.

If she's barking to get your attention, ignore her. If that doesn't work, leave the room and don't allow her to follow you, so you deprive her of your attention. Do this as well if her barking and attention-seeking turns to nipping. Tell her to *"Stop"* in a firm voice - not shouting - remove your hand or leg and, if necessary, leave the room.

As humans, we can use our voice in many different ways: to express happiness or anger, to scold, to shout a warning, and so on. Dogs are the same; different barks and noises give out different messages. **Listen** to your dog and try and get an understanding of Cockapoo language. Learn to recognise the difference between an alert bark, an excited bark, a demanding bark, a high pitched bark, an aggressive bark or a plain "I'm barking 'coz I can bark" bark!

If your dog is barking at other dogs, arm yourselves with lots of treats and spend time calming your dog down. With Cockapoos, this is rarely pure aggression, it is more often a fear response – especially if they are on a lead (leash), as they know they cannot escape so are trying to make themselves look and sound fierce to the other dog or dogs.

Listen to the tone of the bark, a high-pitched bark is usually a sign of fear or nervousness. Ears flattened back on the head is another sign of nerves or fear.

When she starts to bark wildly at another dog while on the lead, distract her by letting her sniff a treat in your hand. Make your dog sit and give a treat. Talk in a gentle manner and keep showing and giving her a treat for remaining calm and not barking. Get her to focus her attention and gaze on you and the treat, not the other dog. There are several videos on YouTube that show how to deal with this problem in the manner described here.

Speak and Shush!

Cockapoos are not good guard dogs, most of them couldn't care less if somebody breaks in and walks off with the family silver – they are more likely to greet with the burglar with a wagging tail and approach for a treat or a pat as the villains make off with your prize possessions!

But if you do have a problem with excessive barking when visitors arrive, the Speak and Shush technique is one way of getting a dog to quieten down. If your Cockapoo doesn't bark and you want her to, a slight variation of this method can also be used to get her to bark as a way of alerting you that someone is at the door. We have used this method very successfully.

When your dog barks at an arrival at your house, gently praise her after the first few barks. If she persists, gently tell her that that is enough. Like humans, some dogs can get carried away with the sound of their own voice, so try and discourage too much barking from the outset. The Speak and Shush technique teaches your dog or puppy to bark and be quiet on command.

Get a friend to stand outside your front door and say "Speak" - or "Woof" or "Alert." This is the cue for your accomplice to knock or ring the bell – don't worry if you both feel like idiots, it will be worth the embarrassment!

When your dog barks, praise her profusely. You can even bark yourself in encouragement! After a few good barks, say "Shush" and then dangle a tasty treat in front of her nose. She will stop barking as soon as she sniffs the treat, because it is physically impossible for a dog to sniff and woof at the same time.

Praise your dog again as she sniffs quietly and then give her the treat. Repeat this routine a few times a day and your Cockapoo will quickly learn to bark whenever the doorbell rings and you ask her to speak.

Eventually your dog will bark AFTER your request but BEFORE the doorbell rings, meaning she has learned to bark on command. Even better, she will learn to anticipate the likelihood of getting a treat following your "Shush" request and will also be quiet on command.

With Speak and Shush training, progressively increase the length of required shush time before offering a treat - at first just a couple of seconds, then three, five, 10, 20, and so on. By alternating instructions to speak and shush, the dog is praised and rewarded for barking on request and also for stopping barking on request.

"Yes, I live on the third floor ... but I have never heard any howling sounds."

If you want your dog to be more vocal, you need to have some treats at the ready, waiting for that rare bark. Wait until she barks - for whatever reason - then say "Speak" or whatever word you want to use, praise her and give her a treat. At this stage, she won't know why she is receiving the treat. Keep praising her every time she barks and give her a treat. After you've done this for several days, hold a treat in your hand in front of her face and say "Speak."

Your dog will probably still not know what to do, but will eventually get so frustrated at not getting the treat that she will bark. At which point, praise her and give her the treat. We trained a Labrador to do this in a week or so and he barked his head off when anybody came to the door or whenever we give him the command: "Speak."

Always use your "encouraging teacher voice" when training; speak softly when instructing your dog to Shush, and reinforce the Shush with whisper-praise. The softer you speak, the more your dog will be likely to pay attention. Cockapoos respond very well to training when it is fun, short and reward-based.

Dealing with Aggression

Some breeds are more prone to aggression than others; fortunately, this issue is not often seen in Cockapoos, so feel free to skip this section. However, given certain situations, any dog can growl, bark or even bite. Sometimes a dog learns unwanted behaviour from another dog or dogs, but often it is because the dog feels insecure or has become too territorial or protective of her owner, toys or food.

NOTE: Puppy biting is not aggression; all puppies bite; they explore the world with their noses and mouths. It is, however, important to train your cute little pup not to bite, as she may cause injury to someone if she continues to bite when fully grown.

Any dog can bite when under stress and, however unlikely it may seem, so can Cockapoos. Here are some different types of aggressive behaviour:

- Growling at you or other people
- Snarling or lunging at other dogs
- Growling or biting if you or another animal goes near her food
- Being possessive with toys

- Growling if you pet or show attention to another animal
- Marking territory by urinating inside the house
- Growling and chasing other small animals
- Growling and chasing cars, joggers or strangers
- Standing in your way, blocking your path
- Pulling and growling on the lead

Tip As well as snarling, lunging, barking or biting, look out for other physical signs, such as raised hackles, top lip curled back to bare the teeth, ears up and tail raised.

One reason for aggression can be that the dog has not been fully socialised, and so feels threatened or challenged. Rather than being comfortable with new situations, other dogs or intrusions, she responds using "the best form of defence is attack" philosophy and displays aggressive behaviour to anything or anyone she is unsure of.

If the aggression is rooted in fear, it may stem from a bad experience the dog has suffered. I know a number of naturally non-aggressive dogs that have started to growl and snarl at other dogs in later life, after they have been the victim of an attack by another dog or dogs.

An owner's treatment of a dog can be a further reason. An owner that shouts, uses physical violence or reprimands the dog too often can cause snapping or other unwanted behaviour from the dog. Aggression breeds aggression. Dogs can also become aggressive or depressed if they are consistently left alone, cooped up, under-fed or under-exercised.

Many dogs are more combative on the lead (leash). This is because they cannot run away; fight or flight. They know they can't escape, and so make themselves as frightening as possible and bark or growl to warn off the other dog or person. Train your dog from an early age to be comfortable walking on the lead. And socialisation is, of course, vital — the first four to five months of a puppy's life is the critical time.

If your dog **suddenly** shows a change of behaviour and becomes aggressive, have her checked out by a vet to rule out any underlying medical reason for the crankiness, such as earache or toothache. Raging hormones can be another reason for aggression or a change in behaviour.

A further reason is they have been spoiled by their owners and have come to believe that the world revolves around them. Not spoiling your Cockapoo and teaching her what is acceptable behaviour in the first place is the best preventative measure. Early training, especially during puppyhood and adolescence - before she develops unwanted habits - can save a lot of trouble in the future.

Professional dog trainers employ a variety of techniques with a dog that has become aggressive. Firstly, they will look at the causes and good trainers use reward-based methods to try and cure aggressive or fearful dogs. *Counter conditioning* is a positive training technique used by many professionals to help change a dog's aggressive behaviour towards other dogs.

A typical example would be a dog that snarls, barks and lunges at other dogs while on the lead. It is the presence of other dogs that is triggering the dog to act in a fearful or anxious manner. Every time the dog sees another dog, she is given a tasty treat to counter the aggression. With enough steady repetition, the dog starts to associate the presence of other dogs with a tasty treat.

Properly and patiently done, the final result is a dog that calmly looks to the owner for the treat whenever she sees another dog while on the lead. Whenever you encounter a potentially aggressive situation, divert your Cockapoo's attention by turning her head away from the other dog and towards you, so that she cannot make eye contact with the other dog.

Aggression Towards People

Desensitisation is the most common method of treating aggression. It starts by breaking down the triggers for the behaviour one small step at a time. The aim is to get the dog to associate pleasant things with the trigger, i.e. people or a specific person whom she previously feared or regarded as a threat.

This is done through using positive reinforcement, such as praise or treats. Successful desensitisation takes time, patience and knowledge. If your dog is starting to growl at people, there are a couple of techniques you can try to break her of this bad habit before it develops into full-blown biting.

One method is to arrange for some friends to come around, one at a time. When they arrive at your house, get them to scatter kibble on the floor in front of them so that your dog associates the arrival of people with tasty treats.

As they move into the house, and your dog eats the kibble, praise your dog for being a good boy or girl. Manage your dog's environment. Don't over-face her.

Most Cockapoos love children, but if yours is at all anxious around them, separate them or carefully supervise their time together in the beginning. Children typically react enthusiastically to dogs and some dogs may regard this as frightening or an invasion of their space.

Some dogs, particularly spoiled ones, may show aggression towards people other than the owner. Several people have written to our website on this topic and it usually involves a partner or husband. Often the dog is jealous of the attention the owner is giving to the other person, or it could be that the dog feels threatened by him; this is more common with Toy breeds.

If it happens with your Cockapoo, the key is for the partner to gradually gain the trust of the dog. He or she should show that they are not a threat by speaking gently to the dog and giving treats for good behaviour. Avoid eye contact, as the dog may see this as a challenge. If the subject of the aggression lives in the house, then let this person give the dog her daily feeds.

A crate is also a useful tool for removing an aggressive dog from the situation for short periods of time, allowing her out gradually and praising good behaviour. As with any form of aggression, the trick is to take steps to deal with it **immediately.**

In extreme cases, when a dog exhibits persistent bad behaviour that the owner is unable to correct, a canine professional may be the answer. However, this is not an inexpensive option. Far better to spend time training and socialising your dog as soon as you get her.

Coprophagia (Eating Faeces)

It is hard for us to understand why a dog would want to eat her or any other animal's faeces (stools, poop or poo, call it what you will), but it does happen - some dogs love the stuff!

Nobody fully understands why; it may simply be an unpleasant behaviour trait, or there could be an underlying reason. It is thought that the inhumane and useless potty-training technique of *"sticking the dog's nose in it"* when she has eliminated inside the house can also encourage it.

If your dog eats poop from the cat litter tray - a problem several owners have contacted us about - place the litter tray somewhere your dog can't get to it – but the cat can. Perhaps on a shelf, or put a guard around it, small enough for the cat to get through, but not your dog.

Our dog sometimes eats cow or horse poop on walks in the countryside. He usually stops when we tell him to and hasn't suffered any after effects – so far. But the offending material sticks to the fur around his mouth and has to be cleaned off - sometimes he allows himself the treat of rolling in the stuff and then has to be hosed down. You may find that your Cockapoo will roll in fox poo to cover the fox's scent.

 Try and avoid areas you know are frequented by foxes if you can, as their faeces can transmit several diseases, including Canine Parvovirus or worms. Neither of these should pose a serious health risk if your dog is up to date with vaccinations and worming treatments.

Vets have found that canine diets with low levels of fibre and high levels of starch increase the likelihood of coprophagia. If your dog is exhibiting this behaviour, first check that the diet you are feeding is nutritionally complete. Look at the first ingredient on the dog food packet or tin – is it corn or meat? Does she look underweight? Check that you are feeding the right amount.

If there is no underlying medical reason, you will have to try and modify your dog's behaviour. Remove cat litter trays, clean up after your dog and do not allow her to eat her own faeces. If it's not there, she can't eat it. One breeder told us of a dog that developed the habit after being allowed to soil his crate as a pup, caused by the owners not being vigilant in their housetraining. The puppy got used to eating his own faeces and then continued to do it as an adult, when it became quite a problem.

Don't reprimand the dog for eating faeces. A better technique is to cause a distraction while she is in the act and then remove the offending material.

 *Coprophagia is sometimes seen in pups six months to a year old and often disappears after this age.*

....

This chapter provides just a general overview of canine behaviour. If your Cockapoo exhibits persistent problems, particularly if she is aggressive towards people or other dogs, consider seeking help from a reputable canine behaviourist, such as those listed the Association of Professional Dog Trainers, at: http://www.apdt.co.uk (UK) or https://apdt.com (USA).

Check they use positive reinforcement techniques - the old Alpha-dominance theories of forcefully imposing your will on a dog have largely been discredited. Even if they hadn't, Cockapoos do not respond well to this type of treatment.

8. Training a Cockapoo

Training a young dog is not unlike bringing up a child. Put lots of time in early on to work for a better mutual understanding and you'll be rewarded with a well-adjusted, sociable individual who is a joy to live with and you can take anywhere.

Dogs are not clones, some are more strong-willed, independent or have higher energy drives than others. But generally, Cockapoos want to please their owners, they enjoy showing off and are receptive to training.

This won't magically happen overnight; you have to make time for training. Cockapoos are super family dogs and companions, but let yours behave exactly how he or she wants and you could finish up with an attention-seeking adult who rules your life!

Cockapoos are highly motivated by reward — especially praise as well as treats - and this is a big bonus when it comes to training. Your dog WANTS to please you and enjoys learning. All you have to do is spend the time teaching him what you want him to do, then repeat the actions so it becomes second nature. The secret of good training can be summed up in four words:

- ❖ Consistency
- ❖ Praise
- ❖ Patience
- ❖ Reward

Many owners say that Cockapoos have empathy (the ability to pick up on the feelings of others). They respond well to your encouragement and a positive atmosphere; they do not respond well to shouting or heavy-handed training methods.

Cockapoos are certainly *"biddable,"* i.e. willing to learn - provided you make it clear exactly what you want them to do; don't give conflicting signals.

They enjoy socialising and love a challenge. Cockapoos can excel as therapy dogs - see Denise Knightley's story at the end of this chapter on how Cockapoo Carmen Rose is helping young children. They also do well in Obedience and Agility, which not only keeps their bodies exercised, but their minds too.

Police and other service dogs are trained to a very high level with only a ball for reward. Don't always use treats with your Cockapoo; praise or play time is often enough reward. Try getting your pup used to a small piece of carrot or apple as a healthy low-calorie alternative to traditional dog treats.

The Intelligence of Dogs

Psychologist and canine expert Dr Stanley Coren has written a book called *The Intelligence of Dogs* in which he ranks the breeds. He surveyed dog trainers to compile the list and used

Understanding of New Commands and *Obeying First Command* as his standards of intelligence. He says there are three types of dog intelligence:

- 🐾 Adaptive Intelligence (learning and problem-solving ability). This is specific to the individual dog and is measured by canine IQ tests
- 🐾 Instinctive Intelligence. This is specific to the individual dog and is measured by canine IQ tests
- 🐾 Working/Obedience Intelligence. This is breed-dependent

He divides dogs into six groups and the brainboxes of the canine world are the 10 breeds ranked in the *"Brightest Dogs"* section of his list. It will come as no surprise to anyone who has ever been into the countryside and seen sheep being worked by a farmer and his right-hand man (his dog) to learn that the Border Collie is the most intelligent of all dogs.

Number Two is the Poodle *(pictured),* followed by the German Shepherd Dog, Golden Retriever, Doberman Pinscher, Shetland Sheepdog, Papillon, Rottweiler and Australian Cattle Dog. All dogs in this class:

- 🐾 Understand New Commands with Fewer than Five Repetitions
- 🐾 Obey a First Command 95% of the Time or Better

The English and American Cocker Spaniels are ranked at Number 21 and 24 respectively, out of 138 breeds. They are both in the second group, Excellent Working Dogs, Understanding of New Commands: 5 to 15 repetitions, Obey First Command: 85% of the time or better. The full list can be seen here: https://en.wikipedia.org/wiki/The_Intelligence_of_Dogs

By the author's own admission, the drawback of this rating scale is that it is heavily weighted towards obedience-related behavioural traits, which are often found in working dogs, rather than understanding or creativity (found in hunting dogs).

As a result, some dogs, such as the Bully breeds – Bulldogs, Mastiffs, Bull Terriers, Pugs, French Bulldogs, etc. - are ranked quite low on the list, due to their independent or stubborn nature.

Both the Poodle and the Cocker Spaniel are willing to learn: the Poodle to show off his fearsome intelligence and the Cocker Spaniel to please you. Your Cockapoo will be a mixture of the two.

FACT ❭ *If your Cockapoo has more of a Poodle brainbox, not only has he the capacity to learn very quickly, but you will also have to find ways of challenging that active mind. Boredom can lead to mischief.*

Whichever breed your Cockapoo takes after, it's true to say that you are starting out with a dog that has the intelligence to pick up new commands quickly and the desire to please you. All you have to do is convince him that good things will happen when he obeys your commands!

Five Golden Rules

1. Training must be reward-based, not punishment based.
2. Keep sessions short or your dog will get bored.
3. Never train when you are in a rush or a bad mood.
4. Training after exercise is fine, but never train when your dog is exhausted.
5. Keep sessions fun; *give your Cockapoo a chance to shine!*

Energetic or independent Cockapoos may try to push the boundaries when they reach adolescence, i.e. as they come out of puppyhood and before they mature into adults, and some may act like spoiled children if allowed to.

 If you have a high spirited, high energy Cockapoo, you have to use your brain to think of ways to make training challenging and to persuade your dog that what you want him to do is actually what HE wants to do!

He will come to realise that when he does what you ask of him, something good happens – verbal praise, pats, play time, treats, etc. You need to be firm with a strong-willed or stubborn dog, but all training should still be carried out using positive techniques.

Establishing the natural order of things is not something forced on a dog through shouting or violence; it is brought about by mutual consent and good training.

Cockapoos are happiest and behave best when they are familiar and comfortable with their place in the household. If you have adopted an older dog, you can still train her, but it will take a little longer to get rid of bad habits and instil good manners. Patience and persistence are the keys here.

Socialisation is a very important aspect of training. Your puppy's breeder should have already begun this process with the litter and then it's up to you to keep it going when puppy arrives home. Young pups can absorb a great deal of information, but they are also vulnerable to bad experiences.

They need exposing – in a positive manner - to different people, other animals and situations. If not, they can find them very frightening when they do finally encounter them later. They may react by cowering, urinating, barking, growling or even snapping.

If they have a lot of good experiences with other people, places, noises, situations and animals before four or five months old, they are less likely to either be timid or nervous or try to establish dominance later. Don't just leave your dog at home in the early days, take him out and about with you, get him used to new people, places and noises. Dogs that miss out on being socialised can pay the price later.

All pups are chewers. If you are not careful, some young pups and adolescents will chew through anything – wires, phone chargers, remote controls, bedding, rugs, etc. Young dogs are not infrequent visitors to veterinary clinics to have *"foreign objects"* removed from their stomachs. Train your young pup only to chew the things you give – so don't give him your old slippers, an old piece of carpet or anything that resembles something you don't want him to chew, he won't know the difference between the old and the new. Buy purpose-made long-lasting chew toys.

Jumping up is another common issue. Cockapoos are generally enthusiastic about life, so it's often a natural reaction when they see somebody. You don't, however, want your dog to jump up on Grandad when he has just come back from a romp through the muddy woods and a swim in a dirty pond (your dog, not Grandad!). While still small, teach your dog not to jump up!

A puppy class is one of the best ways of getting a pup used to being socialised and trained. This should be backed up by short sessions of a few minutes of training a day back home.

 Some Cockapoo puppies, especially those with a lot of working instinct, can be "full-on" and very "mouthy." Do not give your young pup too much attention, and choose training times when he is relaxed, perhaps slightly tired, but not exhausted.

Cockapoos are a good choice for first-time dog owners, and anybody prepared to put in a fair bit of time can train one. But if you do need some professional one-on-one tuition (for you and the dog), choose a trainer registered with the Association of Professional Dog Trainers (APDT) or other positive reward-based training school, as the old Alpha-dominance theories have gone out the window.

When you train your dog, it should never be a battle of wills; it should be a positive learning experience for you both. Bawling at the top of your voice or smacking should play NO part in training any dog, but especially one as sensitive and loving as the Cockapoo.

15 Training Tips

1. **Start training and socialising straight away**. Like babies, puppies learn quickly and it's this learned behaviour that stays with them through adult life. Puppy training should start with just a few minutes a day a couple of days after arriving home.

2. **Your voice is a very important training tool.** Your dog has to learn to understand your language and you have to understand him. Commands should be issued in a calm, authoritative voice - not shouted. Praise should be given in a happy, encouraging voice, accompanied by stroking or patting. If your dog has done something wrong, use a stern voice, not a harsh shriek. This applies even if your Cockapoo is unresponsive at the beginning.

3. **Avoid giving your dog commands you know you can't enforce.** Every time you give a command you don't enforce, he learns that commands are optional.

   One command equals one response. Give your dog only one command - twice maximum - then gently enforce it. Repeating commands will make him tune out, and teach him that the first few commands are a bluff.

Telling your dog to *"SIT, SIT, SIT, SIT!!!"* is neither efficient nor effective. Say a single *"SIT,"* gently place him in the Sit position and praise him.

4. **Train your dog gently and humanely.** Cockapoos are sensitive by nature and do not respond well to being shouted at or hit. Keep training sessions short and upbeat so the whole experience is enjoyable for you and for him. If obedience training is a bit of a bore, pep things up a bit by *"play training"* by using constructive, non-adversarial games.

5. **Do not try to dominate your dog.** Training should be mutual, i.e. your dog should do something because he WANTS to do it and he knows that you want him to do it. As one breeder said, in all her years of raising Cockapoos, she had never once come across an Alpha Cockapoo. Cockapoos are not interested in dominating you — although they might try and push the boundaries.

6. **Begin training at home around the house and garden/yard.** How well your dog responds at home affects his behaviour away from the home as well. If he doesn't respond well at home, he certainly won't respond any better out and about where there are 101 distractions, e.g. interesting scents, people, food scraps, other dogs and small animals or birds.

7. **Mealtimes are a great time to start training.** Teach Sit and Stay at breakfast and dinner, rather than just putting the dish down and letting him dash over immediately. At first, he won't know what you mean, so gently place him into the sit position while you say *"Sit."* Place a hand on his chest during the Stay command - gradually letting go — and then give him the command to eat, followed by encouraging praise - he'll soon get the idea.

8. **Use his name often and in a positive manner** so he gets used to the sound of it. He won't know what it means at first, but it won't take long before he realises you're talking to him.

9. **DON'T use his name when reprimanding, warning or punishing.** He should trust that when he hears his name, good things happen. He should always respond to his name with enthusiasm, never hesitancy or fear. Use words such as *"No," "Ack!"* or *"Bad Boy/Girl"* in a stern (not shouted) voice instead.

   Some parents prefer not to use "No" with their dog, as they use it so often around the kids that it can confuse the pup! When a puppy is corrected by his mother, e.g. – if he bites her – she growls to warn him not to do it again. Using a short sharp sound like *"Ack!"* can work surprisingly well; it does for us.

10. **Don't give your dog lots of attention (even negative attention) when he misbehaves.** Cockapoos love attention and if yours gets lots when he jumps up on you, you are inadvertently reinforcing bad behaviour. If he jumps up demanding your attention, push him away, use the command *"No"* or *"Down"* and then ignore him. If necessary, leave the room so he learns that when he has displeased you, he is deprived of your presence.

11. **Timing is critical.** When your puppy does something right, praise him immediately. If you wait a while, he will have no idea what he has done right. Similarly, when he does something wrong, correct him straight away.

12. **If he has an "accident" in the house, don't shout and definitely don't rub his nose in it.** This will only make things

worse and encourage your dog to fear you. He may even start hiding and peeing or pooping behind the couch or other inappropriate places. If you catch him in the act, use your *"No!"* or *"Ack!"* sound and immediately carry him out of the house.

Then use your toilet command and praise or give a treat when he performs. If your pup is constantly eliminating indoors, you are probably not keeping a close enough eye on him or not picking up on the signs.

13. **In the beginning, give your dog attention when YOU want to – not when he wants it.** When you are training, give your puppy lots of positive attention when he is good. But if he starts jumping up, nudging you constantly or barking to demand your attention, ignore him.

    Don't give in to the demands. Wait a while and pat him when you are ready and AFTER he has stopped demanding your attention.

14. **You can give a Cockapoo TOO MUCH attention in the beginning.** This may create a rod for your own back when they grow into needy adults that are over-reliant on you. They may even develop Separation Anxiety, which is stressful for both dog AND owner.

15. **Start as you mean to go on.** In terms of training, treat your cute little pup as though he were fully-grown. Introduce the rules you want him to live by as an adult. If you don't want your dog to take over your couch or bed or jump up at people when he is an adult, train him not to do it while still young. You can't have one set of rules for a pup and one set for a fully-grown dog; he won't understand.

Also make sure that everybody in the household sticks to the same set of rules. If the kids let him jump on the couch and you don't, your dog will not know what is allowed and what isn't.

Teaching Basic Commands

The Three Ds

The three Ds – **Distance, Duration** and **Distraction** – are the cornerstone of a good training technique.

Duration is the length of time your dog remains in the command.

Distance is how far you can walk away without your dog breaking the command.

Distraction is the number of external stimuli - such as noise, scents, people, other animals, etc. - your dog can tolerate before breaking the command.

Only increase one of the Three Ds at a time. For example, if your new pup has just learned to sit on command, gradually increase the time by a second or two as you go along. Moving away from the dog or letting the kids or the cat into the room would increase the Distance or Distraction level and make the command too difficult for your pup to hold.

If you are teaching the Stay, gradually increase EITHER the distance OR the time (s)he is in the Stay position; don't increase both at once. Start off by training your dog in your home before moving into the garden or yard where there are more distractions - even if it is quiet and you are alone, outdoor scents and sights will be a big distraction for a young dog. Once you have mastered the commands in a home environment, progress to the park.

The key to successful training is to implement the Three Ds progressively and slowly. Don't expect too much too soon. Work within your dog's capabilities, move forward one tiny step at a time and thereby set your dog up to consistently succeed, not fail.

The Sit

Teaching the Sit command to your Cockapoo is relatively easy. Teaching a young pup to sit still for any length of time is a bit more difficult! If your little protégé is very distracted and/or high energy, it may be easier to put him on a lead (leash) to hold his attention in the beginning.

Stand facing each other and hold a treat between your thumb and fingers just an inch or so above his head and let him sniff it.

Don't let your fingers and the treat get much further away or you might have trouble getting him to move his body into a sitting position. In fact, if your dog jumps up when you try to guide him into the Sit, you're probably holding your hand too far away from his nose. If your dog backs up, you can practise with a wall behind him.

As he reaches up to sniff it, move the treat upwards and back over the dog towards his tail at the same time as saying *"Sit."* Most dogs will track the treat with their eyes and follow it with their noses, causing their snouts to point straight up.

As his head moves up toward the treat, his rear end should automatically go down towards the floor. TaDa! (drum roll!).

The second he sits, say *"Yes!"* Give him the treat and tell your dog he's a good boy/girl. Stroke and praise him for as long as he stays in the sitting position. If he jumps up on his back legs and paws you while you are moving the treat, be patient and start all over again. At this stage, don't expect your bouncy little pupil to sit for more than a nanosecond!

NOTE: For positive reinforcement, use the words *Yes!, Good Boy!* or *Good Girl!*

Another method is to put one hand on his chest and with your other hand, gently push down on his rear end until he is sitting, while saying *"Sit."* Give him a treat and praise; even though you have made him do it, he will eventually associate the position with the word "sit."

Once your dog catches on, leave the treat in your pocket (or have it in your other hand). Repeat the sequence, but this time your dog will just follow your empty hand. Say *"Sit"* and bring your empty hand in front of your dog's nose, holding your fingers as if you had a treat. Move your hand exactly as you did when you held the treat. When your dog sits, say *"Yes!"* and then give him a treat from your other hand or your pocket.

Gradually lessen the amount of movement with your hand. First, say *"Sit"* then hold your hand eight to 10 inches above your dog's face and wait a moment. Most likely, he will sit. If he doesn't, help

him by moving your hand back over his head, like you did before, but make a smaller movement this time. Then try again. Your goal is to eventually just say *"Sit"* without having to move or extend your hand at all.

Once your dog reliably sits on cue, you can ask him to sit whenever you meet and talk to people (it may not work straight away, but it might help to calm him down a bit).

The key is anticipation. Give your dog the cue before he gets too excited to hear you and before he starts jumping up on the person just arrived. Generously reward him the instant he sits. Say *"Yes"* and give treats/praise every few seconds while he holds the Sit.

Whenever possible, ask the person you're greeting to help you out by walking away if your dog gets up from the sit and lunges or jumps towards them. With many consistent repetitions of this exercise, your dog will learn that lunging or jumping makes people go away, and polite sitting makes them stay and give attention. You may need to have him on a lead (leash) to begin with.

You can practise training your bouncy Cockapoo not to jump up by arranging for a friend to visit, then for him or her to come in and out of the house several times. Each time, show the treat, give the "Sit" command (initially, don't ask your dog to hold the sit for any length of time), and then allow him to greet your friend. Ask your friend to reach down to pat your dog, rather than standing straight and encouraging the dog to jump up for a greeting.

If your dog is still jumping up, you can use a harness and lead inside the house to physically prevent him from jumping up at people, while still training him to sit when someone arrives. Treats and praise are the key. You can also use the *"Off"* command - and reward with praise or a treat for success - when you want your dog NOT to jump up at a person, or not to jump up on furniture.

"Sit" is a useful command and can be used in a number of different situations. For example, when you are putting his lead on, while you are preparing his food, when he returns the ball you have just thrown, when he is jumping up, demanding attention or getting over-excited.

The Stay

This is a very useful command, but it's not so easy to teach a lively and distracted young Cockapoo pup to stay still for any length of time. Here is a simple method to get your dog to stay; if you are training a young dog, don't ask him to stay for more than a few seconds at the beginning.

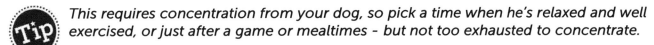

This requires concentration from your dog, so pick a time when he's relaxed and well exercised, or just after a game or mealtimes - but not too exhausted to concentrate.

1. Tell your dog to sit or lie down, but instead of giving a treat as soon as he hits the floor, hold off for one second. Then say *"Yes!"* in an enthusiastic voice and give him a treat. If your dog bounces up again instantly, have two treats ready. Feed one right away, before he has time to move; then say *"Yes!"* and feed the second treat.

2. You need a release word or phrase. It might be *"Free!"* or *"Here!"* or a word that you only use to release your dog from this command. Once you've given the treat, immediately give your release cue and encourage your dog to get up. Then repeat the exercise, perhaps up to a dozen times in one training session, gradually wait a tiny bit longer before releasing the treat. (You can delay the first treat for a moment if your dog bounces up).

3. A common mistake is to hold the treat high and then give the reward slowly. As your dog doesn't know the command yet, he sees the treat coming and gets up to meet the food. Instead, bring the treat toward your dog quickly - the best place to deliver it is right between his front paws. If you're working on a Sit-Stay, give the treat at chest height.

4. When your dog can stay for several seconds, start to add a little distance. At first, you'll walk backwards, because your dog is more likely to get up to follow you if you turn away from him. Take one single step away, then step back towards your dog and say *"Yes!"* and give the treat. Give him the signal to get up immediately, even if five seconds haven't passed. The stay gets harder for your dog depending on how long it is, how far away you are, and what else is going on around him.

5. Remember **DISTANCE, DURATION, DISTRACTION.** For best success in teaching a Stay, work on one factor at a time. Whenever you make one factor more difficult, such as distance, ease up on the others at first, then build them back up. So, when you take that first step back from your dog, adding distance, you should cut the duration of the stay.

6. Once he's mastered the Stay with you alone, move the training on so that he learns to do the same with distractions. Have someone walk into the room, or squeak a toy or bounce a ball once. A rock-solid stay is mostly a matter of working slowly and patiently to start with. Don't go too fast - the ideal scenario is that your Cockapoo never breaks out of the Stay position until you release him.

If he does get up, take a breather and then give him a short refresher, starting at a point easier than whatever you were working on when he cracked.

If you think he's tired or had enough, leave it for the day and come back later – just finish off on a positive note by giving one very easy command you know he will obey, followed by a reward.

Don't use the Stay command in situations where it is unpleasant for your dog. For instance, avoid telling him to stay as you close the door behind you on your way to work. Finally, don't use Stay to keep a dog in a scary situation.

Cockapoos can do so much more than sit and stay, so don't underestimate your dog! They are biddable and their great desire to please their owners means that they can be trained in different fields. Their love of people makes them suitable for therapy work; they can also be trained for Agility, Fly Ball, Rallying, Obedience and other canine competitions.

Down

There are a number of different ways to teach this command, which here means for the dog to lie down. (If you are teaching this command, then use the *"Off"* command to teach your dog not to jump up). This does not come naturally to a young pup, so it may take a little while to master the Down command.

Don't make it a battle of wills and, although you may gently push him down, don't physically force him down against his will. This will be seen as you asserting dominance in an aggressive manner and your Cockapoo will not like it.

1. Give the Sit command.

2. When your dog sits, don't give him the treat immediately, but keep it in your closed hand. Slowly move your hand straight down toward the floor, between his front legs. As your dog's nose follows the treat, just like a magnet, his head will bend all the way down to the floor.

3. When the treat is on the floor between your dog's paws, start to move it away from him, like you're drawing a line along the floor. (The entire luring motion forms an L-shape).

4. At the same time say *"Down"* in a firm manner.

5. To continue to follow the treat, your dog will probably ease himself into the Down position. The instant his elbows touch the floor, say *"Yes!"* and immediately let him eat the treat. If your dog doesn't automatically stand up after eating the treat, just move a step or two away to encourage him to move out of the Down position. Then repeat the sequence above several times. Aim for two short sessions of five minutes per day.

If your dog's back end pops up when you try to lure him into a Down, quickly snatch the treat away. Then immediately ask your dog to sit and try again. It may help to let your dog nibble on the treat as you move it toward the floor. If you've tried to lure your dog into a Down, but he still seems confused or reluctant, try this trick:

1. Sit down on the floor with your legs straight out in front of you. Your dog should be at your side. Keeping your legs together and your feet on the floor, bend your knees to make a 'tent' shape.

2. Hold a treat right in front of your dog's nose. As he licks and sniffs the treat, slowly move it down to the floor and then underneath your legs. Continue to lure him until he has to crouch down to keep following the treat.

3. The instant his belly touches the floor, say *"Yes!"* and let him eat the treat. If your dog seems nervous about following the treat under your legs, make a trail of treats for him to eat along the way.

Some dogs find it easier to follow a treat into the Down from a standing position.

❖ Hold the treat right in front of your dog's nose, and then slowly move it straight down to the floor, right between his front paws. His nose will follow the treat

❧ If you let him lick the treat as you continue to hold it still on the floor, your dog will probably plop into the Down position

❧ The moment he does, say *"Yes!"* and let him eat the treat (some dogs are reluctant to lie on a cold, hard surface. It may be easier to teach yours to lie down on a carpet). The next step is to introduce a hand signal. You'll still reward him with treats, though, so keep them nearby or hidden behind your back.

Method Two

1. Start with your dog in a Sit.

2. Say *"Down."*

3. Without a treat in your fingers, use the same hand motion you did before.

4. As soon as your dog's elbows touch the floor, say *"Yes!"* and immediately get a treat to give him. Important: Even though you're not using a treat to lure your dog into position, you must still give him a reward when he lies down. You want your dog to learn that he doesn't have to see a treat to get one.

5. Clap your hands or take a few steps away to encourage him to stand up. Then repeat the sequence from the beginning several times for a week or two. When your dog readily lies down as soon as you say the cue and then use your new hand signal, you're ready for the next step.

   You probably don't want to keep bending all the way down to the floor to make your Cockapoo lie down. To make things more convenient, you can gradually shrink the signal so that it becomes a smaller movement. To make sure your dog continues to understand what you want him to do, you'll need to progress slowly.

6. Repeat the hand signal, but instead of guiding your dog into the Down by moving your hand all the way to the floor, move it almost all the way down. Stop moving your hand when it's an inch or two above the floor. Practise the Down exercise for a day or two, using this slightly smaller hand signal. Then you can make your movement an inch or two smaller, stopping your hand three or four inches above the floor.

7. After practising for another couple of days, you can shrink the signal again. As you continue to gradually stop your hand signal farther and farther from the floor, you'll bend over less and less. Eventually, you won't have to bend over at all. You'll be able to stand up straight, say *"Down,"* and then just point to the floor.

Your next job is a bit harder - it's to practise your dog's new skill in many different situations and locations so that he can lie down whenever and wherever you ask him to. Practise in calm places at first, like different rooms in your house or in your garden/yard when there's no one else around. Then increase the distractions; so, do some sessions at home when family members are moving around, on walks and then at friends' houses, too.

The Recall

This basic command is perhaps the most important command of all and one that you can teach right from the beginning. If your dog won't come back, you are limiting both your lives. A dog who responds quickly and consistently can enjoy freedoms that other dogs cannot. Although you might spend more time teaching this command than any other, the benefits make it well worth the investment. Cockapoos love to run free, but you can't allow that until he or she has learned the recall.

FACT ❯ *Whether you're teaching a young puppy or an older Cockapoo, the first step is always to establish that coming to you is the BEST thing he can do. Any time your dog comes to you whether you've called him or not, acknowledge that you appreciate it. You can do this with praise, affection, play or treats. This consistent reinforcement ensures that your dog will continue to "check in" with you frequently.*

1. Start off a short distance away from your dog.

2. Say your dog's name followed by the command *"Come!"* in an enthusiastic voice. You'll usually be more successful if you walk or run away from him while you call. Dogs find it hard to resist chasing after a running person, especially their owner.

3. He should run towards you.

Often, especially outdoors, a young dog will start running towards you but then get distracted and head off in another direction. Pre-empt this situation by praising your puppy and cheering him on when he starts to come to you and **before** he has a chance to get distracted.

Your praise will keep him focused so that he'll be more likely to come all the way to you. If he stops or turns away, you can give him feedback by saying *"Oh-oh!"* or *"Hey!"* in a different tone of voice (displeased or unpleasantly surprised). When he looks at you again, smile, call him and praise him as he approaches you.

4. When your puppy comes to you, give him the treat BEFORE he sits down or he may think that the treat was earned for sitting, not coming to you.

5. Another method is to use two people. You hold the treats and let your dog sniff them while the accomplice holds on to the dog by his harness. When you are about 10 or 15 yards away, get your helper to let the dog go, and once he is running towards you, say *"COME!"* loudly and enthusiastically. When he reaches you, stop, bend down and make a fuss of him before giving a treat. Do this several times. The next step is to give the Come command just BEFORE you get your helper to release the dog, and by doing this repetitively, the dog begins to associate the command with the action.

 "Come" or a similar word is better than "Here" if you intend using the "Heel" command, as "Here" and "Heel" sound too similar.

Progress your dog's training in baby steps. If he's learned to come when called in your kitchen, you can't expect him to be able to do it straight away at the park, in the woods or on the beach when surrounded by distractions. When you first use the recall outdoors, make sure there's no one around to distract your dog. It's a good idea to consider using a long training lead - or to do the training within a safe, fenced area. Only when your dog has mastered the recall in a number of locations and in the face of various distractions can you expect him to come to you regularly.

Puppy Biting and Chewing

All puppies spend a great deal of time chewing, playing, and investigating objects. And it's natural for them to explore the world with their mouths and needle-sharp teeth. When puppies play with people, they often bite, chew, nip and mouthe on people's hands, limbs and clothing. Play biting is normal for puppies; they do it all the time with their littermates. They also bite moving targets with their sharp teeth; it's a great game.

 **FACT** *All retrieving breeds are mouthy as pups - and both Spaniels and Poodles were originally bred to retrieve.*

But when they arrive in your home, they have to be taught that human skin is sensitive and body parts are not suitable biting material. Biting is not acceptable, not even from a puppy, and can be a real problem initially, especially if you have children.

When your puppy bites you or the kids, he is playing and investigating; he is NOT being aggressive. Even though the Cockapoo has a reputation for being non-aggressive, a lively young pup can easily get carried away with energy and excitement. Deal with puppy biting from the beginning. Every time you have a play session, have a soft toy nearby and when he starts to chew your hand or feet, clench your fingers (or toes!) to make it more difficult and distract him with a soft toy in your other hand.

Keep the game interesting by moving the toy around or rolling it around in front of him. (He may be too young to fetch it back if you throw it). He may continue to chew you, but will eventually realise that the toy is far more interesting and livelier than your boring hand.

If he becomes over-excited and too aggressive with the toy, if he growls a lot, stop playing and walk away. When you walk away, don't say anything or make eye or physical contact with your puppy. Simply ignore him, this is extremely effective and often works within a few days.

If your pup is more persistent and tries to bite your legs as you walk away, thinking this is another fantastic game, stand still and ignore him. If he still persists, say *"No!"* in a very stern voice, then praise him when he lets go.

If you have to physically remove him from your trouser leg or shoe, leave him alone in the room for a while and ignore demands for your attention if he starts barking.

 Try not to put your pup in a crate when he is being naughty, or he will associate the crate with punishment. Remove yourself or the pup from the room instead - or put him in a pen. Wait until he has stopped being naughty before you put him in his crate.

Although you might find it quite cute and funny if your puppy bites your fingers or toes, it should be discouraged at all costs. You don't want your Cockapoo doing this as an adolescent or adult, when he can inadvertently cause real injury.

Here are some tips to deal with puppy biting:

- Puppies growl and bite more when they are excited. Don't allow things to escalate, so remove your pup from the situation before he gets too excited by putting him in a crate or pen

- Don't put your hand or finger into your pup's mouth to nibble on; this promotes puppy biting

- Limit your children's play time with pup - and always supervise the sessions in the beginning. Teach them to gently play with and stroke your puppy, not to wind him up

- Don't let the kids (or adults) run around the house with the puppy chasing – this is an open invitation to nip at the ankles

- If your puppy does bite, remove him from the situation and people – never smack him

> **Tip** *Cockapoos are people-loving dogs and another tried and tested method is to make a sharp cry of "OUCH!" when your pup bites your hand – even when it doesn't hurt.*

This has worked very well for us. Most pups will jump back in amazement, surprised to have hurt you. Divert your attention from your puppy to your hand. He will probably try to get your attention or lick you as a way of saying sorry. Praise him for stopping biting and continue with the game. If he bites you again, repeat the process. A sensitive dog should soon stop biting you.

You may also think about keeping the toys you use to play with your puppy separate from other toys. That way he will associate certain toys with having fun with you and will work harder to please you. Cockapoos are playful and you can use this to your advantage by teaching your dog how to play nicely with you and the toy and then by using play time as a reward for good behaviour.

As mentioned, puppies explore the world by putting things into their mouths. Other reasons for chewing is that it is a normal part of the teething process, and some adolescent and adult dogs chew because they are bored - usually due to lack of exercise and/or mental stimulation.

If puppy chewing is a problem it is because your pup is chewing on something you don't want him to. So, the trick is to keep him, his mouth and sharp little teeth occupied with something he CAN chew on, such as a durable toy – see **Chapter 3. Bringing Puppy Home** for more information.

You might also consider freezing peanut butter and/or a liquid inside a Kong toy. Put the Kong into a mug, plug the small end with peanut butter and fill it with gravy before putting it into the freezer. (Check the peanut butter doesn't contain the sweetener xylitol as this can is harmful to dogs).

Don't leave the Kong and your Cockapoo on your precious Oriental rug! This will keep your pup occupied for quite a long time. It is also worth considering giving the dog a frozen Kong or Lickimat when you leave the house if your dog suffers from separation anxiety. There are lots of doggie recipes for Kongs and other treats online.

When asked how she dealt with puppy chewing, American owner Arleen Stone King said: "Not well! Two of my friends lost shoes, we lost a check, I lost a good coat, slippers and shoes, countless quilts and comforters, the spindles on a stairway bannister, a leather couch, two pairs of eye glasses, and (this was funny) the older one, Murphy, ate his graduation diploma from puppy school! Obviously, we dealt with it by not dealing with it effectively!!"

Clicker Training

Clicker training is a method of training that uses a sound - a click - to tell an animal when he does something right. The clicker is a tiny plastic box held in the palm of your hand, with a metal tongue that you push quickly to make the sound. The clicker creates an efficient language between a human trainer and a trainee.

First, a trainer teaches a dog that every time he hears the clicking sound, he gets a treat. Once the dog understands this, the click becomes a powerful reward. When this happens, the trainer can use the click to mark the instant the dog performs the right behaviour.

For example, if a trainer wants to teach a dog to sit, he or she will click the instant the dog's rump hits the floor and then deliver a tasty treat. With repetition, the dog learns that sitting earns rewards.

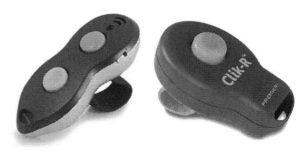

So, the **Click** takes on huge meaning. To the animal it means: "What I was doing the moment my trainer clicked, that's what he wants me to do." The clicker in animal training is like the winning buzzer on a game show that tells a contestant he's just won the money! Through the clicker, the trainer communicates precisely with the dog, and that speeds up training.

Although the clicker is ideal because it makes a unique, consistent sound, you do need a spare hand to hold it. For that reason, some trainers prefer to keep both hands free and instead use a one-syllable word like *"Yes!"* or *"Good!"* to mark the desired behaviour. In the steps below, you can substitute the word in place of the click to teach your pup what the sound means.

It's easy to introduce the clicker to your Cockapoo. Spend half an hour or so teaching him that the sound of the click means *"Treat!"* Here's how:

1. Sit and watch TV or read a book with your dog in the room. Have a container of (healthy) treats within reach.

2. Place one treat in your hand and the clicker in the other. (If your dog smells the treat and tries to get it by pawing, sniffing, mouthing or barking at you, just close your hand around the treat and wait until he gives up and leaves you alone).

3. Click once and immediately open your hand to give your dog the treat. Put another treat in your closed hand and resume watching TV or reading. Ignore your dog.

4. Several minutes later, click again and offer another treat.

5. Continue to repeat the click-and-treat combination at varying intervals, sometimes after one minute, sometimes after five minutes. Make sure you vary the time so that your dog doesn't know exactly when the next click is coming. Eventually, he'll start to turn toward you and look expectantly when he hears the click - which means he understands that the sound of the clicker means a treat is coming his way.

If your dog runs away when he hears the click, you can make the sound softer by putting it in your pocket or wrapping a towel around your hand that's holding the clicker. You can also try using a different sound, like the click of a retractable pen or the word *"Yes!"*

Once your dog understands the connection between the click and the treat, you're ready to start:

1. Click just once, right when your pup does what you want him to do. Think of it like pressing the shutter of a camera to take a picture of the behaviour.

2. Remember to follow every click with a treat. After you click, deliver the treat to your puppy's mouth as quickly as possible.

3. It's fine to switch between practising two or three behaviours within a session, but work on one command at a time. For example, say you're teaching your dog to sit, lie down and raise his paw. You can do 10 repetitions of sit and take a quick play break. Then do 10 repetitions of down and take another quick break. Then do 10 repetitions of stay, and so on. Keep training sessions short and stop before you or your dog gets tired of the game.

 Always set your dog up to succeed, not fail. If he has been struggling with a new command, end training sessions on a good note with something he CAN do.

Collar, Harness and Lead (Leash) Training

You have to train your dog to get used to a collar and/or harness and lead (leash) and then to walk nicely beside you. Teaching these manners can be challenging because young Cockapoos are lively and don't necessarily want to walk at the same pace as you!

All dogs will pull on a lead initially. It's not because they want to show you who's boss, it's simply that they are excited to be out and are forging ahead.

Many owners prefer to use a body harness instead. Harnesses work very well with Cockapoos; they take the pressure away from the dog's sensitive neck area and distribute it more evenly around the body. Many owners use harnesses, although the dogs may also have a collar with an ID tag. Harnesses with a chest ring for the lead can be effective for training. When your dog pulls, the harness turns him around.

Another option is to start your dog on a small lightweight collar and then change to a harness once he has learned some lead etiquette. Some dogs don't mind collars, some will try to fight them, while others will slump to the floor! You need to be patient and calm and proceed at a pace comfortable to her; don't fight your dog and don't force the collar on.

1. If you start your puppy off with a collar, you need a small, lightweight one - not one he is going to grow into. You can buy one with clips to start with, just put it on and clip it together, rather than fiddling with buckles, which can be scary when he's wearing a collar for the first time. Stick to the principle of positive reward-based training and give a treat or praise once the collar is on, not after you have taken it off. Then gradually increase the length of time you leave the collar on.

 If you leave your dog in a crate, or leave him alone in the house, take off the collar. He is not used to it and it may get caught on something, causing panic or injury.

2. Put the collar on when there are other things that will occupy him, like when he is going outside to be with you, or in the home when you are interacting with him. Or put it on at mealtimes or when you are doing some basic training. Don't put the collar on too tight, you want him to forget it's there; **you should be able to get two fingers underneath.**

   Some pups may react as if you've hung a two-ton weight around their necks, while others will be more compliant. If yours scratches the collar, get his attention by encouraging him to follow you or play with a toy to forget the irritation.

3. Once your puppy is happy wearing the collar, introduce the lead. Many owners prefer an extending or retractable lead for their Cockapoo, but consider a fixed-length one to start training him to walk close to you. Begin in the house or garden; don't try to go out and about straight away.

 Think of the lead as a safety device to stop him running off, not something to drag him around with. You want a dog that doesn't pull, so don't start by pulling him around; you don't want to get into a tug-of-war contest.

4. Attach the lead and give him a treat while you put it on. Use the treats (instead of pulling on the lead) to lure him beside you, so that he gets used to walking with the collar and lead on. You can also make good use of toys to do exactly the same thing - especially if your dog has a favourite. Walk around the house with the lead on and lure him forwards with the toy.

It might feel a bit odd but it's a good way for your pup to develop a positive relationship with the collar and lead with the minimum of fuss. Act as though it's the most natural thing in the world for you to walk around the house with your dog on a lead — and just hope the neighbours aren't watching!

Some dogs react the moment you attach the lead and they feel some tension on it — a bit like when a horse is being broken in for the first time. Drop the lead and allow him to run around the house or yard, dragging it behind, but be careful he doesn't get tangled and hurt himself.

Try to make him forget about it by playing or starting a short fun training routine with treats. Treats are a huge distraction for most young dogs. While he is concentrating on the new task, occasionally pick up the lead and call him to you. Do it gently and in an encouraging tone.

5. The most important thing is not to yank on the lead. If it gets tight, just lure him back beside you with a treat or a toy while walking. All you're doing is getting him to move around beside you. Remember to keep your hand down (the one holding the treat or toy) so your dog doesn't get the habit of jumping up at you. If you feel he is getting stressed when walking outside on a lead, try putting treats along the route you'll be taking to turn this into a rewarding game: good times are ahead... That way he learns to focus on what's ahead of him with curiosity and not fear.

Take collar and lead training slowly. Let him gain confidence in you, the lead and himself. Some dogs sit and decide not to move! If this happens, walk a few steps away, go down on one knee and encourage him to come to you, then walk off again.

For some pups, the collar and lead can be restricting and they will react with resistance. Some dogs are perfectly happy to walk alongside you off-lead, but behave differently when they have one on. Proceed in tiny steps if that is what your puppy is happy with, don't over face him, but stick at it if you are met with resistance. With training and patience, your puppy will learn to walk nicely on a lead; it is a question of when, not if.

Walking on a Lead

There are different methods, but we have found the following one to be successful for quick results. Initially, the lead should be kept fairly loose. Have a treat in your hand as you walk, it will encourage your dog to sniff the treat as he walks alongside. He should not pull ahead as he will want to remain near the treat.

Give the command *"Walk"* or *"Heel"* and then proceed with the treat in your hand, keep giving him a treat every few steps initially, then gradually extend the time between treats. Eventually, you should be able to walk with your hand comfortably at your side, periodically (every minute or so) reaching into your pocket to grab a treat to reward your dog.

If your dog starts pulling ahead, first give him a warning, by saying *"No"* or *"Steady"* or a similar command. If he slows down, give him a treat. But if he continues to pull ahead so that your arm becomes fully extended, stop walking and ignore your dog. Wait for him to stop pulling and to look up at you. At this point reward him for good behaviour before carrying on your walk.

If your pup refuses to budge, DON'T drag him. This will ultimately achieve nothing as he will learn to resent the lead. Coax him along with praise and, if necessary, treats so that when he moves forward with you, it is because HE wants to and not because he has been dragged by somebody several times bigger.

Be sure to quickly reward your dog any time he doesn't pull and walks with you with the lead slack. If you have a lively young pup who is dashing all over the place on the lead, try starting training when he is already a little tired, after a play or exercise session – but not exhausted.

Another method is what dog trainer Victoria Stillwell describes as the *"Reverse Direction Technique."* When your dog pulls, say *"Let's Go!"* in an encouraging manner, then turn away from him and walk off in the other direction, without jerking on the lead. When he is following you and the lead is slack, turn back and continue on your original way.

It may take a few repetitions, but your words and body language will make it clear that pulling will not get your dog anywhere, whereas walking calmly by your side - or even slightly in front of you - on a loose lead will get him where he wants to go.

There is an excellent video (in front of her beautiful house!) which shows Victoria demonstrating this technique and highlights just how easy it is with a dog that's keen to please. It only lasts three minutes: https://positively.com/dog-behavior/basic-cues/loose-leash-walking

Harnesses

These are very popular with owners of Cockapoos as they do not put any strain on the neck. There are several different options:

- **Front-clip or training harness** - this has a lead attachment in front of the harness at the centre of your dog's chest. Dog trainers often choose this type as it helps to discourage your dog from pulling on the lead by turning him around

- **Back-clip** – this is generally the easiest for most dogs to get used to and useful for small dogs with delicate throats that are easily irritated by collars. This type is for calm dogs or ones that have already been trained not to pull on the lead

- **Comfort wrap or step-in harness** - lay the harness on the ground, have your dog step in, pull the harness up and around his shoulders and then clip him in; simple!

- **Soft or vest harness** - typically made of mesh and comes in a range of colours and patterns. Some slip over the head and some can be stepped into

- **No-pull harness** - similar to a training harness, designed to help discourage your dog from pulling. The lead attachment ring is at the centre of the dog's chest and the harness tightens pressure if the dog pulls, encouraging him to stay closer to you. Some styles also tighten around the dog's legs

- **Auto or car harness** - these are designed for car travel and have an attachment that hooks into a seat belt

When choosing a harness, decide what its primary purpose will be – is it instead of or in addition to a collar? Do you need one that will help to train your dog, or will a back-clip harness do the job? You want to make sure that it is a snug fit, and if it's a front clip, that it hangs high on your dog's chest. If it dangles too low, it can't help control forward momentum. Make sure the harness isn't too tight or too difficult to get on. It shouldn't rub under your dog's armpits or anywhere else. If possible, take your dog to try on a few options before buying one for the first time.

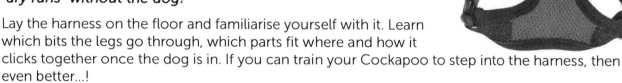

 If you've never used a harness before, it's easy to get tangled up while your pup is bouncing around, excited at the prospect of a walk. It's a good idea to have a few "dry runs" without the dog!

Lay the harness on the floor and familiarise yourself with it. Learn which bits the legs go through, which parts fit where and how it clicks together once the dog is in. If you can train your Cockapoo to step into the harness, then even better...!

....

We strongly recommend that all new owners book their puppy or rescue dog on to a basic training course.

Your Cockapoo will really enjoy the experience and, as well as learning basic obedience, he will learn how to socialise with other dogs. It is also the best, least expensive way for owners to learn how to train their dog properly. Many local veterinary clinics now run puppy training classes.

Once you have mastered the basics, you can go on to learn more and win certificates on the Canine Good Citizen Dog Scheme.

More details are at: www.thekennelclub.org.uk/training/good-citizen-dog-training-scheme in the UK. USA: http://webapps.akc.org/obedience-training-club/#/

GENERAL NOTE: If your puppy is in a hyperactive mood or extremely tired, he is not likely to be very receptive to training.

CREDIT: Thanks to the American Society for the Prevention of Cruelty to Animals for assistance with parts of this chapter. The ASPCA has a lot of good advice and training tips at: www.aspca.org

....

9. Exercise

One thing all dogs have in common – including every Cockapoo ever born - is that they need daily exercise. Even if you have a large garden or back yard where your dog can run free, there are still lots of benefits to daily walks.

Cockapoos love going for walks, but are usually happy to lounge around at home if you have to skip one. Don't think that because yours is happy to snuggle up on the sofa with you that they don't need regular exercise – THEY DO.

Start exercise patterns early so your dog gets used to a routine. **Dogs love routine.** Daily exercise helps to keep your Cockapoo happy, healthy and free from disease. Exercise:

- ❧ Strengthens respiratory and circulatory systems
- ❧ Helps get oxygen to tissue cells
- ❧ Helps keep a healthy heart
- ❧ Wards off obesity
- ❧ Keeps muscles toned and joints flexible
- ❧ Aids digestion
- ❧ Releases endorphins that trigger positive feelings
- ❧ Helps to keep dogs mentally stimulated and socialised

 *Cockapoos' ancestors on both sides were originally bred to run and retrieve all day. One of the main things that surprises many new owners of Cockapoos - especially those that retain a lot of sporting instinct – is how much energy they have, and how much physical and mental activity they need to stop them becoming bored.*

This is one reason for the increase in popularity of the Cavapoo! Lots of people have got to know and love the Cockapoo, but some prefer a less high-energy Doodle. The Cavapoo's forebears are the Poodle and Cavalier King Charles Spaniel, a gentle companion dog which has had a lot of the sporting instinct, or *"drive,"* bred out.

NOTE: Cockapoos bred from American Cocker Spaniels tend to have less drive and lower energy demands, and Cockapoos from show strains of English Cocker Spaniels generally have calmer dispositions than those bred from working English Cockers.

If you have the time, an excellent way of keeping your Cockapoo exercised, mentally stimulated and happy is to take part in an activity, such as Obedience, Agility, Fly Ball, therapy work, or other canine activities that challenge dogs. And even if you don't do any official competitions, Cockapoos love to show off by learning new tricks and commands – or give your dog a chance to shine at home by building your own agility course in the garden!

Lapdogs or Hunters?

The answer is ... a mixture of both! How much hunter and how much lapdog depends largely on your dog's bloodlines. The Cockapoo is part Spaniel, which is a hardy dog bred to flush birds like pheasant, partridge and woodcock from dense undergrowth and then retrieve the game for the guns. A working Spaniel can run all day long with its nose to the ground. Although the Cockapoo has been developed as a companion dog, some still retain a degree of sporting instinct.

The Poodle was originally bred to work as a water retriever, and although its heyday as Europe's working retriever par excellence was a couple of hundred years ago, it is surprising how much instinct is passed down through the generations.

Cockapoos do, however, differ from their hard-working ancestors in that they are far more reliant on humans for their happiness than sporting and working dogs, which tend to be a bit more independent.

How Much Exercise?

The amount of exercise each adult Cockapoo needs varies tremendously from one dog to the next. It depends on various factors, including:

- ❧ Temperament
- ❧ Natural energy levels
- ❧ Bloodline
- ❧ Your living conditions
- ❧ Whether your dog is kept with other dogs
- ❧ What she gets used to

One of the advantages of Cockapoos is that they are happy to fit in with your lifestyle; they enjoy walks but are not bouncing off the walls if they miss one. They are known for being very playful and enjoy toys and games, which help stop them getting bored and mischievous.

Some of your dog's natural temperament and energy level will depend on the bloodline - ask the breeder how much exercise he or she recommends.

A minimum of an hour a day spread over at least two walks will keep your Cockapoo exercised and stimulated - although dogs with sporting instincts will take as much exercise as you can give them - even all-day hikes - once they have built up to it.

Owning more than one dog - or having friends with dogs - is a great way for them to get more exercise. A couple of dogs running around together will get far more exercise than one on her own. If you already have a Cockapoo and are looking for a second dog, consider another Doodle, as Poodle crosses seem to have a natural affinity with their own kind.

A fenced garden or yard is a definite advantage for a Cockapoo - but should not be seen as a replacement for daily exercise away from the home, where a dog can experience new places, scents, other people and dogs. Of course, if you live in an apartment, you may have no outside space, so it is doubly important to make the time to give your dog outdoor exercise.

Your Cockapoo will enjoy going for walks on the lead (leash), but will enjoy it far more when she is allowed to run free, following a scent, chasing a ball or going for a swim. If your dog is happy just to amble along beside you, think about playing some games to raise her heartbeat, build muscle and get her fit.

You must make sure it's safe to let her off the lead, away from traffic and other hazards - and only after she has learned the recall. There are reports in both the UK and North America about increasing numbers of dog attacks, even in dog parks and public parks. If you are at all worried, avoid popular dog walking areas and find other places where your dog can exercise safely.

If you want to hike or take part in agility with your dog, build up time and distance gradually. Exercise within your dog's limits - on both land and water - this loyal breed WILL want to keep up with you, regardless of how fit she is, and you don't want your beloved pooch to struggle.

Mental Stimulation

Without mental challenges, dogs can become bored, unresponsive, destructive, attention-seeking and/or depressed. Cockapoos are known for being playful. Combine this with the intelligence of the Poodle and you have a dog that enjoys a mental as well as physical challenge. Have plenty toys and chews and factor in some regular play time with your dog – even gentle play time for old dogs.

If your dog's behaviour deteriorates, ask yourself: *"Is she getting enough exercise?"* and *"Am I leaving her alone for too long?"*

Cockapoos are natural retrievers, i.e. they love fetching things back to you. As well as throwing a toy or ball, you can make it more interesting by hiding the object and training your dog to find it. Try and avoid sticks, which can splinter in the mouth. Playing in the garden or yard with toys or balls is also a good way to let off steam. If you play Frisbee, don't overdo it - especially with young, growing dogs, as this can lead to joint damage.

A Cockapoo at the heart of the family getting regular exercise and mental stimulation is a happy dog and loving companion second to none.

Cockapoos and Water

All Cockapoos are part Poodle, which was originally bred as a water dog. Many Cockapoos have inherited a love of water. If your dog does enjoy swimming, it is an excellent way to exercise; many veterinary clinics now use water tanks not only for remedial therapy, but also for canine recreation. It is also a great way for high energy Cockapoos to blow off some steam.

Remember that swimming is a lot more strenuous for a dog than walking or even running. Don't constantly throw that ball into the water for long periods - your Cockapoo will fetch it back until she drops. Your dog should exercise within her limits; overstretching could place a strain on the heart. Don't forget to gently dry under your Cockapoo's ear flaps after swimming to reduce the risk of ear infections.

Start off by getting the feet wet and paddling in the shallows, NOT by throwing a ball into water. Allow a young dog to build up confidence. Once used to getting wet feet, throw an object (preferably not one that will float into deep water) into the shallows and encourage your Cockapoo to fetch.

You can even get into the shallow water yourself to give encouragement. Then gradually throw the object into slightly deeper water. All of this should be done over a period of time on separate visits, not in a single day. Avoid very cold weather and choppy water.

NOTE: Not all Cockapoos like water and not all are natural swimmers – yours might not have inherited *"the water gene!"* Some dogs have a natural fear of water. Never force a dog into water that doesn't want to go; you will only make her even more fearful. If you live near water and/or want your dog to enjoy it, introduce her while still a puppy.

Like a child, if a young dog gets frightened of water or loses confidence, she is unlikely to want to go swimming as an adult. If you are regularly near water, you might want to get a life vest, which will keep your dog afloat even when exhausted.

....

Establish a Routine

Establish an exercise regime early in your dog's life. If possible, get your dog used to a walk or walks at the same time every day, at a time that fits in with your daily routine and gradually build that up as the puppy reaches adulthood. For example, take your dog out after her morning feed, then again in the afternoon and a toilet trip last thing at night. Whatever routine you decide on, stick to it.

A dog that has been used to an hour or two of exercise a day will soon become bored and unhappy if your routine changes and she's only getting a couple of 10-minute walks a day.

 If you don't feel you have enough time to give your Cockapoo the exercise she needs, consider employing a daily dog walker, if you can afford it, or take her to doggie day care once or twice a week. As well as the exercise, she will love the interaction with other dogs.

To those owners who say their dog is happy and getting enough exercise playing in the yard or garden, just show her the lead (leash) and see how she reacts. Do you think she is excited at the prospect of leaving the home and going for a walk? Of course she is. Cockapoos are very curious and love investigating interesting new scents and places, which is why you need to plug every little gap in your fence – they will be off given half a chance!

Older dogs still need exercise to keep their body, joints and systems functioning properly. They need a less strenuous regime – they are usually happier with shorter walks, but still enough to keep them physically and mentally active. Again, every dog is different; some are willing and able to keep on running to the end of their lives, others slow right down. If your old or sick dog is struggling, she will show you that she's not up to it by stopping and looking at you or sitting/lying down and refusing to move. If she's healthy and does this, she is just being lazy!

Regular exercise can add months or even years to a dog's life.

Many Cockapoos love snow, but it can sometimes present problems with clumps of snow and ice building up on paws, ears, legs and tummy. Salt or de-icing products on roads and pathways can also cause irritation – particularly if she tries to lick it off - as they can contain chemicals that are poisonous to dogs. If your dog gets iced up, you can bathe paws and anywhere else affected in lukewarm - NOT HOT - water.

If your dog spends a lot of time in snow, you might invest in a quality paw wax or a pair of canine snow boots *(pictured)*, which are highly effective in preventing snow and ice balls forming on paws – provided you can get the boots to stay on!

Exercising Puppies

There are strict guidelines to stick to with puppies. It's important not to over-exercise young pups as their bones and joints are still soft and cannot tolerate a lot of stress. Too much impact can cause permanent damage. So, playing Fetch or Frisbee for hours on end with your young Cockapoo is definitely not a good plan, nor is allowing a pup to freely run up and down stairs in your home. You'll end up with an injured dog and a pile of vet's bills.

Just like babies, puppies have different temperaments and energy levels; some will need more exercise than others. Start slowly and build it up. The worst combination is over-exercise and overweight.

Don't take your pup out of the yard or garden until the all-clear after the vaccinations - unless you carry her around to start the socialisation process. Begin with daily short walks on the lead. Puppies have enquiring minds. Get yours used to being outside the home environment and experiencing new situations as soon as possible. The general guideline for exercise is:

Five minutes of on-lead exercise per month of age

So, a total of 15 minutes when three months (13 weeks)

30 minutes when six months (26 weeks) old, etc.

This applies until around one year to 18 months old, when most of their growing has finished. Slowly increase the time as she gets used to being exercised and this will gradually build up muscles and stamina.

It is OK for your young pup to have free run of your garden or yard, provided it has a soft surface such as grass. This does not count in the five minutes per month rule.

If the yard is stone or concrete, limit the time your dog runs around on it, as the hard surface will impact joints. It is also fine for your pup to run freely around the house to burn off energy - although not up and down stairs or jumping on and off furniture.

A pup will take things at her own pace and stop to sniff or rest. If you have other dogs, restrict the time pup is allowed to play with them, as she won't know when she's had enough. When older, your dog can go out for much longer walks.

One breeder added: "For the first 18 months whilst the puppy's bones are soft and developing, it's best not to over-exert and put strain on the joints. Daily gentle walking is great, just not constant fast and hard running/chasing in the puppy stage, as too much is a big strain."

And when your little pup has grown into a beautiful adult Cockapoo with a skeleton capable of carrying her through a long and healthy life, it will have been worth all the effort:

A long, healthy life is best started slowly

Cockapoo Exercise Tips

- Don't over-exercise puppies or allow them to race up and down stairs

- Aim for at least one walk away from the house every day

- Vary your exercise route – it will be more interesting for both of you

- Triple check the fencing around your garden or yard to prevent The Great Escape

- If you want your dog to retrieve, don't fetch the ball or toy back yourself or she will never learn. Train her by giving praise or a treat when she brings the ball or toy back to your feet

- Do not throw a ball or toy repeatedly for a dog if she shows signs of over-exertion. Your Cockapoo will fetch to please you and because it's great fun. Stop the activity after a while - no matter how much she begs you to throw it again

- The same goes for swimming, which is an exhausting exercise for a dog. Ensure any exercise is within your dog's capabilities – look out for heavy panting. Gentle swimming, if your dog enjoys it, is an excellent activity for Cockapoos. It's also beneficial for older dogs as it is low impact on joints

- Don't strenuously exercise your dog straight after or within an hour of a meal as this can cause Bloat. More normally seen in deep-chested dogs, Canine Bloat can affect any breed and is extremely serious, if not fatal. See **Chapter 11. Cockapoo Health** for details

- Cockapoos need play time as well as walk time. It keeps their minds exercised – and they love the interaction with their beloved owner

- Exercise old dogs more gently - especially in cold weather when it is harder to get their bodies moving. Have a cool-down period after exercise to reduce stiffness and soreness; it helps to remove lactic acids from the dog's body. Our 13-year-old loves a body rub

- If you throw a stick, don't let your dog chew it to bits, as splinters can get lodged in the mouth – or worse

- Make sure your dog has constant access to fresh water. Dogs can only sweat a tiny amount through the pads of their paws, they need to drink water to cool down

Showing off her retrieving instinct is this young Cockapoo bred by Julie Shearman, of Crystalwood Cockapoos, Devon, UK.

Admittedly, when it is pouring down with rain, freezing cold (or scorching hot), the last thing you want to do is to venture outdoors with your dog. And in all likelihood, your Cockapoo may not be too keen either!

But make the effort; the lows are more than compensated for by the highs. Don't let your dog dictate if she doesn't want to go out, it will only make her lazier and less sociable with others. Exercise helps you bond with your dog, keep fit, see different places and meet new companions - both canine and human. In short, it enhances both your lives.

Socialisation

Your adult dog's character will depend largely on two things: inherited temperament and environment, or **NATURE AND NURTURE**. And one absolutely essential aspect of nurture is socialisation.

FACT ▶ *Scientists now realise the importance that socialisation plays in a dog's life. There is a fairly small window that is regarded as the optimum time for socialisation - and this is up to the age of four to five months.*

Socialisation actually begins from the moment the puppy is born and the importance of picking a good breeder cannot be over-emphasised. Not only will he or she breed for good temperament and health, but the canine mother will be well-balanced, friendly and unstressed and the pup will learn a lot in this positive environment.

Learning When Young Is Easiest

Most young animals, including dogs, are naturally able to get used to their everyday environment until they reach a certain age. When they reach this age, they become much more suspicious of things they haven't yet experienced. This is why it often takes longer to train an older dog.

When you think about it, humans are not so different. Babies and children have a tremendous capacity to learn, we call this early period our *"formative years."* As we age, we can still learn, but not at the speed we absorbed things when very young. Also, as we get older we are often less receptive to new ideas or new ways of doing things.

This age-specific natural development allows a puppy to get comfortable with the normal sights, sounds, people and animals that will be a part of her life. It ensures that she doesn't spend her life jumping in fright, snapping, or growling at every blowing leaf. The suspicion that dogs develop later also ensures that they react with a healthy dose of caution to new things that could really be dangerous - Mother Nature is clever!

Socialisation means *"learning to be part of society,"* or *"integration."* This means helping dogs become comfortable within a human society by getting them used to different people, environments, buildings, traffic, sights, noises, smells, animals, other dogs, etc.

It is essential that your dog's introductions to new things are all **positive**. Negative experiences lead to a dog becoming fearful and untrusting.

Your dog may already have a wonderful temperament, but she still needs socialising to avoid her thinking that the world is tiny and it revolves around her. Cockapoos demand enough of your attention without developing a *"Little Emperor"* complex as well!

Good socialisation helps puppies — whether bold or timid - learn their place in society and become more relaxed and integrated adults. It gives your dog confidence and the ultimate goal of socialisation is to have a happy, well-adjusted dog that you can take anywhere. Ever seen a therapy dog in action and noticed how incredibly well-adjusted to life they are? This is no coincidence.

These dogs have been extensively socialised and are ready and able to deal in a calm manner with whatever situation they encounter. They are relaxed and comfortable in their own skin - just like you want your dog to be.

Start socialising your puppy as soon as you bring her home; start around the house and garden and, if it is safe, carry her out of the home environment. Regular socialisation should continue until your dog is around 18 months of age. After that, don't just forget about it; socialisation isn't only for puppies, it should continue throughout life. As with any skill, if it is not practised, your dog will become less proficient at interacting with other people, animals, noises and new situations.

Developing the Well-Rounded Adult Dog

Dogs that have not been properly integrated are more likely to react with fear or aggression to unfamiliar people, animals and experiences. Cockapoos who are relaxed around strangers, other dogs, honking horns, cats, farm animals, cyclists, veterinary examinations, traffic, crowds and noise are easier to live with than dogs who find these situations challenging or frightening. And if you are planning on taking part in canine competitions, get yours used to the buzz of these events early on.

 *Well-socialised dogs live more relaxed, peaceful and happy lives than dogs that are constantly stressed by their environment.*

Socialisation isn't an *"all or nothing"* project. You can socialise a puppy a bit, a lot, or a whole lot. The wider the range of positive experiences you expose her to when young, the better her chances are of becoming a more relaxed adult. Don't over-face your little puppy.

Socialisation should never be forced, but approached systematically and in a manner that builds confidence and curious interaction. If your pup finds a new experience frightening, take a step back, introduce her to the scary situation much more gradually, and make a big effort to do something she loves during the situation or right afterwards.

For example, if your puppy seems to be frightened by noise and vehicles at a busy road, a good method would be to go to a quiet road, sit with the dog away from - but within sight of - the traffic. Every time she looks towards the traffic say *"YES!"* and reward her with a treat. If she is still stressed, you need to move further away. When your dog takes the food in a calm manner, she is becoming more relaxed and getting used to traffic sounds, so you can edge a bit nearer - but still just for short periods until she becomes totally relaxed. Keep each session short and *POSITIVE.*

Meeting Other Dogs

When you take your gorgeous and vulnerable little pup out with other dogs for the first few times, you are bound to be a bit apprehensive. To begin with, introduce your puppy to just one other dog – one that you know to be friendly, rather than taking her straight to the park where there are lots of dogs of all sizes racing around, which might frighten the life out of your timid little darling.

On the other hand, your puppy might be full of confidence right from the off, but you still need to approach things slowly. If your puppy is too cocksure, she may get a warning bite from an older dog, which could make her more anxious when approaching new dogs in the future.

Always make initial introductions on neutral ground, so as not to trigger territorial behaviour. You want your Cockapoo to approach other dogs with friendliness, not fear.

From the first meeting, help both dogs experience good things when they're in each other's presence. Let them sniff each other briefly, which is normal canine greeting behaviour. As they do, talk to them in a happy, friendly tone of voice; never use a threatening tone.

Don't allow them to sniff each other for too long as this may escalate to an aggressive response. After a short time, get the attention of both dogs and give each a treat in return for obeying a simple command, e.g. *"Sit"* or *"Stay."* Continue with the *"happy talk,"* and rewards.

Learn to spot the difference between normal rough and tumble play and interaction that may develop into fear or aggression. Here are some signs of fear to look out for when your dog interacts with other canines:

- Running away or freezing on the spot
- Licking the lips or lips pulled back
- Trembling or panting, which can be a sign of stress or pain
- Frantic/nervous behaviour, e.g. excessive sniffing, drinking or playing frenetically with a toy
- A lowered body stance or crouching
- Lying on her back with paws in the air – this is submissive, as is submissive urination
- Lowering of the head or turning the head away, when you may see the whites of the eyes as the dog tries to keep eyes on the perceived threat
- Growling and/or hair raised on her back (raised hackles)
- Tail lifted in the air or ears high on the head

Some of these responses are normal. A pup may well crouch on the ground or roll on to her back to show other dogs she's not a threat. If the situation looks like escalating, calmly distract the dogs or remove your puppy – don't shout or shriek. Dogs will pick up on your fear and this in itself could trigger an unpleasant situation.

Try not to be over-protective; your puppy has to learn to interact with other dogs. Don't be too quick to rush in and pick her up, as she will sense your anxiety. The same is true when walking your dog on a lead – don't be nervous every time you seen another dog – your Cockapoo will pick up on it and react.

Always follow up a socialisation experience with praise, petting, a fun game or a special treat. One positive sign from a dog is the *"play bow"* (pictured), when she goes down on to her front elbows but keeps her backside up in the air.

This is a sign that she's feeling friendly towards the other dog and wants to play. Relaxed ear and body position and wagging tail are other positive signs.

One sign to look out for is eyeballing. In the canine world, staring a dog in the eyes is a challenge and may cause an aggressive response. This is more relevant to adult dogs, as a young pup will soon be put in her place by bigger or older dogs; it is how they learn. The rule of thumb with puppy socialisation is to keep a close eye on your pup's reaction to whatever you expose her to, so you can tone things down if she seems at all frightened.

Although Cockapoos are not naturally aggressive dogs, aggression is often grounded in fear, and a dog that mixes easily is less likely to be combative. Similarly, without frequent and new experiences, some Cockapoos can become timid and nervous.

Take your new dog everywhere you can. You want her to feel relaxed and calm in any situation, even noisy and crowded ones. Take treats with you and praise her when she reacts calmly to new situations.

Once settled into your home, introduce her to your friends and teach her not to jump up. If you have young children, it is not only the dog that needs socialising! Youngsters also need training on how to act around dogs, so both parties learn to respect the other.

An excellent way of getting your new puppy to meet other dogs in a safe environment is at a puppy class. We highly recommend this for all puppies. Ask around locally if any classes are being run. Some vets and dog trainers run classes for very junior pups who have had all their vaccinations. These help pups get used to other dogs of a similar age.

Walkies!

We asked some Cockapoo breeders and owners how much exercise they gave their dogs and how easy they thought Cockapoos were to train. Here is what they said, starting in the UK:

Breeder Karol Watson Todd says that she finds Cockapoos "excellent" to train.

Pictured, wearing her harness for a romp in the fields, is Amber, bred by Karol and owned by Christine Grey, who says: "One thing that we have discovered is how much exercise Amber needs.

"We give her at least two hours a day (two or three walks) and she seems to have a never-ending supply of energy! Not a problem for us as we love walking, but anyone unable or unprepared for this commitment should probably think twice before parenting a Cockapoo!"

Keith and Diane Raymond own Zippy, also bred by Karol. They added: "To any potential owners of Cockapoos, you need to think very hard about why you want one. They are not dogs for just sitting at your feet all day long. They need plenty of exercise. Our Zippy has up to two or three hours a day and she always wants more."

Breeder Pat Pollington says: "Our dogs have their own field they run in and a concrete yard. They then go for a walk twice a day. We believe every dog needs at least one good walk a day. They also need time off-lead in an area where they can run and use their natural instincts.

"If your dog is unable to go off-lead, there are places that have fully secure fields for dogs to just run and they will need this a good once a week. If they can go off-lead in the playing field and play with other dogs, all the better.

"If you put the work into a Cockapoo, they are very easy to train. They are very loyal dogs, so they always want to please their owner. There are a lot of training classes for puppies and it is always a good idea to book into one of these. A lot of our puppies have learnt sit, paw and stay in just a couple of days of being in their new home. The best time to use is feed time. Make them ask for their food, i.e. sit and paw. Never let a Cockapoo get away with anything just because they are a puppy. If you allow this, then they will want the same when they are adults, and it is a lot harder to train an older dog."

Julie Shearman: "We exercise our Cockapoos for a minimum of an hour "off-lead" each day. Although, if there's a foot of snow, or if you are ill and can't walk the dog, Cockapoos are calm indoors and quite happy to cuddle up with their master. They are the fastest breed we have ever trained! Reports from new owners confirm this, stating that they are top of the obedience class and often picked out to use as demonstration dogs."

Eileen Jackson: "My Cockapoos are from both show and working stock. The difference is in the size; the temperament is much the same. They all need stimulation i.e. games, or hiding toys either in the garden or in the house. They make ideal dogs for Flyball and love their walks."

Owner Stacy Robinson: "We go for 30 to 45-minute walks every day. I used to be a runner and Mabel kept up, no problem. She loves to go hiking in the mountains as well. We went to PetSmart for obedience training and I wouldn't say Mabel was in the top of her class! I threatened to send her to military school, but with patience and time she caught on." *Mabel is pictured here lending a hand in the garden.*

Mike Peyton runs the Cockapoo HQ website at www.cockapoohq.com and owns F1 Luna. He says: "The amount of exercise totally varies every day. Luna is in day care Tuesday and Thursdays, so is not walked on those days. Monday, Wednesday and Friday she gets one long walk of an hour, either morning or evening, and then we play ball with her in the garden for 30 minutes or so. On the weekends, we will do a long walk on one of the days and then maybe on the Sunday we will all have a lazy day together and she won't go out at all. I think she quite enjoys this!

"I think a lot of people are shocked by how much exercise Cockapoos need, especially when they are younger. With Luna being from a show Cocker I think she needs less than a working Cocker."

This is what the North American breeders said, starting with Jeanne Davis: "I exercise my Cockapoos regularly and daily; they do not need to be worn-out like some high performance/high energy dogs. They are extremely easy to obedience train."

Jessica Sampson: "My Cockapoos get one or two good 20 to 30-minute walks each day; also, they get lots of play time in the yard to chase balls and just be dogs! They are also adept swimmers and enjoy spending lots of time in the water."

Jackie Stafford: "Cockapoos are easy apartment dwellers as they conform to the regimen of their owners. They should be allowed to exercise at least 30 minutes a day. Cockapoos are usually very easy to obedience train by repetition. They can be taught to sit in just a few minutes with treats and repetitive commands."

Rebecca Mae Goins, who mainly breeds from American Cockers, says: "Exercising your Cockapoo is fairly simple; you can get a few interactive toys that can help occupy them if you are busy or away. If you have a fenced-in yard, take your Cockapoo out for a game of fetch that lasts around 15 to 20 minutes. If you do not have a fenced yard, take your Cockapoo for walks." *Photo courtesy of Rebecca.*

She added: "I have found that Cockapoos are very intelligent and very fast learners, but the time required to obedience train a Cockapoo depends on the time devoted to this by the breeder and the new family. I start my puppies on manners and basic obedience training as soon as they are up walking around. The sooner you teach them to accept a human handling them, the sooner they'll start learning what you are trying to teach them."

Tiff Atkinson, owner of 23lb four-year-old Cockapoo Dolce, says: "Her energy level is very high, I didn't know what to expect but I knew she would be very playful. She exercises throughout the day. We walk around our neighbourhood a couple of times a day, but mainly she loves just running around the house - so many squirrels to chase!

"Our Dolce picked up obedience training fast, because we were consistent and kept rewarding her. For new owners, consistency is key. Reward good behaviour, train daily, and be very patient. What surprises me the most is Dolce's smarts. I wasn't expecting her to learn so many tricks and command words so fast, and understanding what furniture she can be on versus which furniture she can't be on. I just didn't know how friendly and happy a Cockapoo can be; she really has a huge personality."

Beth Ratkowski has owned two Cockapoos, F2 Louie and 16-month-old F1 Rudy. Sadly, Louie died of liver cancer aged six years, possibly due to inbreeding, according to the vet. Beth says: "I have a fenced quarter-acre yard, so Rudi runs with both my Golden Retrievers; he is very energetic. Louie was a little hunter and would help chase rabbits with my Goldens. He would flush the rabbit and the Goldens would catch it!"

Experienced dog owner Arleen Stone King, of Wisconsin, USA, has F1s Murphy (7) and Daisy (4), and says: "I would say, yes, they have more energy than we had expected. They typically go on two half-hour walks a day. Cockapoo puppies are THE cutest little things, playful, loving, quick learners, and even after they reach adulthood, they still have that cute puppy look.

"I dislike one of their cutest attributes...they get bored easily and ours tend to get somewhat destructive. But part of their charm is that they are mischievous."

Murphy and Daisy are pictured ruling the roost at Arleen's.

"At seven and four years old, they are still *"in training"* on obedience. It's a life-long process; and the thing I believe is key is for everyone involved with the dog to be on exactly the same page...consistency and follow-through. I think dogs typically do better with another one - although it doubles the work for the owner!

They entertain and play with each other, and this takes some of the pressure off of trying to entertain them constantly - and Cockapoos seem to get bored real fast!"

10. Cockapoo Health

Health has a major impact on an animal's quality of life and should always be a consideration when choosing and raising a dog. The first step is to select a puppy from a breeder who produces Cockapoos that are sound in both body and temperament – and this involves health screening - and secondly, to play your part in keeping your dog healthy throughout his or her life.

NOTE: This chapter is intended to be used as a medical encyclopaedia to help you to identify potential health issues and act promptly in the best interests of your dog. Please don't read it thinking your Cockapoo will get lots of these ailments – he or she WILL NOT! The Cockapoo is generally regarded as a fairly robust dog health-wise.

The Importance of Health Testing

It is becoming increasingly evident that genetics can have a huge influence on a person's health and life expectancy – which is why so much time and money is currently being devoted to genetic research. A human is more likely to suffer from a hereditary illness if the gene - or genes - for that disorder is passed on from parents or grandparents. That person is said to have a 'predisposition' to the ailment if the gene(s) is in the family's bloodline. Well, the same is true of dogs – crossbreeds as well as pure breeds.

There is not a single breed without the potential for some genetic weakness. For example, German Shepherd Dogs are more prone to hip problems than many other breeds, and 30% of Dalmatians have problems with their hearing. If you get a German Shepherd or a Dalmatian, your dog will not automatically suffer from these issues, but if he comes from unscreened parents, the dog will statistically be more likely to have them than a dog from a breed with no history of the complaint.

FACT ▷ *Faulty genes carrying genetic illnesses can be inherited along with all the good genes that you love, like those for cute face, colour, good temperament and fluffy coat.*

Many people make the mistake of thinking that if they get a Cockapoo, he or will *automatically* be healthier than a pedigree (pure bred) dog because the gene pool is larger and two separate breeds are involved. This is simply not true; you still have to make sure that both parents are healthy.

It is true that an F1 Cockapoo comes from two totally different gene pools – the Cocker Spaniel and the Poodle. So, compared with many purebreds, there is a bigger gene pool with no inbreeding - and this is a good thing. It can result in something called *hybrid vigour,* which means that the dog is robust – see **Chapter 1.** for more details. However, a Poodle with defective genes bred to a Cocker Spaniel with defective genes will produce a Cockapoo puppy with health issues.

For example, if you breed a Poodle with Progressive Retinal Atrophy (PRA) to a Cocker Spaniel with PRA, the likelihood of the Cockapoo puppy being born with PRA is 100%. If the parents are both carriers, but don't actually have the eye disease themselves, the resulting Cockapoo puppies will have a 25% of being born with PRA, a 50% chance of carrying the disease and only a 25% chance of being completely free of it. This is why getting a puppy from health-tested parents is so important – and it's not just PRA, there are other diseases a Cockapoo's parents should be tested for.

 Just because a puppy's parents are registered with the Kennel Club in the UK or AKC in the USA and have pedigree certificates, it does NOT mean that they have passed any health tests. When choosing a puppy, base your decision on what's going on INSIDE the puppy as well as external appearance - do this by asking to see any health certificates for the puppy's parents.

A pedigree certificate's only guarantee is that the puppy's parents can be traced back several generations and the ancestors were all purebred Cocker Spaniels or Poodles. Many purebred dogs have indeed passed health tests, but prospective buyers should always find out *exactly* what health screening the sire and dam (mother and father) have undergone. Ask to see original certificates - and what, if any, health guarantees the breeder is offering with the puppy.

FACT ❯ *"Vet Checked" does NOT mean health tested. It means that a vet has given the puppy a fairly brief once-over and everything seems to be fine. Health tests are scientific DNA tests that breeding dogs undergo to prove they do not have hereditary diseases.*

Fortunately, the Cockapoo is currently a relatively healthy crossbreed. Responsible breeders are playing their part in producing healthy pups from healthy breeding stock.

However, there is so much money to be made breeding Cockapoos, that unscrupulous breeders have sprung up. And buying a puppy from these people will ultimately lead to more health issues entering the Cockapoo gene pool.

Potential hereditary issues are eye problems and hip dysplasia, and Cockapoos are at medium risk of suffering from cataracts and other eye issues. Cockapoos often live into their teens – but this does not mean that by choosing one you are guaranteed a healthy dog. It is, however, true that your chance of getting a puppy with no hereditary problems is greatly increased if you buy from a breeder who DNA health tests her dogs.

The Cockapoo Club of GB states: "Within the gene pool that affects Cockapoo breeding, there are some known genetic diseases that can cause serious illness later in life that will not be apparent as puppies. The Cockapoo Club of GB is promoting health testing awareness and following procedures to minimise the occurrence of the diseases now and in future Cockapoos in this country."

The American Cockapoo Club's Code of Ethics for registered breeders, Point 7, states: "Use for breeding only those dogs which they believe to be healthy and free from serious congenital and hereditary defects."

Cockapoo Insurance

Insurance is another point to consider for a new puppy or adult dog. The best time to get pet insurance is BEFORE you bring your Cockapoo home and before any health issues develop. Don't wait until you need to seek veterinary help - bite the bullet and take out annual insurance. If you can afford it, take out life cover. This may be more expensive, but will cover your dog throughout his lifetime - including for chronic (recurring or long term) ailments, such as eye, heart or joint problems, ear infections and cancer.

Insuring a healthy puppy or adult dog is the only sure-fire way to ensure vets' bills are covered before anything unforeseen happens - and you'd be a rare owner if you didn't use your policy at least once during your dog's lifetime.

According to the UK's Bought By Many, monthly cover for a healthy nine-week-old Cockapoo puppy varies from around £20 to £30, depending on where you live, how much excess you are willing to pay and the amount of total vets' bills covered per year. In the UK, Bought By Many offers policies from insurers More Than at: https://boughtbymany.com/offers/cockapoo-insurance

They get groups of single breed owners together, so you have to join the Cockapoo Group, but it claims you'll get a 10% saving on normal insurance. We are not on commission - just trying to save you some money! There are numerous companies out there offering pet insurance. Read the small print and the amount of excess; a cheap policy may not always be the best long-term decision.

I ran a few examples for US pet insurance on a nine-week-old Cockapoo pup and came back with quotes from $30 to $45, depending on location, amount of coverage in dollars and deductible. With advances in veterinary science, there is so much more vets can do to help an ailing dog - but at a cost. Surgical procedures can rack up bills of thousands of pounds or dollars.

According to www.PetInsuranceQuotes.com and www.embracepetinsurance.com these are some treatment costs: Progressive Retinal Atrophy (PRA) $2,000-$3,000 per eye, Cataracts $2,500-

$5,000, Luxating Patella $1,500-$3,000, IVDD (Intervertebral Disc Disease) $2,500-$7,000, and Epilepsy $200-$15,000.
($1.30 = approximately £1 at the time of writing).
PetInsuranceQuotes rates insurance companies based on coverage, cost, customer satisfaction and the company itself and came up with the top eight: 1.Healthy Paws, 2.Embrace, 3.Trupanion, 4.ASPCA, 5.Petplan, 6.Nationwide, 7.PetsBest, 8.Figo.

Of course, if you make a claim, your monthly premium will increase, but if you have a decent insurance policy BEFORE a recurring health problem starts, your dog should continue to be covered if the ailment returns. You'll have to decide whether the insurance is worth the money. On the plus side, you'll have peace of mind if your beloved Cockapoo falls ill and you'll know just how much to fork out every month.

Another point to consider is that dogs are at increasing risk of theft by criminals, including organised gangs. With the purchase price of puppies rising, dognapping has shot up. More than 1,900 dogs were stolen in the UK in 2017. Some 49% of dogs are snatched from owners' gardens and 13% from people's homes. Check that theft is included on the policy. Although nothing can ever replace your favourite companion, good insurance will ensure you are not out of pocket.

···

Three Health Tips

1. **Buy a well-bred puppy** - A responsible breeder selects their stock based on:

   - General health and DNA testing of the parents
   - Conformation (physical structure)
   - Temperament

Although well-bred puppies are not cheap, believe it or not, committed Cockapoo breeders are not doing it for the money, often incurring high bills for health screening, stud fees, veterinary costs, specialised food, etc. The main concern of a good breeder is to produce healthy, handsome puppies with good temperaments that are "fit for function."

Better to spend time beforehand choosing a good puppy than to spend a great deal of time and money later when your wonderful pet bought from an online advert or pet shop develops health problems due to poor breeding, not to mention the heartache that causes. **Chapter 3. Bringing Puppy Home** has detailed information on how to find him and the questions to ask.

- Don't buy from a pet shop - no reputable breeder allows her pups to end up in pet shops

- Don't buy a puppy from a small ad on a general website

- Don't buy a pup or adult dog unseen with a credit card - you are storing up trouble and expense for yourself. (If you have selected a reputable breeder located many states away in the USA and can't travel to see the puppy, make sure you ask lots of questions)

2. **Get pet insurance as soon as you get your dog -** Don't wait until your dog has a health issue and needs to see a vet. Most insurers will exclude all pre-existing conditions on their policies. When choosing insurance, check the small print to make sure that all conditions are covered and that if the problem is recurring, it will continue to be covered year after year. When working out costs, factor in the annual or monthly pet insurance fees and trips to a vet for check-ups, annual vaccinations, etc.

   Some breeders provide free insurance for the first few weeks in their Puppy Pack - ask yours if this is the case.

3. **Find a good vet -** Ask around your pet-owning friends, rather than just going to the first one you find. A vet that knows your dog from his puppy vaccinations and then right through their life is more likely to understand your dog and diagnose quickly and correctly when something is wrong. If you visit a big veterinary practice, ask for the vet by name when you make an appointment.

We all want our dogs to be healthy - so how can you tell if yours is? Well, here are some positive things to look for in a healthy Cockapoo:

....

Signs of a Healthy Cockapoo

1. **Eyes -** A Cockapoo's eyes should not be too prominent or too close together. They should be round in shape and dark brown with very dark rims. Paleness around the eyeball (conjunctiva) could be a sign of underlying problems. A red swelling in the corner of one or both eyes could be cherry eye. Sometimes the dog's third eyelid (the nictating membrane) is visible at the eye's inside corner - this is normal. There should be no thick, green or yellow discharge from the eyes. A cloudy eye could be a sign of cataracts.

2. **Nose –** A dog's nose is an indicator of health symptoms. Normal nose colour is black, although some Cockapoo pups are born with pink patches that usually turn black during the first year, sometimes called a *"butterfly nose."* Regardless of colour, the nose should be moist and cold to the touch as well as free from clear, watery secretions.

Any yellow, green or foul-smelling discharge is not normal - in younger dogs this can be a sign of canine distemper. A pink nose or *"snow nose"* may appear in winter due to a lack of Vitamin D, but the nose usually returns to a darker colour during summer – it happens more often with lighter coloured Cockapoos.

A *"Dudley nose"* or *"putty nose"* is one where the nose, the area around the eyes and the feet lack any pigment from birth to old age and appear pink. Some dogs' noses turn pinkish with age; this is because their bodies are producing less pigment and is not a cause for concern.

Avoid getting a Cockapoo puppy with small, pinched nostrils, as these may cause breathing difficulties.

3. **Ears** – If you are choosing a puppy, gently clap your hands behind the pup (not so loud as to frighten him) to see if he reacts. If not, this may be a sign of deafness. Also, ear infections – sometimes known as "otitis" - can be a problem with Cockapoos and other breeds with floppy, hairy ears. A pricked-up ear allows air to circulate, while a folded ear flap creates a warm, moist haven for mini horrors such as bacteria and mites.

    The ear flap can also trap dirt and dust and should be inspected during your regular grooming routine. An unpleasant smell, redness or inflammation are all signs of infection. Some wax inside the ear – usually brown or yellowy - is normal; excessive wax or crusty wax is not. Tell-tale signs of an infection are scratching the ears, rubbing them on the floor or furniture, or shaking the head a lot, often accompanied by an unpleasant smell.

4. **Mouth** – Gums should be a healthy pink or black colour, or a mixture. A change in colour can be an indicator of a health issue. Paleness or whiteness can be a sign of anaemia or lack of oxygen due to heart or breathing problems (this is hard to tell with black gums). Blue gums or tongue are a sign that a dog is not breathing properly. Red, inflamed gums can be a sign of gingivitis or other tooth disease. Again, your dog's breath should smell OK. Young dogs will have sparkling white teeth, whereas older dogs will have darker teeth, but they should not have any hard white, yellow, green or brown bits.

5. **Coat and Skin** – These are easy-to-monitor indicators of a healthy dog. Any dandruff, bald spots, a dull lifeless coat, a discoloured or oily coat, or one that loses excessive hair, can all be signs that something is amiss. Skin should be smooth without redness. If a puppy or adult dog is scratching, licking or biting himself a lot, he may have a condition that needs addressing before he makes it worse. Open sores, scales, scabs, red patches or growths can be a sign of a problem. Signs of fleas, ticks and other external parasites should be treated immediately. Check there are no small black specks, which may be fleas, on the coat or bedding.

6. **Weight –** A general rule of thumb is that your dog's stomach should be above the bottom of his rib cage when standing, and you should be able to feel his ribs beneath his coat without too much effort. If the stomach is level or hangs below, your dog is overweight - or may have a pot belly, which can also be a symptom of other conditions.

7. **Temperature** – The normal temperature of a dog is 101°F to 102.5°F. (A human's is 98.6°F). Excited or exercising dogs may run a slightly higher temperature. Anything above 103°F or below 100°F should be checked out. The exceptions are female dogs about to give birth that

will often have a temperature of 99°F. If you take your dog's temperature, make sure he is relaxed and **always** use a purpose-made canine thermometer.

8. **Stools** - Poo, poop, business, faeces - call it what you will - it's the stuff that comes out of the less appealing end of your Cockapoo on a daily basis! It should be firm and brown, not runny, with no signs of worms or parasites. Watery stools or a dog not eliminating regularly are both signs of an upset stomach or other ailments. If it continues for a couple of days, consult your vet. If puppies have diarrhoea they need checking out much quicker as they can quickly dehydrate.

9. **Energy** – Cockapoos are lively, engaged dogs. Yours should have good amounts of energy with fluid and pain-free movements. Lack of energy or lethargy – if it is not the dog's normal character – could be a sign of an underlying problem.

10. **Smell** – If there is a musty, 'off' or generally unpleasant smell coming from your Cockapoo's body, it could be a sign of a yeast infection. There can be a number of reasons for this; often the ears require attention or it can sometimes be an allergy to a certain food. Another not uncommon cause is that one of the anal glands has become blocked and needs expressing, or squeezing - a job best left to the vet or groomer unless you know what you are doing! Whatever the cause, you need to get to the root of the problem as soon as possible before it develops into something more serious.

11. **Attitude** – A generally positive attitude is a sign of good health. Cockapoos are playful, so symptoms of illness may include one or all of the following: a general lack of interest in his surroundings, tail not wagging, lethargy, not eating food and sleeping a lot (more than normal). The important thing is to look out for any behaviour that is out of the ordinary for your individual dog.

So now you know some of the signs of a healthy dog – what are the signs of an unhealthy one? There are many different symptoms that can indicate your canine companion isn't feeling great. If you don't yet know your dog, his habits, temperament and behaviour patterns, then spend some time getting acquainted with them.

What are his normal character and temperament? Lively or calm, playful or serious, a joker or an introvert, bold or nervous, happy to be left alone or loves to be with people, a keen appetite or a fussy eater? How often does he empty his bowels, does he ever vomit? (Dogs will often eat grass to make themselves sick, this is perfectly normal and a natural way of cleansing the digestive system).

FACT 〉 *You may think your Cockapoo can't talk, but he can! If you really know your dog, his character and habits, then he CAN tell you when he's not well. He does this by changing his patterns.*

Some symptoms are physical, some emotional and others are behavioural. It's important to be able to recognise these changes as soon as possible. Early treatment can be the key to keeping a simple problem from snowballing into something more serious. If you do think your dog is unwell, keep an accurate and detailed account of his symptoms to give to the vet, perhaps even film him on your mobile phone. This will help your vet to correctly diagnose and treat your dog.

Four Vital Signs of Illness

1. **Temperature** - A new-born puppy has a temperature of 94-97°F. This reaches the normal adult body temperature of 101°F at about four weeks old. Anything between 100°F and 102.5°F is regarded as normal for an adult. The temperature is normally taken via the rectum. If you do this, be very careful. It's easier if you get someone to hold your dog while you do

this. Digital thermometers are a good choice, but **only use one specifically made for rectal use,** as normal glass thermometers can easily break off in the rectum.

Ear thermometers *(pictured)* are widely available from Amazon and Walmart, among others, making the task much easier, although they can be expensive and don't suit all dogs' ears. Non-touch ear and forehead thermometers are another option, slightly less accurate than a rectal thermometer, but very easy to use and great for nervous dogs.

Remember that exercise or excitement can cause the temperature to rise by 2°F to 3°F when your dog is actually in good health, so wait until he is relaxed before taking his temperature. If it is above or below the norms and he seems off-colour, give your vet a call.

2. **Respiratory Rate -** Another symptom of illness is a change in breathing patterns. This varies a lot depending on the size and weight of the dog. An adult dog will have a respiratory rate of 15-25 breaths per minute when resting. You can easily check this by counting your dog's breaths for a minute with a stopwatch handy. Don't do this if he is panting; it doesn't count.

3. **Heart Rate -** You can feel your dog's heartbeat by placing your hand on his lower ribcage – just behind the elbow. Don't be alarmed if the heartbeat seems irregular compared to that of a human; it IS irregular in some dogs. Your Cockapoo will probably love the attention, so it should be quite easy to check his heartbeat. Just lay him on his side and bend his left front leg at the elbow, bring the elbow in to his chest and place your fingers on this area and count the beats.

   - Tiny dogs have a heartbeat of up to 160 or 180 beats per minute
   - Small to medium dogs have a normal rate of 90 to 140 beats per minute. (A Cockapoo's heartbeat should be between 70 and 120 beats per minute)
   - Dogs weighing more than 30lb have a heart rate of 60 to 120 beats per minute; the larger the dog, the slower the normal heart rate
   - A young puppy has a heartbeat of around 220 beats per minute
   - An older dog has a slower heartbeat

4. **Behaviour Changes -** Classic symptoms of illness are any inexplicable behaviour changes. If there has NOT been a change in the household atmosphere, such as another new pet, a new baby, moving home, the absence of a family member or the loss of another dog, then the following symptoms may well be a sign that all is not well:

- Tiredness - sleeping more than normal or not wanting to exercise

- Depression

- Anxiety or trembling

- 🐾 Falling or stumbling
- 🐾 Loss of appetite
- 🐾 Walking in circles
- 🐾 Being more vocal - grunting, whining or whimpering
- 🐾 Aggression
- 🐾 Abnormal posture

Your dog may normally show some of these signs, but if any of them appear for the first time or worse than usual, you need to keep him under close watch for a few hours or even days. Quite often he will return to normal of his own accord. Like humans, dogs have off-days too.

If he is showing any of the above symptoms, then don't over-exercise him, and avoid stressful situations and hot or cold places. Make sure he has access to clean water. There are many other signals of ill health, but these are four of the most important. Keep a record for your vet, if your dog does need professional medical attention, most vets will want to know:

WHEN the symptoms first appeared in your dog

WHETHER they are getting better or worse, and

HOW FREQUENT the symptoms are - intermittent, continuous or increasing?

What the Breeders Say

The Cockapoo Handbook asked breeders about Cockapoo health and this is what some of them said, starting in North America with Jeanne Davis, of Wind Horse Offering, Maryland, who believes that in general the Cockapoo is a healthy dog: "I have not had long-term experience with any on-going health issues, although I have heard of ear problems. I have not had any soundness issues."

Jessica Sampson, of Legacy Cockapoos, Ontario, Canada: "For American Cockapoos, PRA-prcd (Progressive Retinal Atrophy-Progressive Rod Cone Degeneration) and Luxating Patella are the big ones. But we also test their hips/eyes and DNA test for glycogen storage disease VII/PFK Deficiency, Degenerative Myelopathy, Exercise-Induced Collapse, and von Willebrand Disease. The current biggest threat to the Cockapoo is uneducated breeders and lack of health/DNA screenings of breeding stock."

Jackie Stafford, of Dj's Cockapoos, Rusk, Texas, added: "The biggest problem I have seen in Cockapoos is luxated patellas. Usually the smaller the dog, the more prevalent it can be."

Rebecca Goins, of Moonshine Babies Cockapoos, agrees: "The main health issues with Cockapoos would be Patella Luxation - Poodles are susceptible to this. Progressive Retinal Atrophy (PRA) is another issue as both parent breeds are susceptible, although the rate of incidence is currently lower in Cockapoos than it is for either Poodles or Cockers."

Photo of this healthy pair courtesy of Rebecca.

"Ear infections also occur, with both Poodles and Cockers being susceptible to ear infections. The Cocker's long ears prevent air flow, as does the hair growth in the ear canal of the Poodle. If this is not kept trimmed on the underside of the ear and the hair plucked from the inside of the ear canal, warm moist conditions can result which can promote fungal and bacterial growth."

UK breeder Pat Pollington, of Polycinders Cockapoos, Devon, outlines some of the extensive health testing that responsible breeders undertake: "The main problem with crossbreeds is that you are putting two different breeds together and both have their own health problems. The most important thing when buying any puppy is that both parents are fully health tested. The good thing with F1 crossbreeds is that because you have two different breeds, there is no interbreeding."

Pictured is Pat's healthy and beautiful F1, Cherry.

She continued: "The main health issue with Cockapoos is prcd–PRA. This is a disease in the eye that will make your dog go blind at a very young age. You need to buy from health-tested parents. Always make sure both parents are tested and that one parent is clear. The English Cocker Spaniel also needs to be FN (Familial Nephropathy) tested. This is a kidney disorder that will kill the dog around the age of two.

"Both of these diseases are well documented in Cockapoos, and they are both very cruel. Poodles should also be BVA (British Veterinary Association) eye-tested. This is an annual test necessary because Poodles are susceptible to Glaucoma. Miniature Poodles should also be hip scored.

"There are some other tests that you can have done, but they are tests for any breed and are highly uncommon. As long as one parent is prcd-PRA clear, the Cocker is FN clear and the Poodles are BVA clear and hip scored, then the breeder has done everything to make sure the puppy has no health issues from the start."

Karol Watson Todd, of KaroColin Cockapoos, Sleaford, Lincolnshire, UK, added: "The biggest threat to health is PRA, as both parent breeds have this as a possibility. I think some of the health testing is irrelevant as neither parent breed greatly show the issues, e.g. hip testing.

"However, luxating patella is an issue and should be tested for, but is not a requirement. As my vet stated: we are testing for things most of the dogs should pass, so not testing for the real issues. As you get into F2s and further, then health testing should be more stringent."

Eyes

There is a range of eye conditions that can affect Cocker Spaniels and Poodles - and therefore Cockapoos. Many of them can be carefully managed with medication and extra care from the owner. All breeding dogs should be examined annually by certified veterinary ophthalmologists. Ask to see the parents' up-to-date certificates if you are buying a Cockapoo puppy.

PRA (Progressive Retinal Atrophy)

PRA is the name for several progressive diseases that lead to blindness. First recognised at the beginning of the 20th century in Gordon Setters, this inherited condition has been documented in over 100 breeds and some mixed breeds. Miniature and Toy Poodles, English Cocker Spaniels, American Cocker Spaniels, Labrador Retrievers, Cockapoos, Labradoodles and Goldendoodles are all recognised as being among the breeds and crossbreeds that can be affected by the disease. Puppies are born with normal eyesight and this generally begins to deteriorate from around the age of three to five in Cockapoos.

The specific genetic disorder that can affect Cockapoos is called prcd-PRA - progressive rod-cone degeneration PRA. (It is sometimes also called GPRA - General Progressive Retinal Atrophy). It causes cells in the retina at the back of the eye to degenerate and die, even though the cells seem to develop normally early in life. The rod cells operate in low light levels and are the first to lose normal function, and so the first sign is night blindness.

Then the cone cells gradually lose their normal function in full light situations. Most affected dogs will eventually go blind. (Conditions that might look like prcd-PRA could be another disease and might not be inherited. Not all retinal disease is PRA and not all PRA is the prcd form of PRA). Annual eye exams by a veterinary ophthalmologist will build a history of eye health that will help to diagnose disease.

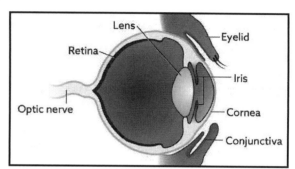

Prcd-PRA is inherited as a recessive trait. This means that the faulty gene must be inherited **from both parents** in order to cause disease in an offspring. In other words, for a puppy to get the disease, both its father and mother were either a carrier or sufferer. A dog that inherits only one copy of the abnormal gene will have no signs of the disease, but will be a carrier and may pass the gene on to any future offspring. Testing for prcd-PRA is mandatory for all Cockapoos registered with The Cockapoo Club of GB (Great Britain). One parent must show Normal/Clear.

Sadly, there is no cure, but prcd-PRA can be avoided in future generations by DNA testing of breeding dogs. If your Cockapoo is affected, it may be helpful to read other owners' experiences of living with blind dogs at www.eyevet.org and www.blinddogs.com.

Eye Testing

In North America, OFA (Orthopedic Foundation for Animals) runs the CAER Eye Certification Registry, which records the results of tested dogs. Breeders using the Optigen laboratory test get one of three results:

CLEAR: these dogs have two normal copies of DNA. Clear dogs will not develop PRA as a result of the mutation

CARRIER: these dogs have one copy of the mutation and one normal copy of DNA. These dogs will not develop PRA themselves as a result of the mutation, but they will pass the mutation on to half of their offspring.

GENETICALLY AFFECTED: these dogs have two copies of the mutation and will almost certainly develop PRA during their lifetime.

In the UK there is the British Veterinary Association (BVA) Eye Scheme, run in conjunction with the Kennel Club. Annual eye tests should be carried out, due to the fact some diseases have a late onset. After a BVA eye test, an Eye Examination Certificate is issued which records the inherited eye disease status as either *"clinically unaffected"* or *"clinically affected."*

If you are buying a puppy, it is highly advisable to check that the parents have been eye-tested and given the all-clear. Always ensure the breeder lets you see the original certificate, which is white in the UK, and not a photocopy. In the US, OFA statistics show that 9.4% of all Poodles tested were carriers for PRA, as were 1.9% of Cocker Spaniels. Identifying dogs that carry the diseased genes and NOT breeding from them is the key to eradicating the problem, and it is mandatory for all members of the Cockapoo Club of GB to test their breeding dogs for PRA.

Other Eye Conditions

Glaucoma

This is a condition that puts pressure on the eye, and if the condition becomes chronic or continues without treatment, it will eventually cause permanent damage to the optic nerve, resulting in blindness. All types of Cocker Spaniel are listed as being susceptible as well as Poodles.

A normal eye contains a fluid called aqueous humour to maintain its shape, and the body is constantly adding and removing fluid from inside of the eye to maintain the pressure inside the eye at the proper level. Glaucoma occurs when the pressure inside the eyeball becomes higher than normal. Just as high blood pressure can damage the heart, high pressure inside the eye can damage the eye, and unless glaucoma is treated quickly, temporary loss of vision or even total blindness can result.

Secondary glaucoma means that it is caused by another problem, such as a wound to the eye. Primary glaucoma is normally inherited and this is the type of glaucoma that Cockapoos should be tested for. Even though a puppy may carry the faulty gene, primary glaucoma does not usually develop in a Cockapoo until at least two to three years old. With primary glaucoma, rarely are both eyes equally affected or at the same time; it usually starts in one eye several months or even years before it affects the second one.

Symptoms - Glaucoma is a serious disease and it's important for an owner to be able to recognise initial symptoms immediately:

- ❧ Pain
- ❧ A dilated pupil or one pupil looks bigger than the other *(Our photo shows an extremely dilated pupil)*
- ❧ Rapid blinking
- ❧ Cloudiness in the cornea at the front of the eye
- ❧ The whites of an eye look bloodshot
- ❧ One eye looks larger or sticks out further than the other one
- ❧ Loss of appetite, which may be due to headaches
- ❧ Change in attitude, less willing to play, etc.

Most dogs will not display all of these signs at first, perhaps just one or two. A dog rubbing his eye with his paw, against the furniture or carpet or your leg is a common - and often unnoticed- early sign. Some dogs will also seem to flutter the eyelids or squint with one eye. The pupil of the affected eye will usually dilate (get bigger) in the early stages. It may still react to all bright light, but only very slowly. If the pupil in one eye is larger than in the other, something is definitely wrong and it could be glaucoma.

If you suspect your dog has glaucoma, get him to the vet as soon as possible, i.e. **immediately,** not the day after, this is a medical emergency. If treatment is not started within a few days - or even hours in some cases - the dog will probably lose sight in that eye. A vet will carry out a manual examination and test your dog's eye pressure using a tonometer on the surface of the eye.

There is still a fair chance that the dog may lose sight in this eye, but a much better chance of saving the second eye with the knowledge and preventative measures learned from early intervention. Treatment revolves around reducing the pressure within the affected eye, draining the aqueous humour and providing pain relief, as this can be a painful condition for your dog. There are also surgical options for the long-term control of glaucoma. As yet it cannot be cured.

Cataracts

The purpose of the transparent lens is to focus the rays of light to form an image on the retina. A cataract occurs when the lens becomes cloudy. Less light enters the eye, images become blurry and the dog's sight diminishes as the cataract becomes larger. If the cataract is small, it won't disturb the dog's vision too much, but owners must monitor cataracts because the thicker and denser they become, the more likely it is they will lead to glaucoma and/or blindness.

Cockapoos are not known to be susceptible to hereditary cataracts, so the more common reasons are old age - late onset cataracts may develop any time after the age of six years - eye injury or disease. In less severe cases, dogs can live a perfectly normal life with daily eye drops and vigilance on the part of the owner.

 Beware of miracle cures! If you do try drops, look for some containing the effective ingredient N-Acetyl Carnosine, or NAC. There is a relatively inexpensive product called Cataract Clear, available from Costcuttersrus.com

Left: eye with cataracts. Right: same eye with artificial lens

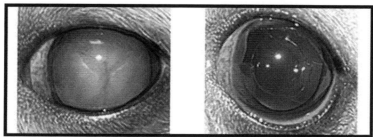

Depending on the cause, severity and type of cataract, surgery is an option for some dogs; the lens is removed and replaced with a plastic substitute. It costs around £2,500-£3,500 per eye (around $2,700-$4,000 in the US), but if the dog is a suitable candidate, it is successful in 90% of cases.

As well as a cloudy eye, other signs are the dog bumping into things, especially in dimly-lit situations, squinting or pawing at the eye, eye redness or an inflamed eye socket, or a bulging eye. If you suspect your Cockapoo has cataracts, get him to the vet for an examination as soon as possible. Early intervention can prevent complications such as glaucoma developing.

Cherry Eye

This can develop in dogs of all breeds, particularly young dogs. Humans have two eyelids, but dogs have a third eyelid, called a *nictating membrane.* This is a thin, opaque tissue with a tear gland that rests in the inner corner of the eye. It provides extra protection for the eye and spreads tears over the eyeball. Usually it is retracted and therefore you can't see it, although you may notice it when your dog is relaxed and falling asleep.

Cherry Eye, *pictured,* is a collapse of the gland of the third eyelid, thought to be due to a weakness of the fibrous tissue that attaches the gland to the surrounding eye. The gland falls down, exposing it to dry air, irritants and bacteria, when it can become infected and begin to swell.

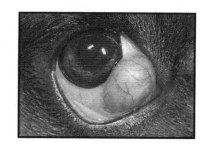

There is sometimes a mucous discharge and if the dog rubs or scratches it, he can further damage the gland and even possibly create an ulcer on the surface of the eye. Although it looks sore, it is not generally painful. Mild cases are treated with a steroid ointment to try and get the gland back to its normal position, and antibiotics to prevent infection. If that doesn't work, surgery to reposition the gland should be considered. A simple stich or two can tack the gland down into the conjunctiva.

Retinal Dysplasia

This is an inherited eye disease that affects some Spaniels when the cells and layer of retinal tissue at the back of the eye do not develop properly. One or both eyes may be affected. It can be detected by a vet using an ophthalmoscope when the puppy is six weeks old or even younger. Most cases of retinal dysplasia do get worse after puppyhood.

Retinal Dysplasia occurs when the two layers of the retina do not form together, causing folds. The disorder causes small blind spots that are probably not even noticed by the dog. However, the more serious geographic dysplasia may lead to large blanks in the visual field, and dogs with retinal detachments are completely blind. Severely affected puppies may have symptoms such as a reluctance to walk into dark areas, bumping into things and obvious sight problems. There is sadly no treatment for the condition.

FACT > *Eye conditions can be caused or worsened by irritants and injury. Remove or trim low, spiky plants in your garden or yard. And although it may look super cute when your Cockapoo sticks his head out of the open car window with the wind whistling through his ears, remember that dust, insects and dirt particles can hit and damage his eyes.*

NOTE: The BVA has an excellent PDF on the subject, visit www.BVA.com and navigate to *Canine Health Schemes,* then scroll down to *Hereditary eye disease leaflet.*

....

Luxating Patella

Luxating Patella, also called *"floating kneecap," "loose knee"* or *"slipped stifle,"* can be a painful condition akin to a dislocated kneecap in humans; the most common cause is genetic and it affects some Miniature and Toy Poodles.

A groove in the end of the femur (thigh bone) allows the knee cap to glide up and down when the knee joint is bent, while keeping it in place at the same time. If this groove is too shallow, the knee cap may luxate – or dislocate.

It can only return to its natural position when the quadriceps muscle relaxes and increases in length, which is why a dog may have to hold his leg up for some time after the dislocation. The condition ranges from Grade 1 to Grade 4. In mild cases (Grade 1) the kneecap may pop back into

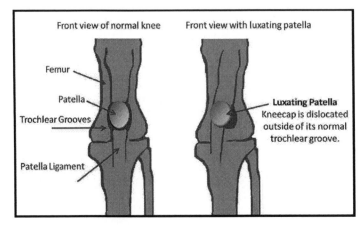

its socket of its own accord, or be manipulated back into place by a vet. In severe cases the patella is permanently out of place and the dog has extreme difficulty extending the knees.

He walks with bent knees virtually all the time - often with the whole leg angled and rotated out. Severe cases are usually dealt with by surgery. Sometimes the problem can be caused – and is certainly worsened - by obesity, the excess weight putting too much strain on the joint – another good reason to keep your Cockapoo's weight in check.

Symptoms - A typical sign would be if your dog is running across the park when he suddenly pulls up short and yelps with pain. He might limp on three legs and then after a period of about 10 minutes, drop the affected leg and start to walk normally again. Another sign is that you might notice him stretching out a rear leg quite often or *"skipping"* once in a while when walking or running. If the condition is severe, he may hold up the affected leg up for a few days.

Dogs that have a luxating patella on both hind legs may change their gait completely, dropping their hindquarters and holding the rear legs further out from the body as they walk. In the most extreme cases they might not even use their rear legs, but walk like a circus act by balancing on their front legs so their hindquarters don't touch the ground.

Typically, many sufferers are middle-aged dogs with a history of intermittent lameness in the affected rear leg or legs, although the condition may appear as early as four to six months old.

FACT ❯ *There is a DNA test that can tell if the parents are clear of the disease. It's run by the OFA in the USA and by qualified veterinary clinics in the UK; ask to see screening certificates for the puppy's parents.*

Treatment - If moderate to severe cases are left untreated, the groove will become even shallower and the dog will become progressively lamer, with arthritis prematurely affecting the joint. This will cause a permanently swollen knee and reduce your dog's mobility. It is therefore important to get your dog in for a veterinary check-up ASAP if you suspect he may have a luxating patella.

Surgery is often required for Grade III and IV luxation. In these cases, known as a **trochlear modification,** the groove at the base of the femur is surgically deepened to better hold the knee cap in place. The good news is that dogs generally respond well, whatever the type of surgery, and are usually completely recovered within two months.

Hip Dysplasia

Canine Hip Dysplasia, or CHD, is the most common cause of hind leg lameness in dogs; dysplasia means **abnormal development.** It is also the most common heritable orthopaedic problem seen in dogs, affecting virtually all breeds, but is more common in large breeds. The condition develops into degenerative osteoarthritis of the hip joints.

CHD is more common in large breeds, but is also known in Cocker Spaniels - both English and American – as well as Poodles, although it's not common in Toys. Some 11.7% of Poodles and 6.4% of Cocker Spaniels tested by OFA in the USA had abnormal hips.

The hip is a ball and socket joint. Hip dysplasia is caused when the head of the femur (thigh bone) fits loosely into a shallow and poorly-developed socket in the pelvis. Most dogs with dysplasia are born with normal hips, but due to their genetic make-up - and possibly other factors such as diet - the surrounding soft tissues develop abnormally.

The joint carrying the weight of the dog becomes loose and unstable, muscle growth lags behind normal development and is often followed by degenerative joint disease or osteoarthritis. Early diagnosis gives your vet the best chance to tackle the problem as soon as possible, minimising the chance of arthritis developing. Symptoms range from mild discomfort to extreme pain. A puppy with canine hip dysplasia usually starts to show signs between five and 13 months old.

Symptoms are: lameness in the hind legs, particularly after exercise, difficulty or stiffness when getting up or climbing uphill, a *"bunny hop"* gait, a waddling or strange rear leg gait, or a reluctance to jump, exercise or climb stairs.

Canine hip dysplasia is usually inherited, but there are also factors that can trigger or worsen the condition, including overfeeding, especially on a diet high in protein, calcium or calories, and either extended periods without exercise or too much vigorous exercise - especially in young dogs.

 With young Cockapoos, high-impact activities that apply a lot of force to the joint, such as jumping and catching Frisbees, jumping on and off furniture or running up and down stairs, should be avoided as they often cause damage to soft bones and tissue.

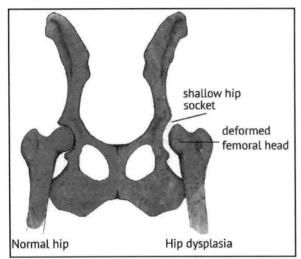

shallow hip socket

deformed femoral head

Normal hip   Hip dysplasia

As usual, early diagnosis leads to a better outcome. Your vet will take X-rays to make a diagnosis. Various medical and surgical treatments are available, which one depends upon factors such as the dog's age, how bad the problem is and, sadly, how much money you can afford to spend on treatment.

Managing CHD usually consists of restricting exercise, supplements, keeping body weight down and managing pain with drugs; cortisone injections may sometimes be used. In severe cases, surgery may be an option, with costs starting at around £1,500 or $2,000 per hip.

Hip Scoring - Ask if the dam and sire of your puppy have been *hip scored* - or tested - for hip dysplasia by the BVA in the UK, or OFA in the USA. The hip score is the total number of points given for each hip examined by X-ray, *the lower the score the better.* The best score for each hip is 0 and the worst is 53 and, as a dog has two hips, the total score will be between 0 and 106.

 *The suggested mean (average) score for Cockapoos should be around 12-13. It is not essential that Cockapoo breeding stock is hip scored, but it's good news if a breeder has had her breeding dogs tested and the score is less than 13.*

Familial Nephropathy (FN)

Familial Nephropathy is an inherited disease that leads to early kidney failure and death. Around 11% of English Cocker Spaniels – both show and working - are carriers of the genetic mutation responsible, but American Cockers are not affected.

There is a 99% reliable FN DNA test to determine affected dogs, and these should not be used for breeding. Without testing, an unsuspecting breeder can mate a male carrier and a female carrier without knowing it and produce a litter containing affected puppies.

The test is mandatory for breeders registered with the Cockapoo Club of GB. Results show if the dog is *Clear, Carrier* or *Affected*, and if one parent has a *Clear* result, the puppy will not inherit the disease, as the gene is recessive.

If you are buying a Cockapoo puppy where English Cockers are in the bloodline, ask to see the parents' certificates for FN. Sadly, the disease usually affects puppies and young dogs between the age of six months and two years. Symptoms are:

- Weight loss
- Excessive thirst
- Excessive urine
- A slowdown in growth
- Reduced appetite
- Vomiting and diarrhoea

All are signs of the kidneys packing up, which leads to the death of the dog, usually at a young age. All members of the Cockapoo Club of GB must test their English Cocker Spaniels for FN.

PFK Deficiency

PFK, or Phosphofructokinase Deficiency is a hereditary metabolic disorder affecting American Cocker Spaniels and their offspring, but not English Cocker Spaniels. It prevents the glucose metabolising into energy. Phosphofructokinase is the name of the enzyme responsible for this metabolic action.

PFK is an **autosomal recessive genetic disease**, so dogs that are carriers show no signs of PFK deficiency, but can pass the faulty gene on to their puppies, thereby spreading the disease. Some 10% of American Cockers are thought to be affected, but both parents have to be **Carriers** or **Affected** for the puppy to inherit PFK deficiency.

Symptoms vary depending on how serious the condition is, but typical signs are: exercise intolerance, lethargy, general weakness, muscle wasting and cramping, blood in the dog's urine, fever, depression, and pale gums.

Affected dogs have persistent mild anaemia (low levels of red blood cells), but can usually compensate for this. They also have intermittent bouts of red blood cell breakdown, called **haemolysis,** when they become lethargic and weak and may even bleed. This usually happens after intense exercise, excessive barking or panting.

The dog's gums are pale or jaundiced and he usually has a high fever. The dog's urine may turn brown, due to blood breakdown products in the urine. If this happens, the dog needs to see a vet.

A vet will examine the dog and take blood tests before diagnosing PFK Deficiency. There is no specific treatment, but the condition can be managed. Owners have to play their part by keeping on the lookout for symptoms and avoiding certain situations, such as increased stress, strenuous exercise, excitement that causes lots of barking, and very hot weather.

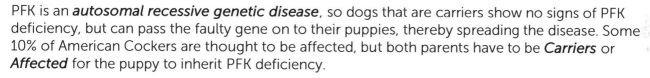

von Willebrand's Disease

Von Willebrand's Disease, or vWD, is the most common inherited bleeding disorder in dogs; it's similar to haemophilia in humans The Cockapoo Club of GB says it is advisable, rather than compulsory, for members to test for Type 1 vWD.

A dog with the disease lacks a substance, called **von Willebrand's factor,** that helps to form blood clots. Dogs that show symptoms of the disease bleed excessively as their blood does not clot properly. However, many diagnosed dogs show no symptoms, or none until later life.

Certain breeds have a higher incidence of vWD than others - including Miniature and Standard Poodles. They can inherit Type 1 von Willebrand's, which is the least severe form of the disease. It is named after Erik Adolf von Willebrand *(pictured),* a Finnish doctor who documented and studied a rare bleeding disorder in an isolated group of people in 1924. He showed that the disease was inherited, rather than caught by infection.

It was thought that the faulty gene(s) was recessive, meaning BOTH parents had to have it for the puppy to be affected. Latest research shows that it may be possible for one affected parent to pass the disease on to a puppy.

The main symptom is excessive bleeding, including nosebleeds, blood in the faeces (black or bright red blood), bloody urine, bleeding from the gums, females bleeding excessively from the vagina, bruising of the skin, and excessive bleeding after surgery or trauma.

Without treatment, an affected dog can bleed to death after surgery or what otherwise might normally be considered a less than life-threatening injury. The only proven way to treat vWD is with transfusions of blood collected from healthy dogs.

Sadly, as yet there is no permanent cure for von Willebrand's Disease. The only way to stop the spread of the disease is to DNA test dogs and to stop breeding from affected animals. A drug called DDAVP can help some dogs with bleeding episodes, but it cannot be given on a regular basis.

Some dogs with von Willebrand's Disease are also *hypothyroid,* meaning they have lower than normal levels of the hormone thyroid. These dogs benefit from thyroid hormone replacement therapy.

Heart Problems

Cockapoos are not particularly prone to heart problems, but they are relatively common among the canine population in general. Heart failure, or congestive heart failure (CHF), occurs when the heart is not able to pump enough blood around the dog's body.

The heart is a mechanical pump. It receives blood in one half and forces it through the lungs, then the other half pumps the blood through the entire body. The two most common forms of heart failure in dogs are Degenerative Valvular Disease (DVD) and Dilated Cardiomyopathy (DCM), also known as an *enlarged heart.*

FACT *In humans, heart disease often results in a heart attack, whereas in dogs, hardening of the arteries and heart attacks are very rare. Canine heart disease IS common, but rather than happening suddenly, it is a slow and insidious process that happens over months or years.*

In dogs, the heart muscles *"give out,"* usually caused by one chamber or side of the heart being required to do more than it is physically able to do. Over time the muscles weaken when excessive force is required to pump the blood through an area. In these cases, symptoms usually worsen until the dog is placed on treatment.

Heart failure in older dogs is often due to problems with the mitral valve, when the valve doesn't close properly and some blood flows backwards. It occurs most commonly in smaller breeds, including small Poodles, Yorkshire Terriers, Lhasa Apsos and Pomeranians.

Symptoms of Heart Disease

- Tiredness and decreased activity levels
- Restlessness, pacing around instead of settling down to sleep

🐾 Intermittent coughing - especially during exertion or excitement – which is often the first sign of mitral valve disorder. It often occurs at night or first thing in the morning and is an attempt to clear fluid in the lungs

If it worsens, other symptoms may appear:

🐾 Lack of appetite

🐾 Rapid breathing

🐾 Abdominal swelling due to fluid

🐾 Noticeable loss of weight

🐾 Fainting (syncope)

🐾 Paleness of the gums

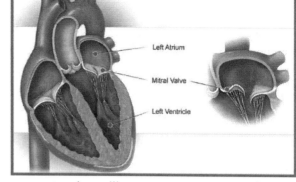

If your dog has some of these symptoms, he needs to see a vet, who will carry out tests to make a diagnosis. These may include listening to the heart, chest X-rays, blood tests, electrocardiogram (a record of your dog's heartbeat) or an echocardiogram (heart ultrasound).

If the problem is due to an enlarged heart or valve disease, the condition cannot be reversed, so treatment focuses on managing the symptoms with various medications. The vet may prescribe a special diet low in salt, as sodium, found in salt, determines the amount of water in the blood. The amount of exercise your dog has will also have to be controlled. Vitamin and other supplements can be beneficial.

The prognosis for dogs with congestive heart failure depends on the cause and severity, as well as their response to treatment.

CHF is progressive, so your dog can never recover from the condition. But once diagnosed, he can live a longer, more comfortable life with the right medication and regular check-ups.

Heart Murmurs

Heart murmurs are not uncommon in dogs. We had a dog diagnosed with a Grade 2 murmur many years ago and, of course, your heart sinks when the vet gives you the terrible news. But once the shock is over, it's important to realise that there are several different severities of the condition and, at its mildest, it is no great cause for concern. Our dog lived a happy and active life until the age of 13 when he succumbed to old age.

Literally, a heart murmur is a specific sound heard through a stethoscope; it results from the blood flowing faster than normal within the heart itself or in one of the two major arteries. Instead of the normal *"lubb dupp"* noise, an additional sound can be heard that can vary from a mild *"pshhh"* to a loud *"whoosh."* The different grades are:

♦ Grade 1—barely audible

♦ Grade 2—soft, but easily heard with a stethoscope

♦ Grade 3—intermediate loudness; most murmurs related to the mechanics of blood circulation are at least Grade 3

♦ Grade 4—loud murmur that radiates widely, often including opposite side of chest

♦ Grade 5 and Grade 6—very loud, audible with stethoscope barely touching the chest; the vibration is also strong enough to be felt through the animal's chest wall

Murmurs are caused by a number of factors; it may be a problem with the heart valves or could be due to some other condition, such as hyperthyroidism, anaemia, or heartworm.

In puppies, there are two major types of heart murmurs, and they will probably be detected by your vet at the first or second vaccinations. The most common type is called an *"innocent heart murmur."* This type of murmur is soft - typically Grade 2 or less - and is not caused by underlying heart disease and typically disappears by four to five months of age.

However, if a puppy has a loud murmur - Grade 3 or louder - or if the heart murmur is still easily heard with a stethoscope after four or five months of age, the likelihood of the puppy having an underlying congenital heart problem becomes much higher. The thought of this is extremely worrying for an owner, but it is important to remember that the disease will not affect all puppies' life expectancy nor quality of life.

A heart murmur can also develop suddenly in an adult dog with no prior history of the problem. This is typically due to age, which in Toy and small breeds is often due to thickening and degeneration of the mitral valve. (This is the type our dog had).

This thickening of the valve prevents it from closing properly and as a result it starts to leak; this is known as **Mitral Valve Disease** or MVD. The more common type of heart disease affecting larger dog breeds in middle age is **Dilated Cardiomyopathy** (DCM). The best way to investigate the cause of the heart murmur is with an ultrasound examination.

 *Good dental care and supplements, such as fatty acids and antioxidants, can help to prevent heart disease.*

Dental Issues

Veterinary studies show that by the age of three, 80% of dogs exhibit signs of dental disease – and Toy Poodles, some Miniature Poodles and dogs with small mouths are more likely than other breeds to have issues with their teeth.

Problems start with plaque, which can lead to a build-up of tartar on the teeth within days. This in turn often leads to *gingivitis* - infection of the gums - and *periodontal disease* - infections around the teeth and their roots.

If no action is taken, dogs can lose their teeth, which is very painful and makes it more difficult to eat. And if the infection travels into the dog's bloodstream it can damage kidneys, liver, heart and joints. Tooth disease can even shorten a dog's life by up to three years. Tell-tale initial signs include:

- Yellow and brown build-up of tartar along the gum line
- Red inflamed gums
- Persistent bad breath

You can give your dog a daily dental stick to help keep his mouth and teeth clean or use natural chews that also clean the teeth, like bully sticks. Teeth cleaning should also become part of your regular maintenance schedule; if neglected some dogs have to have their dog's teeth cleaned under anaesthetic by their local vet. *Our photo shows a dog with healthy teeth and gums.*

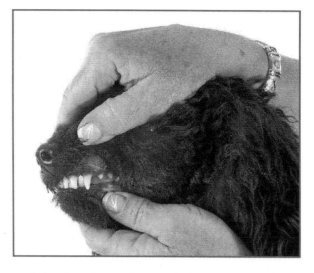

Teeth cleaning at home shouldn't be a chore – although it may start out as a bit of a battle or a game! Take things slowly in the beginning; give lots of praise and many dogs even start to look forward to teeth brushing sessions.

You can start getting your Cockapoo used to a brush and you touching his teeth as soon as he arrives home and has settled in – even before teething. Use a pet toothpaste as the human variety can upset a canine's stomach; many have flavours that your dog will find tasty. One benefit comes from the actual action of the brush on the teeth. Various brushes, sponges and pads are available; the choice depends on factors such as the health of your dog's gums, the size of his mouth and how good you are at teeth cleaning!

Get your dog used to the toothpaste by letting him lick some off your finger. If he doesn't like the flavour, try a different one. Continue this until he looks forward to licking the paste – it might be instant or take days. Put a small amount on your finger and gently rub it on one of the big canine teeth at the front of his mouth.

Then get him used to the toothbrush or dental sponge you will be using, praise him when he licks it – do this for several days. The next step is to actually start brushing. Talk to your dog in an encouraging way and praise him when you're finished.

Lift his upper lip gently, as in the photo, and place the brush at a 45° angle to the gum line. Gently move the brush backwards and forwards. Start just with his front teeth and then gradually do a few more. You don't need to brush the inside of the teeth as his tongue should keep them relatively free of plaque.

Cockapoos love attention and, with a bit of encouragement and patience, it can become an enjoyable task for you both. Brushing your dog's teeth from an early age will help to stave off dental disease – aim to do it once a week, if you can. There are various videos on YouTube that demonstrate how to clean a dog's teeth.

Epilepsy

Cocker Spaniels and Poodles statistically have a slightly higher chance of getting epilepsy than some other breeds, and therefore Cockapoos do as well.

Epilepsy means repeated seizures - also called fits or convulsions - due to abnormal electrical activity in the brain. It can affect any breed of dog and in fact affects around four or five dogs in every 100.

A study carried out in Sweden (Heske et al. 2014), based on data on 35 breeds from insurance companies, found that the Boxer emerged as the breed most likely to be affected by epilepsy, with the Miniature and Toy Poodles ranked fifth. The full results are at:

www.instituteofcaninebiology.org/blog/epilepsy-incidence-and-mortality-in-35-dog-breeds

Seizures often start between the ages of six months and five years. Anyone who has witnessed their dog having a seizure knows how frightening it can be. Seizures are not uncommon, and many dogs only ever have one. If your dog has had more than one, it may be that he is epileptic.

The good news is that, just as with people, there are medications to control epilepsy in dogs, allowing them to live relatively normal lives with normal lifespans.

The type of epilepsy affecting Cockers and Poodles is called *Idiopathic Epilepsy,* which means there is no detectable injury, disease or abnormality. Although yet to be proven, scientists believed that some forms of epilepsy are genetic, and that the type that affects Cockers and small Poodles is *autosomal recessive* – i.e. both parents need the faulty gene(s) for the disease to be passed on.

Affected dogs behave normally between seizures. In some cases, the gap between seizures is relatively constant, in others it can be very irregular with several occurring over a short period of time, but with long intervals between *"clusters."* If they occur because of a problem somewhere else in the body, such as heart disease (which stops oxygen reaching the brain), this is not epilepsy.

Symptoms

Some dogs seem to know when they are about to have a seizure and may behave in a certain way. You will come to recognise these signs as meaning that an episode is likely. Often dogs just seek out their owner's company and come to sit beside them. There are two main types:

Petit Mal, also called a Focal or Partial Seizure, which is the lesser of the two as it only affects one half of the brain. This may involve facial twitching, staring into space with a fixed glaze and/or upward eye movement, walking as if drunk, snapping at imaginary flies, and/or running or hiding for no reason. Sometimes this is accompanied by urination and the dog is conscious throughout.

Grand Mal, or Generalised Seizure, affects both hemispheres of the brain and is more often what we think of when we talk about a seizure. Most dogs become stiff, fall onto their side and make running movements with their legs. Sometimes they will cry out and may lose control of their bowels, bladder or both.

The dog is unconscious once the seizure starts – he cannot hear or respond to you. While it is distressing to watch, **the dog is not in any pain -** even if howling. It's not uncommon for an episode to begin as a focal seizure, but progress into a generalised seizure.

Sometimes, the progression is pretty clear - there may be twitching or jerking of one body part that gradually increases in intensity and progresses to include the entire body – other times the progression happens very fast.

Make a note of the time the seizure starts and ends, or better still, record it on your phone, because it seems to last a lot longer than it actually does. Most seizures last between one and three minutes. If you are not sure if your dog has had a seizure, look on YouTube, where there are many videos of dogs having seizures.

Afterwards dogs behave in different ways. Some just get up and carry on with what they were doing, while others appear dazed and confused for up to 24 hours afterwards. Most commonly, they will be disorientated for only 10 to 15 minutes before returning to their old self.

They often have a set pattern of behaviour after a seizure - for example going for a drink of water or asking to go outside to the toilet. If your dog has had more than one seizure, you may well start to notice a pattern of behaviour that is typically repeated.

Most seizures occur while the dog is relaxed and resting quietly, often in the evening or at night; it rarely happens during exercise. In a few dogs, seizures seem to be triggered by particular events or stress. It is common for a pattern to develop and, should your dog suffer from epilepsy, you will gradually recognise this as specific to your dog.

The most important thing is to **stay calm.** Remember that your dog is unconscious during the seizure and is not in pain or distressed. It is likely to be more distressing for you than for him. Make sure that he is not in a position to injure himself, for example by falling down the stairs, but otherwise do not try to interfere. Never try to put your hand inside his mouth during a seizure or you are likely to get bitten.

It is very rare for dogs to injure themselves during a seizure. Occasionally they may bite their tongue and there may appear to be a lot of blood, but it's unlikely to be serious; your dog will not swallow his tongue. If it goes on for a very long time (more than 10 minutes), his body temperature will rise, which can cause organ damage.

In very extreme cases, some dogs may be left in a coma after severe seizures. Repeated seizures can cause cumulative brain damage, which can result in behavioural changes or early senility, with loss of learned behaviour and housetraining.

When Should I Contact the Vet?

Generally, if your dog has a seizure lasting more than five minutes, or is having more than two or three a day, you should contact your vet. When your dog starts fitting, make a note of the time. If he comes out of it within five minutes, allow him time to recover quietly before contacting your vet.

It is far better for him to recover quietly at home rather than be bundled into the car and carted off to the vet right away.

However, if your dog does not come out of the seizure within five minutes, or has repeated seizures close together, contact your vet immediately, as he or she will want to see your dog as soon as possible.

If this is his first seizure, your vet may ask you to bring him in for a check-up and some routine blood tests. Always call the vet clinic before setting off to be sure that there is someone there who can help when you arrive. There are many things other than epilepsy that cause seizures in dogs.

When your vet first examines your dog, he or she will not know whether your dog has epilepsy or another illness. It's unlikely that the vet will see your dog during a seizure, so it is **vital** that you're able to describe in some detail just what happens.

Your vet may need to run a range of tests to ensure that there is no other cause of the seizures. These may include blood tests, possibly X-rays, and maybe even an MRI scan of your dog's brain. If no other cause can be found, then a diagnosis of epilepsy may be made. If your Cockapoo already has epilepsy, remember these key points:

❧ *Don't change or stop any medication without consulting your vet*

- ❧ *See your vet at least once a year for follow-up visits*
- ❧ *Be sceptical of 'magic cure' treatments*

Treatment

It is not usually possible to remove the cause of the seizures, so your vet will use medication to control them. Treatment will not cure the disease, but it will manage the signs – in some cases even a well-controlled epileptic may have occasional seizures.

As yet there is no cure for epilepsy, so don't be tempted with *"instant cures"* from the internet.

There are many drugs used in the control of epilepsy in people, but very few of these are suitable for long-term use in a dog. Two of the most common are Phenobarbital and Potassium Bromide (some dogs can have negative results with Phenobarbital). There are also a number of holistic remedies advertised, but we have no experience of them or any idea if any are effective.

Other factors that have proved useful in some cases are:

- ❧ Avoiding dog food containing preservatives
- ❧ Adding vitamins, minerals and/or enzymes to the diet
- ❧ Ensuring drinking water is free of fluoride

 *Each epileptic dog is different and treatment plans are all specific to the individual. They are based on the severity and frequency of seizures and how the dog responds to different medications. Many epileptic dogs require a combination of one or more drugs to get the dog onto an even keel and control the seizures.*

Once your dog has been on treatment for a while, he will become dependent on the levels of drug in his blood at all times to control seizures. If you miss a dose of treatment, blood levels can drop and this may be enough to trigger a seizure.

Keep a record of events in your dog's life, note down dates and times of episodes and record when you have given medication. Each time you visit your vet, take this diary along with you so he or she can see how your dog has been since his last check-up.

If seizures are becoming more frequent, it may be necessary to change the medication. The success or otherwise of treatment may depend on YOU keeping a close eye on your Cockapoo to see if there are any physical or behavioural changes.

 You need patience when managing an epileptic pet. It is important that medication is given at the same time each day.

It is not common for epileptic dogs to stop having seizures altogether. However, provided your dog is checked regularly by your vet to make sure that the drugs are not causing any side effects, there is every chance that he will live a full and happy life.

With the proper medical treatment, most epileptic dogs have far more good days than bad ones. Enjoy all those good days.

Remember: *live WITH epilepsy not FOR epilepsy.*

Thanks to www.canineepilepsy.co.uk for assistance with this section. If your Cockapoo has epilepsy, we recommend reading this website to gain a greater understanding of the illness.

Canine Diabetes

Diabetes can affect dogs of all breeds, sizes and both sexes, as well as obese dogs. There are two types:

- **Diabetes mellitus**, caused by a lack of vasopressin, a hormone that controls the kidneys' absorption of water

- **Diabetes insipidus** occurs when the dog's body does not produce enough insulin and cannot successfully process sugars

Dogs, like humans, get energy by converting food into sugars, mainly glucose. This travels in the dog's bloodstream and individual cells remove some glucose from the blood to use for energy. The substance that allows the cells to take glucose from the blood is a protein called *insulin.*

Insulin is created by beta cells located in the pancreas, next to the stomach. Almost all diabetic dogs have Type 1 diabetes; their pancreas does not produce any insulin. Without it, the cells have no way to use the glucose that is in the bloodstream, so the cells 'starve' while the glucose level in the blood rises. A vet takes blood and urine samples to check glucose concentrations in order to diagnose diabetes. Early treatment helps to prevent further complications developing.

Diabetes mellitus (sugar diabetes) is the most common form and, according to UFAW, affects one in 294 dogs in the UK. According to a study of 180,000 insured dogs, Miniature and Toy Poodles ranked 11th out of 46 breeds for the disorder: https://onlinelibrary.wiley.com/doi/pdf/10.1111/j.1939-1676.2007.tb01940.x

Both males and females can develop it; unspayed females have a slightly higher risk. The typical canine diabetes sufferer is middle-aged, female and overweight, with unspayed females being at slightly higher risk, but there are also juvenile cases. The condition is now treatable and need not shorten a dog's lifespan or interfere greatly with his quality of life. Due to advances in veterinary science, diabetic dogs undergoing treatment now have the same life expectancy as non-diabetic dogs of the same age and gender.

Symptoms of Diabetes Mellitus are:

- Extreme thirst

- Excessive urination

- Weight loss

- Increased appetite

- Coat in poor condition

- Lethargy

- Vision problems due to cataracts

If left untreated, diabetes can lead to cataracts and even blindness, increasing weakness in the legs (neuropathy), other ailments and even death.

Treatment and Exercise

Many cases of canine diabetes can be successfully treated with a combination of diet and medication, while more severe cases may require insulin injections. In the newly-diagnosed dog, insulin therapy begins at home.

Normally, after a week of treatment, the dog returns to the vet for a series of blood sugar tests over a 12 to 14-hour period to see when the blood glucose peaks and when it hits its lows. Adjustments are then made to the dosage and timing of the injections. You may also be asked to collect urine samples using a test strip of paper that indicates the glucose levels in urine.

 If your dog is already having insulin injections, beware of a "miracle cure" offered on some internet sites. It does not exist. There is no diet or vitamin supplement that can reduce your dog's dependence on insulin injections, because vitamins and minerals cannot do what insulin does in the dog's body.

If you think that your dog needs a supplement, discuss it with your vet first to make sure that it does not interfere with any other medication.

Managing your dog's diabetes also means managing his activity level. Exercise burns up blood glucose the same way that insulin does. If your dog is on insulin, any active exercise on top of the insulin might cause him to have a severe low blood glucose episode, called *"hypoglycaemia."* Keep your dog on a reasonably consistent exercise routine. Your usual insulin dose will take that amount of exercise into account. If you plan to take your dog out for some demanding exercise, such as running around with other dogs, you may need to reduce his usual insulin dose.

Tips

- You can usually buy specially formulated diabetes dog food from your vet
- You should feed the same type and amount of food at the same time every day
- Most vets recommend twice-a-day feeding for diabetic pets (it's OK if your dog prefers to eat more often). If you have other pets, they should also be on a twice-a-day feeding schedule, so that the diabetic dog cannot eat from their bowls
- Help your dog to achieve the best possible blood glucose control by not feeding table scraps or treats between meals
- Watch for signs that your dog is starting to drink more water than usual. Call the vet if you see this happening, as it may mean that the insulin dose needs adjusting

Remember these simple points:
- ✓ **Food raises blood glucose**
- ✓ **Insulin and exercise lower blood glucose**
- ✓ **Keep them in balance**

For more information on canine diabetes visit www.caninediabetes.org

---

Canine Cancer

This is the biggest single killer and will claim the lives of one in four dogs, regardless of breed. It is the cause of nearly half the deaths of all dogs aged 10 years and older, according to the American Veterinary Medical Association.

A study of more than 15,000 dogs of different breeds found that Miniature and Toys Poodles and Cocker Spaniels are LESS likely than average to contract cancer - which is great news for the Cockapoo.

Detailed cancer statistics by breed can be found at the NCBI (National Center for Biotechnology Information) website: www.ncbi.nlm.nih.gov/pmc/articles/PMC3658424 (Go to the top right of your screen in Google, click the three vertical dots, then click *Find* and type in *"Cocker Spaniel"* or *"Poodle"* - all the references will be highlighted in yellow).

Common Cancer Symptoms

Early detection is really important, and some things to look out for are:

- 🐾 Swellings anywhere on the body or around the anus
- 🐾 Lumps in a dog's armpit or under the jaw
- 🐾 Sores that don't heal
- 🐾 Weight loss
- 🐾 Laboured breathing
- 🐾 Changes in exercise or stamina level
- 🐾 Change in bowel or bladder habits
- 🐾 Increased drinking or urination
- 🐾 Vomiting
- 🐾 Poor appetite, difficulty swallowing or excessive drooling
- 🐾 Bad breath can also sometimes be a sign of cancer

If your dog has been spayed or neutered, there is evidence that the risk of certain cancers decreases. These cancers include uterine and breast/mammary cancer in females, and testicular cancer in males (if the dog was neutered before he was six months old). However, recent studies also show that some dogs may have a higher risk of certain cancers after early neutering. Spaying prevents mammary cancer in female dogs, which is fatal in about 50% of all cases.

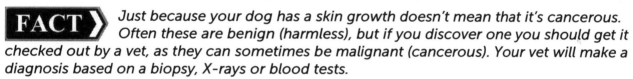

FACT ❯ *Just because your dog has a skin growth doesn't mean that it's cancerous. Often these are benign (harmless), but if you discover one you should get it checked out by a vet, as they can sometimes be malignant (cancerous). Your vet will make a diagnosis based on a biopsy, X-rays or blood tests.*

Many older dogs develop fatty lumps, or *lipomas,* which are often benign, but still need checking out by a vet to make sure.

Canine cancer is growing at an ever-increasing rate, and one of the difficulties is that your dog cannot tell you when a cancer is developing. However, if cancers can be detected early enough through a physical or behavioural change, dogs often respond well to treatment.

Over recent years, we have all become more aware of the risk factors for human cancer. Responding to these by changing our habits is having a significant impact on human health.

Stopping smoking, protecting ourselves from over-exposure to strong sunlight and eating a healthy, balanced diet all help to reduce cancer rates. We know to keep a close eye on ourselves, go for regular health checks and report any lumps and bumps to our doctors as soon as they appear. *The same is true with your dog.*

Reducing the Risk

The success of treatment depends on the type of cancer, the treatment used and, importantly, how early the tumour is found. The sooner treatment begins, the greater the chances of success.

One of the best things you can do for your dog is to keep a close eye on him for any tell-tale signs, which can be done as part of your regular handling and grooming sessions. If you notice any changes or bumps, monitor them over the next few days. If there is a change in size or appearance, see your vet as soon as possible. It might only be a cyst, but better to be safe than sorry. While it is impossible to completely prevent cancer from occurring, the following points may help to reduce the risk:

- Feed a healthy diet with little or, preferably, no preservatives
- Consider adding a dietary supplement, such as antioxidants, Vitamins A, C, E, beta carotene, lycopene or selenium, or coconut oil – check compatibility with any other treatments
- Don't let your Cockapoo get overweight
- Give your dog regular daily exercise
- Keep your dog away from chemicals, pesticides, cleaning products, etc.
- Avoid passive smoking
- Consider using natural flea remedies (check they work) and avoid unnecessary vaccinations
- If your dog has light skin, don't leave him in strong sunshine for extended periods
- Check your dog regularly for lumps and bumps and any other physical or behavioural changes

If your Cockapoo is diagnosed with cancer, there IS hope. Advances in veterinary medicine and technology offer various treatment options, including chemotherapy, radiation and surgery.

Unlike humans, dogs' hair does not fall out with chemotherapy. New, improved treatments are being introduced all the time.

One of our dogs was diagnosed with T-cell lymphoma, a particularly aggressive form of cancer, when he was four years old. We had noticed a small lump on his anus, which grew to the size of a small grape within a couple of days.

We rushed him down to the vet and he had surgery the following day. He died aged 13, having lived a further nine very happy years.

DISCLAIMER: The author is not a vet. This chapter is intended to give owners an outline of some of the health issues and symptoms that may affect Cockapoos. If you have any concerns regarding your dog's health, our advice is always the same: consult a veterinarian.

11. Skin and Allergies

Allergies are a growing concern for owners of many dogs. Visit any busy veterinary clinic these days – especially in spring and summer – and it's likely that one or more of the dogs is there because of some type of sensitivity. There is anecdotal evidence that some Cockapoos, just like other breeds and crossbreeds, can develop food intolerances, seasonal or other allergies.

Any individual dog can have issues. Skin conditions, allergies and intolerances are on the increase in the canine world as well as the human world.

How many children did you hear of having asthma or a peanut allergy when you were at school? Not too many, I'll bet. Yet allergies and adverse reactions are now relatively common – and it's the same with dogs. The reasons are not clear; it could be connected to breeding or feeding – or both, but as yet, there is no clear scientific evidence to back this up.

There are also reports that white or light-coloured dogs of all breeds may have a higher chance of allergies, possibly due to them having less pigment in their skin.

The skin is a complicated topic and a whole book could be written on this subject alone. While many dogs have no problems at all, some suffer from sensitive, itchy, dry or oily skin, hot spots, yeast infections or other skin disorders, causing them to scratch, bite or lick themselves excessively. Symptoms may vary from mild itchiness to a chronic reaction.

In common with other breeds with long, floppy ears, ear infections can also be a cause for concern with Cockapoos – more on these later.

Canine Skin

As with humans, the skin is the dog's largest organ. It acts as the protective barrier between your dog's internal organs and the outside world; it also regulates temperature and provides the sense of touch. Surprisingly, a dog's skin is actually thinner than ours, and it is made up of three layers:

1. **Epidermis** or outer layer, the one that bears the brunt of your dog's contact with the outside world.

2. **Dermis** is the extremely tough layer mostly made up of collagen, a strong and fibrous protein. This is where blood vessels deliver nutrients and oxygen to the skin, and it also acts as your dog's thermostat by allowing his body to release or keep in heat, depending on the outside temperature and your dog's activity level.

3. **Subcutis** is a dense layer of fatty tissue that allows your dog's skin to move independently from the muscle layers below it, as well as providing insulation and support for the skin.

FACT *Human allergies often trigger a reaction within the respiratory system, causing us to wheeze or sneeze, whereas allergies or hypersensitivities in a dog often cause a reaction in his SKIN.*

- ❧ Skin can be affected from the **INSIDE** by things that your dog eats or drinks

- ❧ Skin can be affected from the **OUTSIDE** by fleas, parasites, or inhaled and contact allergies triggered by grass, pollen, man-made chemicals, dust, mould, etc.

Like all dogs, Cockapoos can suffer from food intolerances as well as environmental allergies. Canine skin disorders are complicated. Some dogs can run through fields, digging holes and rolling around in the grass with no after-effects at all. Others may spend a lot of time indoors and have an excellent diet, but still experience severe itching and/or bald spots. Some dogs can eat almost anything and everything with no issues at all, while owners of others spend much of their time trying to find the magic bullet – the ideal food for their dog's sensitive stomach.

It's by no means possible to cover all of the issues and causes in this chapter. The aim here is to give a broad outline of some of the ailments most likely to affect your Cockapoo and how to deal with them. We have also included remedies tried with some success by ourselves (we had a dog with skin issues) and other owners of affected dogs, as well as advice from a holistic specialist. This information is not intended to take the place of professional help; always contact your vet if your dog appears physically unwell or uncomfortable. This is particularly true with skin conditions:

Tip *SEEK TREATMENT AS SOON AS POSSIBLE. If you can find the source(s) of the allergy early, you reduce the chances of it taking hold and causing secondary issues and infections.*

One of the difficulties with skin ailments is that the exact cause is often difficult to diagnose, as the symptoms are similar to other issues. If environmental allergies are involved, specific and expensive tests are available. You'll have to take your vet's advice on this, as the tests are not always conclusive. And if the answer is dust or pollen, it can be difficult – if not downright impossible - to keep your lively Cockapoo away from the triggers while still having a normal life. If the cause is environmental, it is often a question of managing the condition, rather than curing it.

Another issue reported by some dog owners is food allergy or intolerance - there IS a difference. See **Chapter 6. Feeding a Cockapoo** for more information.

Photo of Lincoln enjoying a romp in the field courtesy of Nigel and Julie Houston.

Personal Experiences

Allergies often develop in adolescence or early adulthood, which is often anything from a few months to two or three years old. Our affected dog was perfectly normal until he reached two when he began scratching, triggered by environmental allergies - most likely pollen.

Over the years he was on various different remedies that all worked for a time. As his allergies were seasonal, he normally did not have any medication between October and March. But come spring and as sure as daffodils are daffodils, he started scratching again. Luckily, they were manageable and he lived a happy, active life until he passed away aged 13.

Dolce is a four-year-old F1 Cockapoo who developed allergies when she was one year old. Owner Tiff Atkinson says: "Our Dolce has allergies due to her light coat. Her vet tends to think it is food-related so she eats special treats and food, really anything from the hydrolyzed protein line. We need a special prescription for it, and her symptoms have lessened since I changed her diet.

"Dolce used to get ear infections as the weather changes at the start of summer and late fall or early winter, but now I know the signs, so I can prevent it. Her symptoms were scooting across the floor, biting her paws, biting her butt area (underneath her tail), very bad ear infections and lots of scratching." *Photo: Dolce looking the picture of health.*

"We clean her ears with Douxo Micellar Solution, and as soon as I notice her ear is a little red, we use Otibiotic Ointment so it never develops into an ear infection anymore. Recently, I have been applying Natural Dog Company's Skin Soother to Dolce's itchy areas every two to three days and she has completely stopped scratching! She is a very happy and lively girl."

Karen Howe has two red and white F1 Cockapoos, Rodney and Mabel, and says: "Rodney's allergies all started at around 18 months old. He began licking his paws a lot until he was making them sore. The vet initially prescribed Piriton and diagnosed seasonal allergies, but the Piriton didn't seem to have much effect.

"He was then prescribed steroids, which definitely stopped the licking, but as soon as he finished the course he was back licking again. During this time, I did a lot of Google research and realised that I definitely didn't want him back on steroids again and I also wasn't happy about the next step the vet had suggested, which was to go on Apoquel. This was when I decided to try him on a raw diet and, although it hasn't completely cured him, it has definitely helped and made his paw-licking more manageable.

"I feed raw completes from Naturaw, which contain no vegetables. I also ensure that his treats are all grain-free, as I do notice a flare-up in his licking if he has had treats with grain in them. During the summer months he is definitely more itchy, so I do believe he has seasonal allergies as well."

Our photo, courtesy of Karen, shows Rodney full of beans on a day out at the seaside.

"He therefore has Piriton and an itchy dog supplement added to his dinner. I was never officially offered allergy tests for him, so I don't truly know exactly what he is allergic to, but feel that we are able to manage it well now without the use of drugs with long term side effects.

"I have noticed many benefits of switching them both to a raw diet: their coats are glossy and soft, their teeth are cleaner, they poo less and when they do poo, it is solid and doesn't really smell. They also absolutely love it and clear every bowl. I definitely wouldn't switch back now."

Ann Draghicchio's F1b, Toby, also has allergies. Ann says: "Toby has allergies and requires daily medication.

He is on a daily dose of Apoquel. Prior to that he had been chewing his paws every day and now he no longer does that. We also have him on a chicken-free diet."

Allergies and their treatment can be stressful for dogs and owners alike. The number one piece of advice is that if you suspect your Cockapoo has an allergy or skin problem, try to deal with it right away - either with medication, natural remedies or a combination of the two – before the all-too-familiar scenario kicks in and it develops into a chronic condition.

Whatever the cause, before a vet can make a diagnosis, you'll have to give details of your dog's diet, exercise regime, habits, medical history and local environment. The vet will then carry out a physical examination, possibly followed by further (expensive) tests, before a course of treatment can be prescribed. You'll have to decide whether these tests are worth it and whether they are likely to discover the exact root of the problem.

Types of Allergies

"Canine dermatitis" means inflammation of a dog's skin and it can be triggered by numerous things, but the most common by far is allergies. Vets estimate that as many as one in four dogs they see has some kind of allergy. Symptoms are:

- Chewing his feet
- Rubbing his face on the floor
- Scratching the body
- Scratching or biting the anus
- Itchy ears, head shaking
- Hair loss
- Mutilated skin with sore or discoloured patches or hot spots

A Cockapoo who is allergic to something will show it through skin problems and itching; your vet may call this *"pruritus."* It may seem logical that if a dog is allergic to something inhaled, like certain pollen grains, his nose will run; if he's allergic to something he eats, he may vomit, or if allergic to an insect bite, he may develop a swelling. But in practice this is seldom the case.

FACT *In dogs, the skin is the organ most affected by allergies, often resulting in a mild to severe itching sensation over the body and possibly a recurring ear infection. Reddish coloured tear stains can also be a sign of a yeast infection.*

Dogs with allergies often chew their feet until they are sore and red. You may see yours rubbing his face on the carpet or couch or scratching the belly and flanks. Because the ear glands produce too much wax in response to the allergy, ear infections can occur - with bacteria and yeast (which is a fungus) often thriving in the excessive wax and debris. Cockapoos don't have to suffer from allergies to get an ear infection; the lack of air flow under the floppy hairy ears makes them prone to the condition.

Digestive health can play an important role. Holistic vet Dr Jodie Gruenstern says: "It's estimated that up to 80% of the immune system resides within the gastrointestinal system; building a healthy gut supports a more appropriate immune response. The importance of choosing fresh proteins and healthy fats over processed, starchy diets (such as kibble) can't be overemphasized. Grains and other starches have a negative impact on gut health, creating insulin resistance and inflammation."

An allergic dog may cause skin lesions or **hot spots** by constant chewing and scratching. Sometimes he will lose hair, which can be patchy, leaving a mottled appearance. The skin itself may be dry and crusty, reddened, swollen or oily, depending on the dog. It is very common to get secondary bacterial skin infections due to these self-inflicted wounds.

An allergic dog's body is reacting to certain molecules called **allergens.** These may come from:

- Trees
- Grass
- Pollens
- Specific food or food additives, such as a type of meat, grains, colourings or preservatives
- Milk products
- Fabrics, such as wool or nylon
- Rubber and plastics
- House dust and dust mites
- Mould
- Flea bites
- Chemical products used around the house

(Photolibrary image of a Cockapoo on grass).

These allergens may be **inhaled** as the dog breathes, **ingested** as the dog eats, or caused by **contact** with the dog's body when he walks or rolls. However they arrive, they all cause the immune system to produce a protein (IgE), which causes irritating chemicals like histamine to be released. In dogs, these chemical reactions and cell types occur in sizeable amounts *only within the skin*, hence the scratching. Managing allergies is all about *REDUCING THE (ALLERGEN) LOAD.*

Inhalant Allergies (Atopy)

The most common allergies in dogs are inhalant and seasonal - at least at first; some allergies may develop and worsen. Substances that can cause an allergic reaction in dogs are similar to those causing problems for humans, and dogs of all breeds can suffer from them.

A clue to diagnosing these allergies is to look at the timing of the reaction. Does it happen all year round? If so, this may be mould, dust or some other trigger that is permanently in the environment. If the reaction is seasonal, then pollens may well be the culprit. A diagnosis can be made by one of three methods of *allergy testing.*

The most common is a blood test for antibodies caused by antigens in the dog's blood, and there are two standard tests: a RAST test (radioallergosorbent) and an ELISA test (enzyme-linked immunosorbent assay). According to the Veterinary and Aquatic Services Department of Drs. Foster and Smith, they are very similar, but many vets feel that the ELISA test gives more accurate results.

The other type of testing is intradermal skin testing where a small amount of antigen is injected into the skin of the animal and after a short period of time, the area around the injection site is inspected to see if the dog has had an allergic reaction. This method has been more widely used in the USA than the UK to date. Here is a link to an article written by the owner of a Boxer dog with severe inhalant allergies: www.allergydogcentral.com/2011/06/30/dog-allergy-testing-and-allergy-shots

Our photo shows a Golden Retriever that has undergone intradermal skin testing.

In this particular case, the dog has been tested for more than 70 different allergens, which is a lot. In all likelihood, your vet would test for fewer. The injections are in kits. If you consider this option,

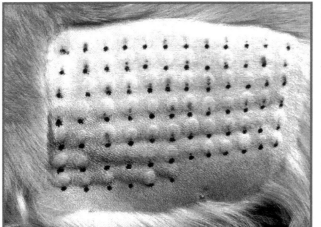

ask the vet or specialist how many allergens are in the kit.

Intradermal skin testing is regarded as *"the gold standard"* of allergy testing for atopy. The dog is sedated and an area on the flank is shaved down to the skin. A small amount of antigen is injected into the skin on this shaved area. This is done in a specific pattern and order. After a short time, the shaved area is examined to detect which antigens, if any, have created a reaction. It may look pretty drastic, but reactions – the visible round bumps - are only temporary and the hair grows back.

Intradermal skin testing works best when done during the season when the allergies are at their worst. The good news is that it is not necessarily much more expensive than blood testing and after a while the dog is none the worse for the ordeal. The procedure is normally carried out by a veterinary dermatologist or a vet with some dermatological experience, and dogs need to be clear of steroids and antihistamines for around six weeks beforehand.

While allergy testing is not particularly expensive, the intradermal method usually requires your dog to be sedated. And there's also no point doing it if you are not going to go along with the recommended method of treatment afterwards - which is immunotherapy, or *"hyposensitisation,"* an expensive and lengthy process. It consists of a series of injections made specifically for your dog and administered over months (or even years) to make him more tolerant of specific allergens. Vets in the US claim that success rates can be as high as 75%.

But before you get to the stage of considering allergy testing, your vet will have had to rule out other potential causes, such as fleas or mites, fungal, yeast or bacterial infections and hypothyroidism. Due to the time and cost involved in skin testing, vets treat most mild cases of allergies with a combination of avoidance, fatty acids, tablets and sometimes steroid injections for flare-ups. Many owners of dogs with allergies also look at changing to an unprocessed diet (raw or cooked) and natural alternatives to long-term use of steroids, which can cause other health issues.

Environmental or Contact Irritations

These are a direct reaction to something the dog physically comes into contact with. It could be as simple as grass, trees, specific plants, dust or other animals. If the trigger is grass or other outdoor materials, the allergies are often seasonal. The dog may require treatment (often tablets, shampoo or localised cortisone spray) for spring and summer, but be perfectly fine with no medication for the other half of the year. This was the case with our dog.

If you suspect your Cockapoo may have outdoor contact allergies, here is one very good tip guaranteed to reduce scratching: get him to stand in a tray or large bowl of water on your return from a walk. Washing the feet and under the belly will get rid of some of the pollen and other allergens, which in turn will reduce the scratching and biting. This can help to reduce the allergens to a tolerable level.

Other possible triggers include dry carpet shampoos, caustic irritants, new carpets, cement dust, washing powders or fabric conditioners. If you wash your dog's bedding or if he sleeps on your bed, use a fragrance-free - if possible, hypoallergenic - laundry detergent and avoid fabric conditioner.

The irritation may be restricted to the part of the dog - such as the underneath of the paws or belly - which has touched the offending object. Symptoms are skin irritation - either general or specific hotspots - itching (pruritus) and sometimes hair loss. Readers of our website sometimes report to us that their dog will incessantly lick one part of the body, often the paws, anus, belly or back.

Flea Bite Allergies

These are a very common canine allergy and affect dogs of all breeds. To compound the problem, many dogs with flea allergies also have inhalant allergies. Flea bite allergy is typically seasonal, worse during summer and autumn - peak time for fleas - and in warmer climates where fleas are prevalent.

This type of allergy is not to the flea itself, but to proteins in flea saliva, which are deposited under the dog's skin when the insect feeds. Just one bite to an allergic Cockapoo will cause intense and long-lasting itching. If affected, the dog will try to bite at the base of his tail and scratch a lot.

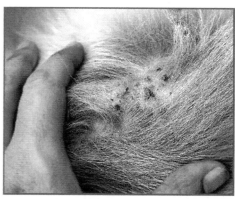

Most of the damage is done by the dog's scratching, rather than the flea bite, and can result in the hair falling out or skin abrasions. Some Cockapoos will develop hot spots. These can occur anywhere, but are often along the back and base of the tail. Flea bite allergies can only be totally prevented by keeping all fleas away from the dog. Various flea prevention treatments are available – see the section on **Parasites**. If you suspect your dog may be allergic to fleas, consult your vet for the proper diagnosis and medication.

Diet and Food Allergies

Food is the third most common cause of allergies in dogs. Cheap dog foods bulked up with grains and other ingredients can cause problems. Some owners have reported their dogs having intolerance to wheat and other grains.

If you feed your dog a dry commercial dog food, make sure that it is high quality, preferably hypoallergenic, and that the first ingredient listed on the sack is *meat or poultry,* not grain. Without the correct food, a dog's whole body - not just the skin and coat - will continuously be under stress and this manifests itself in a number of ways. The symptoms of food allergies are similar to those of most allergies:

- Itchy skin affecting primarily the face, feet, ears, forelegs, armpits and anus
- Excessive scratching
- Chronic or recurring ear infections
- Hair loss
- Hot spots
- Skin infections that clear up with antibiotics, but return after the antibiotics have finished
- Possible increased bowel movements, maybe twice as many as normal

The bodily process that occurs when an animal has a reaction to a particular food agent is not very well understood, but the veterinary profession does know how to diagnose and treat food allergies. As many other problems can cause similar symptoms (and also the fact that many sufferers also have other allergies), it is important that any other conditions are identified and treated before food allergies are diagnosed.

Atopy, flea bite allergies, intestinal parasite hypersensitivities, sarcoptic mange and yeast or bacterial infections can all cause similar symptoms. This can be an anxious time for owners as vets try one thing after another to get to the bottom of the allergy.

The normal method for diagnosing a food allergy is elimination. Once all other causes have been ruled out or treated, then a food trial is the next step — and that's no picnic for owners either - see **Chapter 6. Feeding a Cockapoo** for more information.

In reality, most owners proceed with trial and error, researching online forums and other sources to find out what has worked for other Cockapoos. If this is the route you decide to take, look for a food that is completely natural - without preservatives - either raw or cooked. There are many pre-prepared frozen options available these days - most of which can be delivered to your home. They may not be the cheapest food, but will be worth it if your Cockapoo wolfs it down without any diarrhoea or skin issues.

As with other allergies, dogs may have short-term relief by taking fatty acids, antihistamines, and steroids, but removing the offending items from the diet is the only permanent solution.

Acute Moist Dermatitis (Hot Spots)

Acute moist dermatitis or hot spots are not uncommon. A hot spot can appear suddenly and is a raw, inflamed and often bleeding area of skin. The area becomes moist and painful and begins spreading due to continual licking and chewing. They can become large, red, irritated lesions in a short pace of time. The cause is often a local reaction to an insect bite - fleas, ticks, biting flies or mosquitoes. Other causes of hot spots include:

* Allergies - inhalant allergies and food allergies
* Mites
* Ear infections
* Poor grooming
* Burs or plant awns
* Anal gland disease

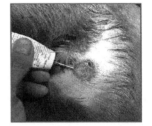

Once diagnosed and with the right treatment, hot spots disappear as soon as they appeared. The underlying cause should be identified and treated, if possible. Check with your vet before treating your Cockapoo for fleas and ticks at the same time as other medical treatment (such as anti-inflammatory medications and/or antibiotics), as he or she will probably advise you to wait.

Treatments may come in the form of injections, tablets or creams — or your dog might need a combination of them. Your vet will probably clip and clean the affected area to help the effectiveness of any spray or ointment and your poor Cockapoo might also have to wear an E-collar until the condition subsides, but usually this does not take long.

Interdigital Cysts

If your Cockapoo gets a fleshy red lump between the toes that looks like an ulcerated sore or a hairless bump, then there's a good chance it is an interdigital cyst - or *interdigital furuncle* to give the condition its correct medical term.

This unpleasant condition can be very difficult to get rid of, since it is often not the primary issue, but a sign of some other problem. The Bully breeds - Bulldogs, French Bulldogs, Pugs, etc. - are most susceptible, but Cockapoos can, like any dog, suffer from them – and often it's those dogs that suffer from other allergies.

 Actually, they are not cysts, but the result of **furunculosis**, a condition of the skin that clogs hair follicles and creates chronic infection. They can be caused by a number of factors, including allergies, poor foot conformation, mites, yeast infections, ingrown hairs or other foreign bodies, and obesity.

These nasty-looking bumps are painful for your dog, will probably cause a limp and can be a nightmare to get rid of. Vets might recommend a whole range of treatments to get to the root cause of the problem. It can be extremely expensive if your dog is having a barrage of tests or biopsies, and even then you are not guaranteed to find the underlying cause.

The first thing he or she will probably do is put your dog in an E-collar to stop him licking the affected area, which will never recover properly as long as it's constantly being licked. This again is stressful for your dog.

Cockapoos are sensitive dogs and some can be resistant to E-collars - they may slump down like you've hung a 10-ton weight on their neck or just become depressed by the whole thing. You might consider putting socks on the affected foot or feet, which will work well while your dog sleeps, but then you'll have to watch him like a hawk when awake to stop the affected areas being licked or bitten.

Here are some remedies your vet may suggest:

- ❧ Antibiotics and/or steroids and/or mite killers
- ❧ Soaking the feet in Epsom salts twice daily to unclog the hair follicles
- ❧ Testing for allergies or thyroid problems
- ❧ Starting a food trial if food allergies are suspected
- ❧ Shampooing the feet
- ❧ Cleaning between the toes with medicated (benzoyl peroxide) wipes
- ❧ A referral to a veterinary dermatologist
- ❧ Surgery (this is a last-resort option)

If you suspect your Cockapoo has an interdigital cyst, get to the vet for a correct diagnosis and then discuss the various options. A course of antibiotics may be suggested initially, along with switching to a hypoallergenic diet if a food allergy is suspected. If the condition persists, many owners get discouraged, especially when treatment may go on for many weeks.

Be wary of going on to steroid injections or repeated courses of antibiotics, as this may mean that the underlying cause of the furuncle has not been diagnosed and will persist.

Before you resort to any drastic action, first try soaking your Cockapoo's affected paw in Epsom salts for five or 10 minutes twice a day. After the soaking, clean the area with medicated wipes, which are antiseptic and control inflammation. In the US these are sold under the brand name Stridex pads, available in the skin care section of any grocery, or from the pharmacy.

If you think the cause may be an environmental allergy, wash your dog's feet and under his belly when you return from a walk, as this will help to remove pollen and other allergens.

Surgery is a drastic option. Although it can be effective in solving the immediate problem, it will not deal with whatever is triggering the interdigital cysts in the first place. Not only is healing after this surgery a lengthy and difficult process, it also means your dog will never have the same foot as before - future orthopaedic issues and a predisposition to more interdigital cysts are a couple of problems that can occur afterwards.

All that said, your vet will understand that interdigital cysts aren't so simple to deal with, but they are always treatable. **Get the right diagnosis as soon as possible**, limit all offending factors and give medical treatment a good solid try before embarking on more drastic cures.

Parasites

Demodectic Mange

Demodectic Mange is also known as *Demodex, red mange, follicular mange* or *puppy mange.* It is caused by the tiny mite Demodex canis – *pictured* - which can only be seen through a microscope. The mites actually live inside the hair follicles on the bodies of virtually every adult dog, and most humans, without causing any harm or irritation. In humans, the mites are found in the skin, eyelids and the creases of the nose...try not to think about that!

The Demodex mite spends its entire life on the host dog. Eggs hatch and mature from larvae to nymphs to adults in 20 to 35 days and the mites are transferred directly from the mother to the puppies within the first week of life by direct physical contact.

FACT ❭ *Dogs with healthy immune systems rarely get full-blown Demodex. However, a small number of dogs with weak immune systems can't combat the mites, and the disease spreads to the face and forelimbs or across the dog's whole body. Affected skin turns blue-grey due to the presence of thousands of blackheads or "comedones." Puppy Mange usually disappears when the pup's immune system kicks in at about 12 months of age.*

Vets currently believe that virtually every mother carries and transfers mites to her puppies, but most are immune to its effects. It is most likely to develop in puppies with parents that have mange, and most lesions develop after four months of age. It can also develop around the time when females have their first season and may be due to a slight dip in their immune systems.

Symptoms – Bald patches are usually the first sign, usually accompanied by crusty, red skin that sometimes appears greasy or wet. Usually hair loss begins around the muzzle, eyes and other areas on the head. The lesions may or may not itch. In localised mange, a few circular crusty areas appear, most frequently on the head and front legs of three to six-month-old puppies. Most will self-heal as the puppies become older and develop their own immunity, but a persistent problem needs treatment.

With generalised mange there are bald patches over the entire coat, including the head, neck, body, legs, and feet. The skin on the head, side and back is crusty, often inflamed and oozes a clear fluid. The skin itself will often be oily to touch and there is usually a secondary bacterial infection. Some puppies can become quite ill and can develop a fever, lose their appetites and become lethargic. If you suspect your puppy has generalised demodectic mange, (as opposed to local, which only affects the face and front legs), get him to a vet straight away.

There is also a condition called pododermatitis, when the mange affects a puppy's paws. It can cause bacterial infections and be very uncomfortable, even painful. The symptoms of this mange include hair loss on the paws, swelling of the paws (especially around the nail beds) and red/hot/inflamed areas that are often infected. Treatment is always recommended, and it can take several rounds to clear it up.

Diagnosis and Treatment – The vet will normally diagnose demodectic mange after taking a skin scraping. As these mites are present on every dog, they do not necessarily mean the dog has mange. Only when the mite is coupled with lesions will the vet diagnose mange. Treatment usually involves topical (on the skin) medication and sometimes tablets. In 90% of cases localised demodectic mange resolves itself as the puppy grows. If the dog has just one or two lesions, these can usually be successfully treated using specific creams and spot treatments. There are also non-chemical treatments, such as the one pictured, to relieve symptoms.

With the more serious generalised demodectic mange, treatment can be lengthy and expensive. The vet might prescribe an anti-parasitic dip every two weeks. Owners should always wear rubber gloves when treating their dog, and it should be applied in an area with adequate ventilation.

Most dogs with a severe issue need six to 14 dips every two weeks. After the first three or four dips, your vet will probably take another skin scraping to check the mites have gone. Dips continue for one month after the mites have disappeared, but dogs shouldn't be considered cured until a year after their last treatment.

FACT ❯ *Some dogs – especially Toy breeds, including some Cockapoos bred from Toy Poodles - can have a bad reaction to anti-parasitic dips. Before proceeding, check with your vet as to whether an anti-parasitic dip is suitable for your dog.*

Other options include the heartworm treatment Ivermectin. This isn't approved by the FDA for treating mange, but is often used to do so. It is usually given orally every one to two days, or by injection, and can be very effective. **Again, some dogs react badly to it.**

Another drug is Interceptor (Milbemycin oxime), which can be expensive as it has to be given daily. However, it is effective on up to 80% of the dogs who did not respond to dips – but should be given with caution to pups under 21 weeks of age.

Dogs that have the generalised condition may have underlying skin infections, so antibiotics are often given for the first several weeks of treatment. Because the mite flourishes on dogs with suppressed immune systems, you should try to get to the root cause of immune system disease, especially if your Cockapoo is older when he develops demodectic mange.

Harvest Mite

Another parasitic mite that can affect dogs and other animals in late summer and autumn is the harvest mite, particularly if you walk your dog through long, grassy fields. The orange, six-legged mite is so small, it is barely visible to the human eye. It attacks warm blooded animals – and humans, as the larvae feed on tissue fluid and can cause considerable discomfort.

The larvae congregate on small clods of earth or vegetation and are particularly active in dry, sunny weather. When a warm-blooded animal comes into contact with them, they swarm on and attach to the skin – especially thin-skinned areas with not much hair.

An individual larva injects a fluid that breaks down skin cells. The mite then sucks on the same place for two or three days before dropping off the host, leaving a red swelling that can itch severely.

The itching usually develops within three to six hours, but can continue for several weeks. The fluid injected by the mite is very irritating, causing the dog to scratch, bite and lick, which can result in further self-inflicted injury. Harvest mite larvae are only active during the day, so if your regular walk is through long, grassy fields, consider going

very early in the morning in warm weather, before the mites become active. And if you do have a problem, wash all clothes you were wearing when you think the mites first attacked.

There are sprays available from your vet that can help, but it is more important to thoroughly wash your dog with a good insecticidal shampoo. *Thornit* is a remedy used for ear mites that can also be used for harvest mites. Thornit is a powder based on Iodoform that can be lightly dusted on to the itchy areas, or in to itchy ears. Relief usually comes within two to five days. *Yumega Plus* for dogs can also help to relieve itching as it has a combination of Omega and Omega 6.

Sarcoptic Mange (Scabies)

Also known as canine scabies, this is caused by the parasite **Sarcoptes scabiei.** This microscopic mite can cause a range of skin problems, the most common of which is hair loss and severe itching. The mites can infect other animals such as foxes, cats and even humans, but prefer to live their short lives on dogs. Fortunately, there are several good treatments for this type of mange and the disease can be easily controlled.

In cool, moist environments, the mites live for up to 22 days. At normal room temperature they live from two to six days, preferring to live on parts of the dog with less hair. These are the areas you may see him scratching, although it can spread throughout the body in severe cases. Diagnosing canine scabies can be somewhat difficult, and it is often mistaken for inhalant allergies.

Once diagnosed, there are a number of effective treatments, including selamectin (Revolution – again, some dogs can have a bad reaction to this), an on-the-skin solution applied once a month which also provides heartworm prevention, flea control and some tick protection. Various Frontline products are also effective – check with your vet for the correct ones.

There is, however, one product that is recommended by many breeders and gets excellent reviews when compared to other flea and tick treatments, both in terms of effectiveness and also the fact that very few dogs have any reaction to it - unlike with many topical applications.

It is the *Seresto Flea Collar, pictured,* which provides full body protection (unlike some other flea collars that only protect the head and neck) against all fleas, ticks, sarcoptic mange, lice and other bloodsucking critters!

The Seresto collar lasts up to eight months and is waterproof – although if your Cockapoo goes swimming regularly, it might need replacing more often. Provided your Cockapoo will keep the collar on, I'd recommend it - but it's not cheap, at around £33 in the UK and $50 in the US.

There are also holistic remedies for many skin conditions. Because your dog does not have to come into direct contact with an infected dog to catch scabies, it is difficult to completely protect him. Foxes and their environment can also transmit the mite so, if possible, keep your Cockapoo away from areas where you know foxes are present.

Fleas

When you see your dog scratching and biting, your first thought is probably: "He's got fleas!" and you may well be right. Fleas don't fly, but they do have very strong back legs and they will take any opportunity to jump from the ground or another animal into your Cockapoo's lovely warm coat. You can sometimes see the fleas if you part your dog's hair.

And for every flea that you see on your dog, there is the stomach-churning prospect of hundreds of eggs and larvae in your house or apartment. So, if your dog gets fleas, you'll have to treat your environment as well as your dog in order to completely get rid of them.

The best form of cure is prevention. Vets recommend giving dogs a preventative flea treatment every four to eight weeks – although the Seresto Flea Collar lasts for eight months. If you do give a regular topical (applied to the skin) treatment, the frequency depends on your climate, the season - fleas do not breed as quickly in the cold - and how much time your dog spends outdoors.

To apply topical insecticides like Frontline and Advantix, part the skin and apply drops of the liquid on to a small area on your dog's back, usually near the neck. Some kill fleas and ticks, and others just kill fleas - check the details.

It is worth spending the money on a quality treatment, as cheaper brands may not rid your Cockapoo completely of fleas, ticks and other parasites. Sprays, dips, shampoos and collars are other options, as are tablets and injections in certain cases, such as before your dog goes into boarding kennels or has surgery. Incidentally, a flea bite is different from a flea bite allergy.

One UK breeder said that many breeders are opposed to chemical flea treatments, such as Spot On or ones from the vet, as so many dogs have been reported as reacting to the area it's applied to on the skin - and in extreme cases some have been known to have seizures. She added that when she found a flea, she simply washed all of her dogs, one after the other, and then washed every last piece of bedding and hadn't seen them since. There are also holistic and natural remedies to chemical flea treatments, discussed later in this chapter.

NOTE: There is also anecdotal evidence from owners of various breeds that the US flea and worm tablet *Trifexis* may cause severe side effects in some dogs. You can read some owners' comments at: www.max-the-schnauzer.com/trifexis-side-effects-in-schnauzers.html In fact, US breeder Rebecca Mae Goins, of Moonshine Babies Cockapoos, even stipulates that new owners should NOT use Trifexis or Comfortis, a flea prevention treatment, in all her Puppy Health Contracts.

Ticks

A tick is not an insect, but a member of the arachnid family, like the spider. There are over 850 types, some have a hard shell and some a soft one. Ticks don't have wings - they can't fly, they crawl. They have a sensor called Haller's organ that detects smell, heat and humidity to help them locate food, which in some cases is a Cockapoo. A tick's diet consists of one thing and one thing only – blood! They climb up onto tall grass and when they sense an animal is close, crawl on.

Ticks can pass on a number of diseases to animals and humans, the most well-known of which is *Lyme Disease*, a serious condition that causes lameness and other problems. Dogs that spend a lot of time outdoors in high risk areas, such as woods, can have a vaccination against Lime Disease.

One breeder added: "We get ticks from sand dunes sometimes and, if removed quickly, they're not harmful. We use a tick tool which has instructions in the packet. You put the forked end either side of the tick and twist it till it comes out."

If you do find a tick on your Cockapoo's coat and are not sure how to get it out, have it removed by a vet or other expert. Inexpertly pulling it out yourself and leaving a bit of the tick behind can be detrimental to your dog's health. Prevention treatment is similar to that for fleas. If your Cockapoo has sensitive skin, he might do better with a natural flea or tick remedy.

Heartworm

Heartworm is a serious and potentially fatal disease affecting pets in North America and many other parts of the world (but not the UK). It is caused by foot-long worms called heartworms that live in the heart, lungs and associated blood vessels of affected animals, causing severe lung disease, heart failure and damage to organs.

The dog is a natural host for heartworms, enabling the worms living inside a dog to mature into adults, mate and produce offspring. If untreated, their numbers can increase; dogs have been known to harbour several hundred worms in their bodies. Heartworm disease causes lasting damage to the heart, lungs and arteries, and can affect the dog's health and quality of life long after the parasites are gone. For this reason, prevention is by far the best option and treatment - when needed - should be administered as early as possible.

The mosquito *(pictured below)* plays an essential role in the heartworm life cycle. When a mosquito bites and takes a blood meal from an infected animal, it picks up baby worms that develop and mature into "infective stage" larvae over a period of 10 to 14 days.

Then, when the infected mosquito bites another dog, cat or susceptible wild animal, the infective larvae are deposited onto the surface of the animal's skin and enter the new host through the mosquito's bite wound. Once inside a new host, it takes approximately six months for the larvae to develop into adult heartworms. Once mature, heartworms can live for five to seven years in a dog. In the early stages of the disease, many dogs show few or no symptoms. The longer the infection persists, the more likely symptoms will develop. These include:

- A mild persistent cough
- Reluctance to exercise
- Tiredness after moderate activity
- Decreased appetite
- Weight loss

As the disease progresses, dogs may develop heart failure and a swollen belly due to excess fluid in the abdomen. Dogs with large numbers of heartworms can develop sudden blockages of blood flow within the heart leading to the life-threatening caval syndrome. This is marked by a sudden onset of laboured breathing, pale gums and dark, bloody or coffee-coloured urine. Without prompt surgical removal of the heartworm blockage, few dogs survive.

Although more common in the south eastern US, heartworm disease has been diagnosed in all 50 states. And because infected mosquitoes can fly indoors, even dogs that spend much time inside the home are at risk. For that reason, the American Heartworm Society recommends that you get your dog tested every year and give your dog heartworm preventive treatment for 12 months of the year. If you live in a risk area, check that your tick and flea medication also prevents heartworm. In the UK, heartworm has only been found in imported dogs.

Thanks to the American Heartworm Society for assistance with the section.

Ringworm

This is not actually a worm, but a fungus and is most commonly seen in puppies and young dogs. It is highly infectious and often found on the face, ears, paws or tail. The ringworm fungus is most prevalent in hot, humid climates but, surprisingly, most cases occur in autumn and winter.

Ringworm infections in dogs are not that common; in one study of dogs with active skin problems, less than 3% had ringworm.

Ringworm is transmitted by spores in the soil and by contact with the infected hair of dogs and cats, which can be typically found on carpets, brushes, combs, toys and furniture. Spores from infected animals can be shed into the environment and live for over 18 months, but fortunately most healthy adult dogs have some resistance and never develop symptoms. The fungi live in dead skin, hairs and nails - and the head and legs are the most common areas affected.

Tell-tale signs are bald patches with a roughly circular shape *(pictured)*. Ringworm is relatively easy

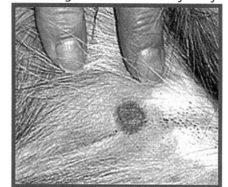

to treat with fungicidal shampoos or antibiotics from a vet. Humans can catch ringworm from pets, and vice versa. Children are especially susceptible, as are adults with suppressed immune systems and those undergoing chemotherapy. Hygiene is extremely important.

If your dog has ringworm, wear gloves when handling him and wash your hands well afterwards. And if a member of your family catches ringworm, make sure they use separate towels from everyone else or the fungus may spread. As a teenager I caught ringworm from horses at the stables where I worked at weekends - much to my mother's horror - and was treated like a leper by the rest of the family until it cleared up!

Bacterial infection (Pyoderma)

Pyoderma literally means *pus in the skin* (yuk!) and fortunately this condition is not contagious. Early signs of this bacterial infection are itchy red spots filled with yellow pus, similar to pimples or spots in humans. They can sometimes develop into red, ulcerated skin with dry and crusty patches.

Pyoderma *(pictured)* is caused by several things: a broken skin surface, a skin wound due to chronic exposure to moisture, altered skin bacteria, or impaired blood flow to the skin. Dogs have a higher risk of developing an infection when they have a fungal infection or an endocrine (hormone gland) disease such as hyperthyroidism, or have allergies to fleas, food or parasites.

Pyoderma is often secondary to allergic dermatitis and develops in the sores on the skin that occur as a result of scratching. Puppies often develop *puppy pyoderma* in thinly-haired areas, such as the groin and underarms. Fleas, ticks, yeast or fungal skin infections, thyroid disease, hormonal imbalances, heredity and some medications can increase the risk.

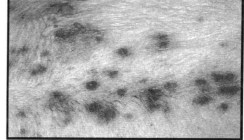

If you notice symptoms, get to the vet quickly before the condition develops from *superficial pyoderma* into *severe pyoderma*, which is very unpleasant and takes a lot longer to treat.

Bacterial infection, no matter how bad it may look, usually responds well to medical treatment, which is generally done on an outpatient basis. Superficial pyoderma will usually be treated with a two to six-week course of antibiotic tablets or ointment. Severe or recurring pyoderma looks awful, causes your dog some distress and can take months of treatment to completely cure. Medicated shampoos and regular bathing, as instructed by your vet, are also part of the treatment. It's also important to ensure your dog has clean, dry, padded bedding.

Canine Acne

This is not that common and - just as with humans - generally affects teenagers, often between five and eight months of age with dogs. Acne occurs when oil glands become blocked causing bacterial infection and these glands are most active in teenagers. Acne is not a major health problem as most of it will clear up once the dog becomes an adult, but it can recur. Typical signs are pimples, blackheads or whiteheads around the muzzle, chest or groin. If the area is irritated, then there may be some bleeding or pus that can be expressed from these blemishes.

Hormonal Imbalances

These occur in dogs of all breeds, are often difficult to diagnose and occur when a dog is producing either too much (hyper) or too little (hypo) of a particular hormone. One visual sign is often hair loss on both sides of the dog's body, which is not usually itchy. Hormone imbalances can be serious as they are often indicators that glands that affect the dog internally are not working properly. However, some types can be diagnosed by special blood tests and treated effectively.

....

Ear Infections

Cockapoos have long, floppy, hairy ears, which can make some dogs susceptible to ear infections. Infection of the external ear canal (outer ear infection) is called *otitis externa* and is one of the most common types seen. One cause is moisture in the ear canal, which in turn allows bacteria to flourish there.

FACT ❯ *The fact that a dog has recurring ear infections does not necessarily mean that the ears are the source of the problem – although they might be. Some dogs have chronic or recurring ear infections due to inhalant or food allergies, or low thyroid function (hypothyroidism). Sometimes the ears are the first sign of allergy.*

The underlying problem must be treated or the dog will continue to have long-term ear problems. Tell-tale signs include your dog shaking his head, scratching or rubbing his ears a lot, or an unpleasant smell coming from the ears.

If you look inside the ears, you may notice a reddy brown or yellow discharge, it may also be red and inflamed with a lot of wax. Sometimes a dog may appear depressed or irritable; ear infections are painful. In chronic cases, the inside of his ears may become crusty or thickened.

Causes of ear problems include:

- ❀ Allergies, such as environmental or food allergies

- ❀ Ear mites or other parasites

- ❀ Bacteria or yeast infections

- ❀ Injury, often due to excessive scratching

- ❀ Hormonal abnormalities, e.g. hypothyroidism

🐾 The ear anatomy and environment, e.g. excess moisture

🐾 Hereditary or immune conditions and tumours

In reality, many Cockapoos have ear infections due to the structure of the ear. The long, hairy ears often prevent sufficient air flow inside the ear. This can lead to bacterial or yeast infections - particularly if there is moisture inside. These warm, damp and dark areas under the ear flaps provide an ideal breeding ground for bacteria.

Treatment depends on the cause and what – if any - other conditions your dog may have. Antibiotics are used for bacterial infections and antifungals for yeast infections. Glucocorticoids, such as dexamethasone, are often included in these medications to reduce the inflammation in the ear. Your vet may also flush out and clean the ear with special drops, something you may have to do daily at home until the infection clears.

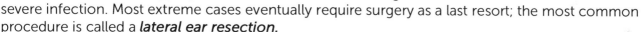

A dog's ear canal is L-shaped, which means it can be difficult to get medication into the lower, or horizontal, part of the ear. The best method is to hold the dog's ear flap with one hand and put the ointment or drops in with the other, if possible tilting the dog's head away from you so the liquid flows downwards **with gravity**.

Make sure you then hold the ear flap down and massage the medication into the horizontal canal before letting go of your dog, as the first thing he will do is shake his head – and if the ointment or drops aren't massaged in, they will fly out. Nearly all ear infections can be successfully managed if properly diagnosed and treated. But if an underlying problem remains undiscovered, the outcome will be less favourable.

Deep ear infections can damage or rupture the eardrum, causing an internal ear infection and even permanent hearing loss. Closing of the ear canal, called **hyperplasia** or **stenosis**, is another sign of severe infection. Most extreme cases eventually require surgery as a last resort; the most common procedure is called a **lateral ear resection.**

Our dog with allergies had a lateral ear resection following years of recurring ear infections and the growth of scar tissue. It was surgery or deafness, the vet said. We opted for surgery and the dog has been free of ear infections ever since. However, it is an **extremely** painful procedure for a dog and should only be considered as a very last resort.

 To avoid or alleviate recurring ear infections, check your dog's ears and clean them regularly. Hair should be regularly plucked from inside your Cockapoo's ears – either by you or a groomer, or both.

When cleaning or plucking your dog's ears, be very careful not to put anything too far inside. Visit YouTube to see videos of how to correctly clean ears without damaging them. DO NOT use cotton buds inside the ear, they are too small and can cause injury. Some owners recommend regularly cleaning the inside of ears with cotton wool and a mixture of water and white vinegar once or twice a week.

You can also consider buying Spaniel food and water bowls **(pictured).** They have higher, narrower tops than normal dog dishes, helping to keep a dog's ears out of his food and water. If your Cockapoo is one of the many that enjoys swimming, great care should be taken to ensure the insides of both ears are thoroughly dry afterwards - and after bathing at home. There is more information in **Chapter 12. Grooming a Cockapoo.**

If your dog appears to be in pain, has smelly ears, or if his ear canals look inflamed, contact your vet straight away. If you can nip the first infection in the bud, there is a chance it will not return. If your dog has a ruptured or weakened eardrum, ear cleansers and medications could do more harm than good. Early treatment is the best way of preventing a recurrence.

Some Allergy Treatments

Treatments and success rates vary tremendously from dog to dog and from one allergy to another, which is why it is so important to consult a vet at the outset. Earlier diagnosis is more likely to lead to a successful treatment. Some owners whose dogs have recurring skin issues find that a course of antibiotics or steroids works wonders for their dog's sore skin and itching. However, the scratching starts all over again shortly after the treatment stops.

NOTE: While a single steroid injection is highly effective in calming down symptoms almost immediately, frequent or long-term steroid use is not a good option as it can lead to serious side effects. Read more at: https://vcahospitals.com/know-your-pet/steroid-treatment-long-term-effects-in-dogs

Food allergies require patience, a change or several changes of diet and maybe even a food trial, and the specific trigger is notoriously difficult to isolate – unless you are lucky and hit on the culprit straight away. With inhalant and contact allergies, blood and skin tests are available, followed by hypersensitisation treatment. However, these are expensive and often the specific trigger for many dogs remains unknown. So, the reality for many owners of Cockapoos with allergies is that they manage the condition, rather than curing it completely.

Our Experience With Max

After corresponding with numerous other dog owners and consulting our vet, Graham, it seems that our experiences with allergies are not uncommon. This is borne out by the dozens of dog owners who have contacted our website about their pet's allergy or sensitivities. According to Graham, more and more dogs are appearing in his waiting room every spring with various types of allergies. Whether this is connected to how we breed our dogs remains to be seen.

Our dog, Max, was perfectly fine until about two years old, when he began to scratch a lot. He scratched more in spring and summer, which meant that his allergies were almost certainly inhalant or contact-based and related to pollens, grasses or other outdoor triggers. One option was a barrage of tests to discover exactly what he was allergic to. We decided not to do this, not because of the cost, but because the vet said it was highly likely that he was allergic to pollens.

Max was an active dog that enjoyed regular outdoor daily exercise. If we had confirmed an allergy to pollens, we were not going to stop taking him outside for walks; his life would have been miserable confined to the house. So, he was treated on the basis of having seasonal inhalant or contact allergies, probably related to pollen.

As already mentioned, it's definitely beneficial to have a shallow bath or hose outside to rinse the dog's paws and underbelly after a walk in the countryside. This is something our vet does with his own dogs and has found that the scratching reduces as a result. Regarding medications, Max was at first put on to a tiny dose of Piriton *(pictured)*, an antihistamine for hay fever sufferers (human and canine) and for the first few springs and summers, this worked well.

Allergies can often change and the dog can also build up a tolerance to a treatment, which is why they can be so difficult to treat. This has been the case with us over the years. The symptoms changed from season to season, although the main ones remained and were: general scratching, paw biting and ear infections. One year he bit the skin under his tail a lot (near the anus) – he would jump around like he had been stung by a bee, but it was just the itching. This was treated effectively with a single steroid injection followed by spraying the area with cortisone once a day at home for a period. This type of spray can be very effective if the itchy area is small, but no good for spraying all over a dog's body.

A few years ago, he started nibbling his paws for the first time - a habit he persisted with - although not to the extent that they become red and raw. Over the years we tried a number of treatments, all of which worked for a while, before he came off the medication in autumn for six months when plants and grasses stop growing outdoors. He managed perfectly fine the rest of the year without any treatment at all.

Not every owner wants to treat their dog with chemicals, nor feed a diet that includes preservatives, which is why this book includes alternatives. Also, 15 years ago, when we were starting out on the *"Allergy Trail,"* there were far fewer options than there are now. If I get another dog that develops allergies, I will explore some of the many other options available.

We fed Max a high quality hypoallergenic dry food. If we were starting again from scratch, knowing what we know now, I would probably investigate earlier a raw or home-cooked diet (which is what he was fed towards the end of his life), if necessary in combination with holistic remedies.

One season the vet put him on a short course of steroids. These worked very well for five months, but steroids are not a long-term solution. Another spring, we were prescribed Atopica, a non-steroid daily tablet sold in the UK only through vets. The active ingredient is **cyclosporine**, which suppresses the immune system. Some dogs can get side effects, although ours didn't, and holistic practitioners believe that it is harmful to the dog. This treatment was expensive, but initially extremely effective – so much so that we thought we had cured the problem completely. However, after a couple of seasons on cyclosporine he developed a tolerance to the drug and started scratching again.

A few years ago, he went back on the antihistamine Piriton, a higher dose than when he was two years old, and this worked very well again. One advantage of this drug is that is it manufactured by the million and is therefore very inexpensive.

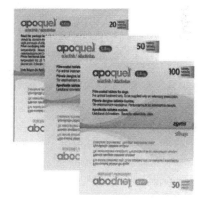

In 2013 the FDA approved **Apoquel** (oclacitinib) to control itching and inflammation in allergic dogs. In some quarters it was hailed a wonder drug for canine allergies. In fact, it proved so popular in the UK and North America that in the following two years there was a shortage of supply, with the manufacturers not being able to produce it fast enough.

We tried Apoquel with excellent results. There was some tweaking at the beginning to get the daily dose right, but it really proved effective. The tablets are administered according to body weight and cost around £1 or $1.50 each. It's not cheap, but Apoquel can be a miracle worker for some dogs.

NOTE: This article from Dogs Naturally magazine recommends NOT giving Apoquel to your dog: www.dogsnaturallymagazine.com/wouldnt-give-dog-new-allergy-drug - make up your own mind what is best for your dog. Allergies are often complex and difficult to treat; you should weigh up the pros and cons in the best interests of your own dog. Max's allergies were manageable; he loved his food, was full of energy and otherwise healthy, and lived a happy life to the age of 13.

Vets often recommend adding fish oils (which contain Omega-3 fatty acids) to a daily feed to keep your dog's skin and coat healthy all year round – whether or not he has problems. We added a liquid supplement called Yumega Plus, which contains Omegas 3 and 6, to one of the two daily feeds all year round. When the scratching got particularly bad, we bathed our dog in an antiseborrheic shampoo called Malaseb, *pictured,* twice a week for a limited time. This also helped, although was not necessary once on Apoquel.

The main point is that most allergies are manageable, although they may change throughout the life of the dog and you may have to alter the treatment. Here are some suggestions:

Bathing - bathing your dog using shampoos that break down the oils that plug the hair follicles. These shampoos contain antiseborrheic ingredients such as benzoyl peroxide, salicylic acid, sulphur or tar. One example is Sulfoxydex shampoo, which can be followed by a cream rinse such as Episoothe Rinse afterwards to prevent the skin from drying out.

Dabbing – Using an astringent such as witch hazel or alcohop on affected areas. We have heard of zinc oxide cream being used to some effect. In the human world, this is rubbed on to mild skin abrasions and acts as a protective coating. It can help the healing of chapped skin and nappy rash in babies. Zinc oxide works as a mild astringent and has some antiseptic properties and is safe to use on dogs, *as long as you do not allow the dog to lick it off.*

Daily supplements - Vitamin E, vitamin A, zinc and omega oils all help to make a dog's skin healthy. Feed a daily supplement that contains some of these, such as fish oil, which provides omega.

Here are some specific remedies from owners. We are not endorsing them; we're just passing on the information. Check with your vet before trying any new remedies. A medicated shampoo with natural tea tree oil has been suggested by one owner. Some have reported that switching to a fish-based diet has helped lessen scratching, while others have suggested home-cooked or raw food is best. Another owner said: "I have been putting a teaspoon of canola (rapeseed) oil in my dog's food every other day and it has helped with the itching. I have shampooed the new carpet in hopes of removing any of the chemicals that could be irritating her. And I have changed laundry detergent. After several loads of laundry everything has been washed."

And from another: "My eight-month-old dog also had a contact dermatitis around his neck and chest. I was surprised how extensive it was. The vet recommended twice-a-week baths with an oatmeal shampoo. I also applied organic coconut oil daily for a few weeks and this completely cured the dermatitis. I also put a capsule of fish oil with his food once a day and continue to give him twice-weekly baths. His skin is great now."

Many owners have tried coconut oil *(pictured)* with some success. Here is a link to an article on the benefits of coconut oils and fish oils, check with your vet first: www.dogsnaturallymagazine.com/the-health-benefits-of-coconut-oil

If you suspect your dog has a skin problem, ear infection or allergy, get him to the vet straight away. You can hopefully nip it in the bud before secondary infections develop – and save a lot of heartache and money in the long run.

The Holistic Approach

As canine allergies become increasingly common, more and more owners of dogs with allergies and sensitivities are looking towards natural foods and remedies to help deal with the issues.

Others are finding that their dog does well for a time with injections or medication, but then the symptoms slowly start to reappear. A holistic practitioner looks at finding the root cause of the problem and treating that, rather than just treating the symptoms.

Dr Sara Skiwski is a holistic vet working in California. She writes here about canine environmental allergies: "Here in California, with our mild weather and no hard freeze in Winter, environmental allergens can build up and cause nearly year-round issues for our beloved pets. Also seasonal allergies, when left unaddressed, can lead to year-round allergies. Unlike humans, whose allergy symptoms seem to affect mostly the respiratory tract, seasonal allergies in dogs often take the form of skin irritation/inflammation.

"Allergic reactions are produced by the immune system. The way the immune system functions is a result of both genetics and the environment: Nature versus Nurture. Let's look at a typical case. A puppy starts showing mild seasonal allergy symptoms, for instance a red tummy and mild itching in Spring. Off to the vet!

"The treatment prescribed is symptomatic to provide relief, such as a topical spray. The next year when the weather warms up, the patient is back again - same symptoms but more severe this time. This time the dog has very itchy skin. Again, the treatment is symptomatic - antibiotics, topical spray (hopefully no steroids), until the symptoms resolve with the season change. Fast forward to another Spring...on the third year, the patient is back again but this time the symptoms last longer, (not just Spring but also through most of Summer and into Fall).

"By Year Five, all the symptoms are significantly worse and are occurring year-round. This is what happens with seasonal environmental allergies. The more your pet is exposed to the allergens they are sensitive to, the more the immune system over-reacts and the more intense and long-lasting the allergic response becomes. What to do?

"In my practice, I like to address the potential root cause at the very first sign of an allergic response, which is normally seen between the ages of six to nine months old. I do this to circumvent the escalating response year after year. Since the allergen load your environmentally-sensitive dog is most susceptible to is much heavier outdoors, I recommend two essential steps in managing the condition. They are vigilance in foot care as well as hair care.

"What does this mean? A wipe down of feet and hair, especially the tummy, to remove any pollens or allergens is key. This can be done with a damp cloth, but my favorite method is to get a spray bottle filled with Witch Hazel and spray these areas.

"First, spray the feet then wipe them off with a cloth, and then spray and wipe down the tummy and sides. This is best done right after the pup has been outside playing or walking. This will help keep your pet from tracking the environmental allergens into the home and into their beds. If the feet end up still being itchy, I suggest adding foot soaks in Epsom salts."

Dr Sara also stresses the importance of keeping the immune system healthy by avoiding unnecessary vaccinations or drugs: "The vaccine stimulates the immune system, which is the last thing your pet with seasonal environmental allergies needs.

"I also will move the pet to an anti-inflammatory diet. Foods that create or worsen inflammation are high in carbohydrates. An allergic pet's diet should be very low in carbohydrates, especially grains.

Research has shown that "leaky gut," or dysbiosis, is a root cause of immune system overreactions in both dog and cats (and some humans). Feed a diet that is not processed, or minimally processed; one that doesn't have grain and takes a little longer to get absorbed and assimilated through the gut. Slowing the assimilation assures that there are not large spikes of nutrients and proteins that come into the body all at once and overtax the pancreas and liver, creating inflammation.

"A lot of commercial diets are too high in grains and carbohydrates. These foods create inflammation that overtaxes the body and leads not just to skin inflammation, but also to other inflammatory conditions, such as colitis, pancreatitis, arthritis, inflammatory bowel disease and ear infections. Also, these diets are too low in protein, which is needed to make blood. This causes a decreased blood reserve in the body and in some of these animals this can lead to the skin not being properly nourished, starting a cycle of chronic skin infections which produce more itching."

After looking at diet, check that your dog is free from fleas and then these are some of Dr Sara's suggested supplements:

✓ **Raw (Unpasteurised) Local Honey** - an alkaline-forming food containing natural vitamins, enzymes, powerful antioxidants and other important natural nutrients, which are destroyed during the heating and pasteurisation processes. Raw honey has anti-viral, anti-bacterial and anti-fungal properties. It promotes body and digestive health, is a powerful antioxidant, strengthens the immune system, eliminates allergies, and is an excellent remedy for skin wounds and all types of infections. Bees collect pollen from local plants and their honey often acts as an immune booster for dogs living in the locality.

Dr Sara says: "It may seem odd that straight exposure to pollen often triggers allergies, but that exposure to pollen in the honey usually has the opposite effect. But this is typically what we see. In honey, the allergens are delivered in small, manageable doses and the effect over time is very much like that from undergoing a whole series of allergy immunology injections."

✓ **Mushrooms** - make sure you choose the non-poisonous ones! Dogs don't like the taste, so you may have to mask it with another food. Medicinal mushrooms are used to treat and prevent a wide array of illnesses through their use as immune stimulants and modulators, and antioxidants. The most well-known and researched are reishi, maitake, cordyceps, blazei, split-gill, turkey tail and shiitake. The mushrooms stabilise mast cells in the body, which have the histamines attached to them. Histamine is what causes much of the inflammation, redness and irritation in allergies. By helping to control histamine production, the mushrooms can moderate the effects of inflammation and even help prevent allergies in the first place.

WARNING! Mushrooms can interact with some over-the-counter and prescription drugs, so do your research as well as checking with your vet first.

✓ **Stinging Nettles** - contain biologically active compounds that reduce inflammation. Nettles have the ability to reduce the amount of histamine the body produces in response to an allergen. Nettle tea or extract can help with itching. Nettles not only help directly to decrease the itch, but also work overtime to desensitise the body to allergens, helping to reprogramme the immune system.

✓ **Quercetin** – is an over-the-counter supplement with anti-inflammatory properties. It is a strong antioxidant and reduces the body's production of histamines.

✓ **Omega-3 Fatty Acids** - these help decrease inflammation throughout the body. Adding them into the diet of all pets - particularly those struggling with seasonal environmental allergies – is very beneficial. If your dog has more itching along the top of their back and on their sides, add in a fish oil supplement. Fish oil helps to decrease the itch and heal skin lesions. The best sources of Omega 3s are krill oil, salmon oil, tuna oil, anchovy oil and other fish body oils, as well as raw organic egg yolks. If using an oil alone, it is important to give a vitamin B complex supplement.

✓ **Coconut Oil** - contains lauric acid, which helps decrease the production of yeast, a common opportunistic infection. Using a fish body oil combined with coconut oil before inflammation flares up can help moderate or even suppress your dog's inflammatory response.

Dr Sara adds: "Above are but a few of the over-the-counter remedies I like. In non-responsive cases, Chinese herbs can be used to work with the body to help to decrease the allergy threshold even more than with diet and supplements alone. Most of the animals I work with are on a program of Chinese herbs, diet change and acupuncture.

"So, the next time Fido is showing symptoms of seasonal allergies, consider rethinking your strategy to treat the root cause instead of the symptom."

With thanks to Dr Sara Skiwski, of the Western Dragon Integrated Veterinary Services, San Jose, California, for her kind permission to use her writings as the basis for *The Holistic Approach.*

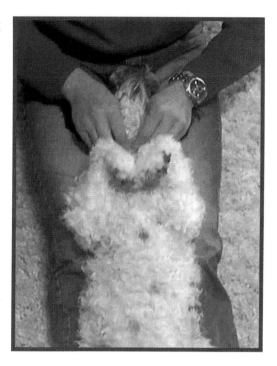

FACT ❭ *Massage can stimulate your dog's immune system and help to prevent or reduce allergies. It's also good for improving your dog's circulation and flexibility, reducing muscle and arthritis pain and other age-related problems. Anybody can do it – we do – and your Cockapoo will love the attention!*

Holistic practitioners believe that acupressure can also specifically help dogs with allergies. Type *"Acupressure for Dogs"* into Google to learn about the theory behind it and how to apply pressure at specific points on your dog's body. Acupressure can also help nervous and elderly dogs.

....

This chapter has only just touched on the complex subject of skin disorders. As you can see, no two dogs are the same and the causes and treatments are many and varied. One thing is true whatever the condition: if your Cockapoo has a skin issue, seek a professional diagnosis as soon as possible before attempting to treat it yourself and it becomes entrenched.

Early diagnosis and treatment give the best chance of a full recovery.

Some skin conditions cannot be completely cured, but they can be successfully managed, allowing your dog to live a happy, pain-free life. Once you have your pup or adult dog, remember that these factors go a long way in preventing or managing skin problems and ear infections in Cockapoos:

🐾 Regular grooming

🐾 A high quality diet

🐾 Attention to ears and cleanliness

12. Grooming the Cockapoo

When dog lovers weigh up all the pros and cons of different breeds before finally deciding on a Cockapoo, one topic which often seems to slip under the radar is ...grooming. Many new owners are very surprised at just how high maintenance the Cockapoo coat is, and Cockapoo forums are full of posts on the subject - not to mention countless photos of shaggy dogs! This chapter gives owners an insight into just what's involved.

....

The Cockapoo Coat

The coat is one of the big attractions of the Cockapoo, with many – but not all - inheriting the low-shedding properties of the Poodle. Although this type of coat is best for allergy sufferers and leaves little or no trace around the house, apart from the odd furball, it comes at a price. Maintenance is time-consuming as well as expensive. Unless you learn to trim your dog yourself, you'll need to visit a professional groomer every six to 12 weeks.

A Cockapoo that has inherited more of the characteristics of the straighter coat of the Cocker Spaniel will shed hair, but these coats are actually easier to look after. Regular brushing at home and the occasional bath are enough to keep the coat clean and shiny.

Although this type of coat does not need overall trimming, some Cocker Spaniel owners do take their dogs to the groomer's every few months for a bath, general tidy up, ear plucking, anal gland squeezing and nail trimming.

FACT ❯ *All Cockapoos are born with a soft, wavy puppy coat, which starts to change to an adult coat at around six to eight or nine months old, a process which can last several months. The texture of an adult coat can vary from wavy to curly like the Poodle to straighter, like the Cocker, depending on genetics. The low-shedding wavy coat (pictured) is the most popular.*

It is around this time of change that a Cockapoo puppy's coat can become matted if it hasn't been regularly brushed. After several weeks or months without attention, the matted coat can become so tangled that it has to be shaved off, which can permanently ruin the coat.

There is no denying that Cockapoo puppies look extremely cute when left with a long, natural coat. But if you ignore grooming for the first few months, your puppy will return traumatised from her first trip to the grooming parlour and you will then have a lifelong battle, as the initial experience was negative. This is why it is so important to get your puppy used to being handled and brushed from the very beginning. Many grooming salons offer *"puppy clips"* and much of the experience is about getting the pup used to visiting the groomer while young.

Professional grooming fees will cost you thousands of pounds or dollars over the lifetime of your Cockapoo! Some owners decide to clip the dogs themselves, and later in this chapter, breeder and former professional dog groomer Jessica Sampson gives advice on how to clip a Cockapoo.

Coat colour is governed by genetics, and although breeders may breed for a certain colour, genetics are complicated and there is no guarantee that all puppies from the same litter will turn out to be the same colour.

Also, coat colour may change or fade between puppyhood and adulthood. It is unlikely that a mature Cockapoo will be exactly the same shade as she was when first seen as a pup. For example, blacks may fade, reds may fade to apricot, some cream puppies may grow up to be almost white, and apricot may lighten. The change often happens by the time the dog is two years old.

Coats also fade as a dog enters her senior years, while injury to the skin - caused by bites, clipper cuts, surgical procedures, etc. – can make the affected area darker. And, like any breed, the Cockapoo can have coat or skin-related health issues. These are covered in detail in **Chapter 10. Cockapoo Health** and **Chapter 11. Skin and Allergies.**

A Big Surprise

Many people get a Cockapoo because they have heard that they are non-shedding. Well, as you've read, there is no thing as a non-shedding dog! It is true that a lot of Cockapoos are low shedding and many of them are compatible for people with allergies.

To make sure of this, you need to spend time with the individual puppy you are thinking of getting – and let the dog lick you; it's often saliva people are allergic to. If that's not possible, at least rub your face with a cloth that the Cockapoo has been lying on and has licked.

With the new IC (Improper Coat) genetic test, it will become easier in future for breeders to produce the highly-desired wavy, low-shedding coat that gives the Cockapoo that cute Teddy bear look.

One of the big surprises for some current owners is just how much their Cockapoo sheds! *Our photo shows a Cockapoo with Spaniel characteristics.*

Mike Payton, of Cockapoo HQ, and owner of F1 Luna, says: "A lot of people are surprised by how much Cockapoos moult. They are sold as being non-shedding, when there's a good chance that yours will moult. Luna sheds a lot! She has more of a Spaniel straight-haired coat, compared to a lot of Cockapoos, and we have recently purchased a special grooming attachment."

Regular Maintenance

Grooming doesn't just mean giving your Cockapoo a quick tickle with a brush every couple of weeks. There are other facets that play a part in keeping your dog clean and skin-related issues at bay. Time spent grooming is also time spent bonding with your dog; this physical and emotional inter-reliance brings us closer to our pets. Routine grooming sessions also allow you to examine your dog's coat, skin, ears, teeth, eyes, paws and nails for signs of problems. And once they have got used to it, most Cockapoos enjoy the attention.

 Most Cockapoos require extensive clipping and grooming throughout their lives, so get your puppy used to being groomed from an early age; adults do not take kindly to being handled if they are not used to it.

You can start gently brushing your Cockapoo puppy a few days after you bring her home, and book an introductory trip to the groomer's as soon as it's safe to do so after vaccinations. Puppy hair is soft and matts easily, so regular grooming early on, i.e. a few times a week, is essential. Don't risk permanently destroying some of the coat qualities by neglecting the task. A slicker or pin brush *(pictured)* is a good tool for brushing your puppy and getting the tangles out. Be careful not to damage the skin.

Other benefits of regular brushing are that it removes dead hair and skin, stimulates blood circulation and spreads natural oils throughout the coat, helping to keep it in good condition.

If your adult Cockapoo has a curly or straight coat, brushing once or twice a week is enough, but the more common soft, wavy, coat requires more time and effort. Cockapoos with low-shedding coats need to be trimmed regularly, which could be anything from every six to 12 weeks. If you are considering full grooming at home, here are some things to consider buying:

- Electric clippers – quality and price vary; cheap ones blunt quicker
- Brush - a slicker brush and/or pin brush
- Steel comb and possibly a de-matting comb
- Pet scissors with rounded ends
- Shampoo formulated for dogs
- Nail clippers or grinder
- Styptic powder to stop bleeding from the quick (nail)
- Eye wipes
- Canine toothbrush and toothpaste
- Ear powder if your Cockapoo has hairy ears

 If your Cockapoo is resisting your grooming efforts, place her on a table or bench - make sure she can't jump off or fasten her on. You'd be surprised what a difference this can make once out of her normal environment - i.e. floor level - and at your level.

A few things to look out for when grooming are:

Acne - Little red pimples on a dog's face and chin means she has got acne. A dog can get acne at any age, not just as an adolescent. Plastic bowls can also trigger the condition, which is why stainless steel ones are often better. Daily washing followed by an application of an antibiotic cream is usually enough to get rid of the problem; if it persists it will mean a visit to your vet.

Dry skin - A dog's skin can dry out, especially with artificial heat in the winter months. If you spot any dry patches, for example on the inner thighs or armpits, or a cracked nose, massage a little petroleum jelly or baby oil on to the dry patch.

Eyes - These should be clean and clear. Cloudy eyes, particularly in an older dog, could be early signs of cataracts. Red or swollen tissue in the corner of the eye could be a symptom of cherry eye, which can affect dogs of all breeds. Ingrowing eyelashes is another issue which causes red, watery eyes. If your dog has an issue, you can start by gently bathing the eye(s) with warm water and cotton wool - but never use anything sharp; a dog can suddenly jump forwards or backwards, causing injury. If the eye is red or watering for a few days or more, get it checked out by a vet.

Tear Stain – This is more noticeable in Cockapoos with light-coloured coats, as it is often reddy-brown. It is usually caused by excessive tear production, but can also be a sign of a yeast infection or an underlying eye problem. There are several widely available products – including natural remedies - which can help the condition.

NOTE: The USA's FDA has sent a letter of warning to three manufacturers of tear stain removal products, including Angels' Eyes, Angels' Glow and Pets' Spark, as they contain the antibiotic tylosin tartrate, which has not been approved for use in dogs or cats.

Ear Cleaning

It is not uncommon for Cockapoos to suffer from ear infections. Breeds with pricked-up ears like the German Shepherd Dog suffer far fewer ear infections than those with long, floppy ears.

An upright ear allows air to circulate inside, whereas covered inner ears are generally warm, dark and moist, making them a haven for bacteria and yeast. This can lead to recurring infections and, in severe cases, the dog going deaf or even needing a surgical operation.

Whether your Cockapoo needs hair plucking out of her ears to allow better air flow depends on:

- 🐾 How hairy the inside of the ear is
- 🐾 How big the ear canal is, and
- 🐾 Whether she sheds naturally

Many Cockapoos love swimming, and this can also cause ear infections if the area under the ear flap remains wet for long periods. The wetness, combined with the warmth of an enclosed space, is an ideal breeding ground for bacteria.

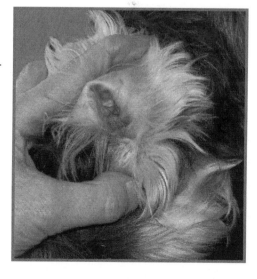

A good habit to get into is to towel dry under the ear flaps after your dog has been swimming. Keep an eye out for redness or inflammation of the ear flap or inner ear, or a build-up of dark wax. Also, wash or hose your dog down after swimming in the sea to keep the coat free from salt – don't forget to dry the ears afterwards.

Some owners with susceptible dogs bathe the inner ear with cotton wool and warm water or a veterinary ear cleaner as part of their regular grooming routine. Whether or not your dog has issues, it is good practice to check her ears and eyes regularly.

Typical signs of an ear infection are: your dog shaking her head a lot, scratching her ears, rubbing her ears on the carpet or ground, and/or an unpleasant smell coming from the ears, which is a sign of a yeast infection.

 If your dog exhibits any of these signs, consult your vet ASAP, as simple routine cleaning won't solve the problem, and ear infections are notoriously difficult to get rid of once your dog's had one.

The best way of avoiding ear infections is to keep your dog's ears clean, dry and free from too much hair right from puppyhood. One method is:

- Buy a good quality ear cleaning solution from the vet, pet shop or online
- Squeeze the cleaner into your Cockapoo's ear canal and rub the ear at the base next to the skull
- Allow your dog to shake her head
- Use a cotton ball to gently wipe out any dirt and waxy build up inside the ear canal

Method Two is to use a baby wipe and gently wipe away any dirt and waxy build up. In both cases it is important to only clean as far down the ear canal as you can see to avoid damaging the eardrum.

The first method is preferred if you are also bathing your dog, as it will remove any unwanted water that may have got down into the ears during the bath. See **Chapter 11. Skin and Allergies** for more information on ear infections.

 *Putting something sharp or narrow - like a cotton bud – inside your dog's ears can cause injury.*

Nail Trimming

If your Cockapoo is regularly exercised on grass or other soft surfaces, the nails may not be getting worn down sufficiently, so they may have to be clipped or filed. Nails should be kept short for the paws to remain healthy. Long nails can interfere with a dog's gait, making walking awkward or painful and they can also break easily, usually at the base of the nail where blood vessels and nerves are located.

Get your dog used to having her paws inspected from puppyhood; it's also a good opportunity to check for other problems, such as cracked pads or interdigital cysts (swellings between the toes, often due to a bacterial infection).

Be warned: many dogs dislike having their nails trimmed, so it requires patience and persistence on your part.

To trim your dog's nails:

1. Use a specially designed clipper. Most have safety guards to prevent you cutting the nails too short.

2. Do it before they get too long; if you can hear the nails clicking on the floor, they're too long.

3. You want to trim only the ends, before *"the quick,"* (hence the expression *"cut to the quick"*), which is a blood vessel inside the nail. You can see where the quick ends on a white nail, but not on a dark nail.

4. Clip only the hook-like part of the nail that turns down. Start trimming gently, a nail or two at a time, and your dog will learn that you're not going to hurt her. If you accidentally cut the quick, stop the bleeding with styptic powder.

Another option is to file your dog's nails with a nail grinder tool. Some dogs may have tough nails that are hard to trim and this may be less stressful for your dog, with less chance of pain or bleeding. The grinder is like an electric nail file and only removes a small amount of nail at a time.

It is harder to cut the quick with a grinder, and many dogs prefer them to a clipper. However, you have to gradually introduce your dog to a grinder - they often don't like the noise or vibration at first. If you find it impossible to clip your dog's nails, or are worried about doing it, take her to the vet or groomer - and ask her to squeeze your dog's anal sacs while she's there!

Anal Sacs

And while we're discussing the less appealing end of your Cockapoo, let's dive straight in and talk about **anal sacs!** Sometimes called scent glands, these are a pair of glands located inside your dog's anus that give off a scent.

 *Dogs explore the world with their noses, which is why you often see dogs that meet for the first time sniffing each other's rear ends.*

You won't want to hear this, but problems with impacted anal glands are not uncommon! When a dog passes firm stools, the glands normally empty themselves, but soft poop can mean that not enough pressure is exerted to empty the glands, causing discomfort. Infected glands result in swelling and pain. In extreme cases one or both anal glands can be removed, although a dog can live perfectly well with one anal gland (one of ours did).

If your dog drags herself along on her rear end - called *"scooting"* - or tries to lick or scratch her anus, she could well have impacted anal glands that need squeezing - also called expressing - either by you, if you know how to do it, your vet or a groomer. She might also have worms. Either way, it pays to keep an eye on both ends of your dog!

....

Keeping Teeth Healthy

Veterinary studies show that by the age of three, 80% of dogs show signs of gum or dental disease. Just like Poodles, some Cockapoos can be affected by dental problems. Symptoms include yellow and brown build-up of tartar along the gum line, red inflamed gums and persistent bad breath (halitosis).

It is important to make the time to take care of your Cockapoo's **teeth** – regular dental care greatly reduces the onset of gum or tooth decay and infection. If left, problems can escalate very quickly.

FACT *Plaque coats dirty teeth and within three to five days this starts to harden into tartar, often turning into gingivitis, or inflammation of the gums. Gingivitis is regularly accompanied by infections around the teeth. This can be serious as it can, in extreme cases, lead to infections of the vital organs, such as heart, liver and kidneys.*

Even if the infection doesn't spread beyond the mouth, bad teeth are very unpleasant for a dog, just as with a human, causing toothache and difficulty chewing. You can give your dog a daily dental treat, such as Dentastix or Nylabone, a bully stick, antler horns, etc. or a large raw bone once in a while to help with dental hygiene.

Start getting your pup used to teeth cleaning as soon as they have settled in. Take things slowly in the beginning and give lots of praise. Cockapoos love your attention and some will start looking forward to tooth brushing sessions - especially if they like the flavour of the toothpaste. *Use a pet toothpaste; dogs don't rinse and spit and the human variety can upset a canine's stomach.*

Get your dog used to the toothpaste by letting her lick some off your finger. If she doesn't like the flavour, try a different one. Continue until she looks forward to licking the paste - it might be instant or take days. Put a small amount on your finger and gently rub it on the big canine teeth at the front of her mouth. Over the next one to two weeks, rub your finger with the toothpaste all over her teeth.

Then get either a finger brush or the right size of three-sided brush for your Cockapoo's mouth and put the toothpaste in between the bristles (rather than on top) so more of it actually gets on to the teeth and gums. Allow her to get used to the toothbrush being in her mouth several times - praise her when she licks it – before you start proper brushing.

Lift her upper lip gently and place the brush at a 45° angle to the gum line. Gently move the brush backwards and forwards. Start just with her front teeth and then gradually do a few more.

Do the top ones first. You don't need to brush the inside of her teeth as the tongue keeps them relatively free of plaque. Regular brushing shouldn't take more than five minutes - well worth the time and effort when it spares your Cockapoo the pain and misery of periodontal disease.

 If your Cockapoo has to be anaesthetised for anything, ask the vet to check and, if necessary, clean the teeth while the dog is under. Prevention is better than cure.

Do-It-Yourself Clipping

In this section, Jessica Sampson, of Legacy Cockapoos, Beaverton, Ontario, Canada, outlines the best methods and equipment for anyone thinking of learning how to clip their Cockapoo themselves. She also gives advice on the best method of bathing a Cockapoo.

Jessica is an approved American Cockapoo Club breeder and breeds F2 and F3 Cockapoos, with coat colours ranging from black, phantom, sable, apricot, red and chocolate to merle and parti. For 15 years she was a professional dog groomer.

Jessica - *pictured with F1 stud Ace (left) and F1 female, Elsa -* starts off by explaining a little about the different generations of Cockapoos:

As far as grooming is concerned, the generation of the Cockapoo generally makes no difference. The only time it does make a difference for grooming and clipping is if your Cockapoo has a smooth/flat coat like a Cocker Spaniel. In this case, they look beautiful in a Cocker-style clip, with full fluffy ear featherings. The smooth coat's brushing requirements are also much lighter in the maintenance department as they have far less coat to contend with.

When breeding Cockapoos, we strive for a soft, silky, full, wavy, fleecy coat type. Smooth/flat and curly coated Cockapoos are considered to have the less desirable coat type. But you can get all three coat types in any given litter. After the third generation, things start to stabilize out and you start seeing less and less of the other coat types.

The majority of F1s have a full, wavy, fleecy coat type, although you will get a few smooth and curly-coated dogs as well. The second generation has the most diversity in coat type. All three coat types can be born to a litter of F2s. By the time you reach F3s, things start to stabilize out.

This is, of course, if you have been selectively breeding only the dogs with the desired coat type. If you continue to breed down your lines with all three coat types, you will continue to have all three coat types. There is little difference in temperament within the generations.

Brushing

Cockapoos require regular grooming to keep their coat healthy and free of matting. One of the most important parts of grooming your Cockapoo is brushing. One thorough brushing a week is usually adequate, but the right tools and technique are very important.

Tools - the most important tools you will ever own are a soft slicker brush, and a fine-tooth steel comb. A de-matting comb can also be useful but, if you are brushing your dog regularly and thoroughly, there should be no need for it.

With these tools and the proper technique, you will be able to achieve a professional quality brush out. I rarely found use for any other type of brushes and found many of them to be a waste of money and time.

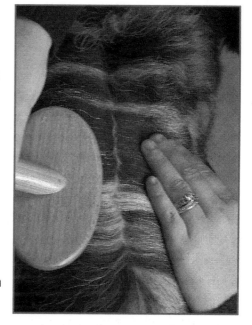

Technique – this is your secret weapon! This is very important to get a thorough brush that penetrates right down to the skin and not just brushes the surface fur. The technique is called *"Line Brushing"* and here's how to do it:

🐾 First separate the hair. Make a line going horizontally along the dog from nose to tail so you can see the skin

🐾 Using your soft slicker brush, brush the hair up across the entire line against the natural lie of the coat

🐾 Separate a new line 1/4 inch below the first line and repeat over the entire dog

🐾 Repeat the line brushing technique with your fine-tooth steel comb as well. Make sure you pay special attention to the armpit, groin and behind the ears, as these are typical spots where matting forms. If the fine-tooth comb does not easily pass through the coat with no hang ups, your dog is not thoroughly brushed and you need to repeat the process where needed

Clipping

Clipping should always be done on a clean dog to preserve the life of your grooming equipment.

When clipping a Cockapoo, the look we are trying to achieve is that of a *"Teddy bear."* Generally, we strive for a clip of about two to three inches in length. The top of the head is the same length as the body. If the tail is docked (USA and Canada), it is clipped the same length as the body. If the dog's tail has been left natural, the tail featherings should be left long and natural.

The face should have hair and a beard, all flowing into one another and trimmed no longer than four inches. The ears should be left long and trimmed even with the bottom of the beard. The face and body should never be shaved. If the dog is not being shown, then a shorter or longer coat is allowed. Remember to keep the eyes clear of fur and well brushed. If you choose to leave your

Cockapoo *"au naturel,"* they tend to resemble a shaggy sheepdog and her coat will require much more maintenance to stay matt-free.

Bathing

The Cockapoo is considered a low odor dog. With regular brushing, the natural oils in the dog's coat tend to repel dirt, leaving her needing very little bathing. You should only bath your Cockapoo when it is needed - and no more than once a month if you bath regularly. Over-bathing will lead to your dog having a dry skin and coat.

To maintain a matt-free coat, make sure you thoroughly brush your Cockapoo before you bath her. Matts stretch when wet and tighten when they dry, resulting in stubborn matts.

Trying to remove them can be very difficult and painful for your dog, and the result is quite often having these matts shaved or clipped out of the coat. Here is the technique I use:

- Put cotton balls into you Cockapoo's ear canals to help prevent water from entering

- Thoroughly wet your Cockapoo. Be very careful not to get any water down the ear canals, which can cause ear infections

- Apply a good quality dog shampoo, NEVER use a human shampoo as this is too harsh for a dog's skin and can lead to skin irritation and/or possible hair loss

- Work up a good lather working the suds deep into the coat

- Rinse and repeat with a second shampoo. The first shampoo quite often does not penetrate all the way to the skin. A second shampoo will leave your Cockapoo smelling fresh and sparkling. This is a groomer's secret! If you've ever wondered why your dog comes home smelling and feeling so much better than when you have bathed her, this is why

- Rinse and then rinse again. This is the most important step in bathing, which many overlook. If your dog is not rinsed thoroughly, her coat will look dull and the skin will become flaky and itchy, making your Cockapoo very uncomfortable. The soap left behind in the hair will also attract dirt, resulting in your dog needing to be bathed once again

- Remove the cotton balls and fill the ear canal with doggy ear cleaner, rub the base of the ears and allow your dog to shake her head. This will remove any water that may have snuck by your cotton balls. Use this opportunity to gently wipe out any waxy build-up in the ear.

CAUTION! Only clean as far as you can see to avoid damaging your dog's eardrum.

- After your Cockapoo is dry, thoroughly brush her again

13. The Birds and the Bees

Judging by the number of questions our website receives from owners who ask about the canine reproductive cycle and breeding their dogs, there is a lot of confusion about the doggy facts of life out there. Some owners want to know whether they should breed their dog, while others ask if and at what age they should have their dog neutered – this term can refer to both the spaying of females and the castration of males.

Owners of females often ask when she will come on heat, how long this will last and how often it will occur. Sometimes they want to know how you can tell if a female is pregnant or how long a pregnancy lasts. So here, in a nutshell, is a chapter on The Facts of Life as far as Cockapoos are concerned.

Females and Heat

Just like all other female mammals, including humans, a female Cockapoo has a menstrual cycle - or to be more accurate, an oestrus cycle (*estrus* in the US). This is the period of time when she is ready (and willing!) for mating and is more commonly called **heat**, being **on heat**, **in heat** or *in season*.

A Cockapoo female has her first cycle at six to nine months old, although there are no hard and fast rules; some may not have their first heat until later. Females may follow the pattern of their mother, so if you are getting a female puppy, it may be worth asking your breeder at what age the dam (mother) first came on heat.

She will then come on heat roughly every six months. There is no season of the year which corresponds to a breeding season, so it could be winter and summer or spring and autumn (fall), etc.

When a young female comes on heat, it is normal for her cycles to be somewhat irregular, and can take up to two years for regular cycles to develop. The timescale also becomes more erratic with old, unspayed females. Unlike women, female dogs do not stop menstruating when they reach middle age, although the heat becomes shorter and lighter. A litter for an older female (over seven years old) is not advisable as it can result in complications – for both mother and pups.

On average, the heat cycle will last around 21 days, but can be anything from seven to 10 days up to four weeks. Within this period there will be several days in the middle of the cycle that will be the optimum time for her to get pregnant. This is the phase called the *oestrus*.

The third phase, called **dioestrus**, begins immediately afterwards. During this time, her body will produce hormones whether or not she is pregnant. Her body thinks and acts like she is pregnant. All the hormones are present; only the puppies are missing. This can sometimes lead to what is known as a "false pregnancy."

The first visual sign of heat that you may notice is that your dog's vulva (external sex organ, or pink bit under her tail) becomes swollen, which she will lick to keep herself clean. If you're not sure, hold a tissue against her vulva — does it turn pink or red? She will then bleed; this is sometimes called spotting. It will be a light red or brown at the beginning of the heat cycle, turning more watery after a week or so. Some females can bleed quite heavily; however, this is not usual with Cockapoos. If you have any concerns, contact your vet to be on the safe side.

Females on heat often urinate more frequently than normal, or may *"mark"* various objects on a walk or even in the home by doing a small pee on them! She may also start to *"mate"* with your leg, other dogs or objects. These are all normal signs. The good news is that both Cocker Spaniels and Poodles generally want to keep themselves clean by licking their rear end when on heat — and this is usually true of Cockapoos too.

If your girl does leave an unwanted trail around the house, cover anything you don't want stained. You might consider using doggy diapers/nappies, also called heat pants, *(pictured).* Some are disposable, others have washable linings and they are all widely available online.

Owners have reported a variety of behavioural changes when their female has her first heat cycle. Some go off their food or start shedding hair. Others may become more clingy - or ignore you and sulk in their beds.

FACT ❯ *When a female is on heat, she produces hormones that attract male dogs. Because dogs have a sense of smell thousands of times stronger than ours, your girl on heat is a magnet for all the neighbourhood males. It is believed that they can detect the scent of a female on heat up to two miles away!*

They may congregate around your house or follow you around the park (if you are brave or foolish enough to venture out there while she is in season), waiting for their chance to prove their manhood — or mutthood in their case.

Don't expect your precious little Cockapoo princess to be fussy. Her hormones are raging when she is on heat and, during **her most fertile days, which are Day 9 to 10 of heat for five or more days,** she is ready, able and ... VERY willing! As she approaches the optimum time for mating, you may notice her tail bending slightly to one side. She will also start to urinate more frequently. This is her signal to all those virile male dogs out there that she is ready for mating.

Although breeding requires specialised knowledge on the part of the owner, it does not stop a female on heat from being extremely interested in attention from any old mutt. To avoid an unwanted pregnancy, you must keep a close eye on your female on heat and not allow her to freely wander where she may come into contact with other dogs - and that includes the garden or yard, unless it is 100% dog proof.

It is amazing the lengths some uncastrated - also called intact or entire - males will go to impregnate a female on heat. Travelling great distances to follow her scent, jumping over barriers, digging under fences, chewing through doors or walls and sneaking through hedges are just some of the tactics employed by canine Casanovas on the loose.

Love is a powerful thing - and canine lust even more so...A dog living in the same house as a female in season has even been known to mate with her through the bars of a crate!

If you do have an intact male, you need to physically keep him in a separate place, perhaps with a friend, separate kennel or even boarding kennels. The desire to mate is all-consuming and can be accompanied by howling or "marking" (urinating) indoors from a frustrated Romeo.

Avoid taking your female out in public places while she is in season, and certainly don't let her run free anywhere that you might come across other dogs. The instinct to mate may trump all of her training. Worst case scenario is your precious and expensive little pooch suddenly becomes deaf to your increasingly panicky calls as she gallops off into the distance with a gleam in her eye and the scruffy mutt from down the road!

During her heat period, you can compensate for these restrictions by playing more indoor or garden games to keep her mentally and physically active. You can also buy a spray which masks the natural oestrus scent of your female. Marketed under such attractive names as *"Bitch Spray,"* these will lessen the scent, but not eliminate it. They might be useful for reducing the amount of unwanted attention, but are not a complete deterrent. There is, however, no canine contraceptive and the only sure-fire way of preventing your female from becoming pregnant is spaying.

There is a *"morning after pill"* – actually a series of oestrogen tablets or an injection - which some vets may administer after an unwanted coupling, but side effects can be severe, including Pyometra (a potentially life-threatening infection of the womb), bone marrow suppression and infertility.

 *Unlike women, female dogs don't go through the menopause and can give birth even when they are quite old – but it is not good for their health.*

Breeding Restrictions

Normally, responsible breeders wait until a female is fully health tested, has had one or two heat cycles and is at least 18 months to two years old before mating. Females should not be used for breeding too early; pregnancy draws on the calcium reserves needed for their own growing bones. If bred too soon, they may break down structurally and have health issues in later life.

Good breeders also limit the number of litters from each female, as breeding can take a lot out of them. To protect females from overbreeding, the UK's Kennel Club has introduced **Breeding Restrictions.** These do not apply to crossbreeds, as they cannot be registered with the Kennel Clubs, but should be adhered to by all responsible breeders, regardless of whether they are producing crossbreeds or pure breeds.

Now the Kennel Club will not register a litter from any female:

1. That has already had four litters.
2. If she is less than one year old at the time of mating.
3. If she is eight years or older when she whelps (gives birth).
4. If the litter is the result of any mating between father and daughter, mother and son or brother and sister.
5. If she has already had two C-Sections (Caesarean Sections).
6. In the UK, the dam has to be resident at a UK address at the date of whelping – this is to try and discourage people buying from foreign puppy farms.

Neutering - Pros and Cons

Once a straightforward subject, this is currently a hot potato in the dog world. Dogs that are kept purely as pets – i.e. not for showing, breeding or working – are often spayed or neutered. There is also the life-threatening risk of *Pyometra* in unspayed middle-aged females.

While early spay/neuter has been traditionally recommended, there is some scientific evidence that, for some breeds, it may be better to wait until the dog is through puberty. (The procedure of removing ovaries or testicles is also known as a gonadectomy).

Armed with the facts, it is for each individual owner to decide what is best for their dog – unless there was a Spay/Neuter clause in your Puppy Contract.

A major argument for neutering of both sexes is that there is already too much indiscriminate breeding of dogs in the world. As you will read in **Chapter 14. Cockapoo Rescue**, it is estimated that 1,000 dogs are put to sleep **every hour** in the USA alone. It is for this reason that rescue organisations in North America, the UK and Australia neuter all dogs that they rehome.

Some areas in the United States, e.g. LA, have even adopted a compulsory sterilisation policy, aimed at: *"reducing and eventually eliminating the thousands of euthanizations conducted in Los Angeles' animal shelters every year."* The RSPCA, along with most UK vets, also promotes the benefits of neutering. It is estimated that more than half of all dogs in the UK are spayed or castrated.

Another point is that you may not have a choice. Some Puppy Contracts from breeders may stipulate that, except in special circumstances, you agree to neuter your Cockapoo as a Condition of Sale. Others may state that you need the breeder's permission to breed your dog.

Scientific Studies

The other side of the coin is that there is recent scientific evidence that neutering – and especially early neutering - can have a detrimental effect on the health of some dogs, especially larger, fast-growing breeds.

In 2013, the University of California, Davis School of Veterinary Medicine published a study revealing that neutered Golden Retrievers and Labradors appear to be at a higher risk of joint disorders and cancers compared with sexually intact dogs of the same breed. Google *"UCDavis early neuter in dogs"* or visit: http://www.aaha.org/blog/NewStat/post/2014/07/17/785809/UC-Davis-study-neutering-Golden-retrievers-Labradors.aspx

A follow-up study involving both males and females (with around a 5% incidence of joint disorders in intact dogs) found that Retrievers that had been neutered before six months of age were four or five times more likely to have joint problems.

The same study looked at cancer. Intact females had a 3% rate of cancer, while females spayed up to eight years old were three to four times more likely to get cancer. Neutering males had "relatively minor effects." Read it at: http://journals.plos.org/plosone/article?id=10.1371/journal.pone.0102241

A 2018 article, published in The IAABC Journal (International Association of Animal Behavior Consultants), highlights the pros and cons of neutering. Written by a vet, it's a bit technical, but worth a read: https://fall2018.iaabcjournal.org/2018/10/31/spay-and-neuter-surgery-effects-on-dogs or Google *IAABC early neuter in dogs.*" The table at the end of the article summarises the pros and cons.

As yet, there are no scientific studies on neutering small and medium-sized dogs such as Miniature or Toy Poodles, Cocker Spaniels or Cockapoos.

....

Spaying

Spaying is the term traditionally used to describe the sterilisation of a female dog so that she cannot become pregnant. This is normally done by a procedure called an *"ovariohysterectomy"* and involves the removal of the ovaries and uterus, or womb. Although this is a routine operation, it is major abdominal surgery and she has to be anaesthetised.

One less invasive option offered by some vets is an *"ovariectomy,"* which removes the ovaries, but leaves the womb intact. It requires only a small incision and can even be carried out by laparoscopy, or keyhole surgery. The dog is anaesthetised for a shorter time and there is less risk of infection or excess bleeding during surgery.

One major reason often given for not opting for an ovariectomy is that the female still runs the risk of Pyometra later in life. However, there is currently little or no scientific evidence of females that have undergone an ovariectomy contracting Pyometra afterwards.

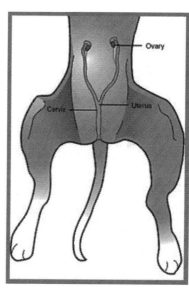

If a female is spayed before her first heat cycle, she will have an almost zero risk of mammary cancer (the equivalent of breast cancer in women). Even after the first heat, spaying reduces the risk of this cancer by 92%. Some vets claim that the risk of mammary cancer in unspayed female dogs can be as high as one in four. There is, however, emerging evidence (with Retrievers) that is it better to wait until a female is four years old.

Spaying is a much more serious operation for females than neutering is for males. It involves an internal abdominal operation, whereas the neutering procedure is carried out on the male's testicles, which are outside his abdomen. As with any major procedure, there are pros and cons.

For:

🐾 Spaying prevents infections, cancer and other diseases of the uterus and ovaries. A spayed female will have a greatly reduced risk of mammary cancer

🐾 Spaying eliminates the risk of Pyometra, which results from hormonal changes in the female's reproductive tract. It also reduces hormonal changes that can interfere with the treatment of diseases like diabetes or epilepsy

🐾 You no longer have to cope with any potential mess caused by bleeding inside the house during heat cycles

- You don't have to guard your female against unwanted attention from males as she will no longer have heat cycles
- Spaying can reduce behaviour problems, such as roaming, aggression towards other dogs, anxiety or fear (not all canine experts agree)
- A spayed dog does not contribute to the pet overpopulation problem

Against:

- Complications can occur, including an abnormal reaction to the anaesthetic, bleeding, stitches breaking and infections; *these are not common*
- Occasionally there can be long-term effects connected to hormonal changes. These include weight gain or less stamina, which can occur years after spaying
- Older females may suffer some urinary incontinence, but it only affects a few spayed females. NOTE: Some younger dogs can also suffer from urinary incontinence after spaying - discuss with your vet
- Cost. This can range from £100 to £250 in the UK, more for keyhole spaying, and approximately $150-$500 at a vet's clinic in the USA, or from around $50 at a low-cost clinic, for those that qualify
- There is early evidence that spaying some Retrievers before six months of age can increase the chance of joint problems developing

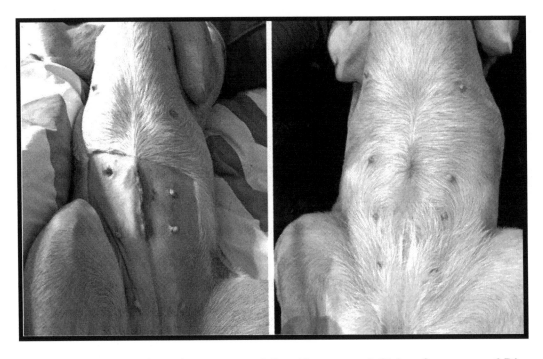

These photographs are reproduced courtesy of Guy Bunce and Chloe Spencer, of Dizzywaltz Labrador Retrievers, Berkshire, England. The left image shows four-year-old Disney shortly after a full spay (ovariohysterectomy). The right one shows Disney a few weeks later.

Neutering

Neutering male dogs involves castration (the removal of the testicles). This can be a difficult decision for some owners, as it causes a drop in the pet's testosterone levels, which some humans – men in particular! - feel affects the quality of their dog's life. Fortunately, dogs do not think like people and male dogs do not miss their testicles or the loss of sex.

 *Dogs working in service or for charities are routinely neutered and this does not impair their ability to perform any of their duties.*

There are countless unwanted puppies, many of which are destroyed. There is also the huge problem of a lack of knowledge from the owners of some dogs, resulting in the production of poor puppies with congenital health or temperament problems.

Technically, neutering can be carried out at any age over eight weeks, provided both testicles have descended. However, recent research is definitely coming down on the side of waiting until the dog is at least one year old.

Surgery is relatively straightforward, and complications are less common and less severe than with spaying. Although he will feel tender afterwards, your dog should return to his normal self within a couple of days.

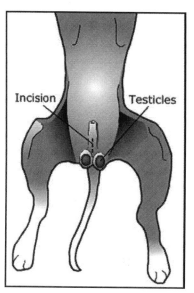

Dogs neutered before puberty tend to grow a little larger than dogs done later. This is because testosterone is involved in the process that stops growth, so the bones grow for longer without testosterone.

When a dog comes out of surgery, his scrotum, or sacs that held the testicles, will be swollen and it may look like nothing has been done. It is normal for these to shrink slowly in the days following surgery. Here are the main pros and cons:

For:

- Castration is a simple procedure, and dogs usually make a swift recovery afterwards
- Behaviour problems such as aggression and roaming can be reduced
- Unwanted sexual behaviour, such as mounting people or objects, is usually reduced or eliminated
- Testicular problems such as infections, cancer and torsion (painful rotation of the testicle) are eradicated
- Prostate disease, common in older male dogs, is less likely to occur
- A submissive un-neutered male dog may be targeted by other dogs. After he has been neutered, he will no longer produce testosterone and so will not be regarded as much of a threat by the other males, so he is less likely to be bullied
- A neutered dog is not fathering unwanted puppies

Against:

- A major scientific study focussed on Retrievers seems to show that some dogs neutered before six months of age are four to five times more likely to have joint problems
- As with any surgery, there can be bleeding afterwards; you should keep an eye on him for any blood loss after the operation. Infections can also occur, generally caused by the dog licking the wound, so try and prevent him doing this. If he persists, use an E-collar. In the **vast majority** of cases, these problems do not occur
- Some dogs' coats may be affected (this also applies to spaying); supplementing the diet with fish oil can compensate for this
- Cost - this starts at around £80 in the UK. In the USA this might cost upwards from $100 at a private veterinary clinic, or from $50 at a low cost or Humane Society clinic

New Techniques

Two other phrases you may hear are *"tubal ligation"* or *"vasectomy." Tubal ligation* is the tying of a female's Fallopian tubes and a **vasectomy** is the clamping shut of the sperm ducts from the male's testicles. Many veterinary papers have been written on these topics, but as yet, not many vets offer them as options, possibly because they have not been trained to carry out these procedures.

In both procedures, the dog continues to produce hormones - unlike with spaying and neutering - but is unable to get pregnant or father puppies. With further evidence of the positive effects of hormones, these operations could become more common in the future — although more vets will have to be trained in these procedures.

There's a new non-surgical procedure to sterilise male dogs called *"Zeutering."* It involves injecting zinc gluconate into the dog's testicles. Dogs are lightly sedated, but not anaesthetised. It's inexpensive, there's little recovery time and no stitches.

However, studies show that Zeutering is only 99% effective, and its long-term effects are still being researched. A downside is that, while it makes dogs sterile, they still retain some of their testosterone. Therefore, habits that usually disappear with traditional castration, such as marking, roaming, following females on heat and aggression towards other males, remain. Zeutering isn't for every dog, but worth discussing with your vet.

Urban Myths

Neutering or spaying will spoil the dog's character - There is no evidence that any of the positive characteristics of your dog will be altered. He or she will be just as loving, playful and loyal. Neutering may reduce aggression or roaming, especially in male dogs, because they are no longer competing to mate with a female.

A female needs to have at least one litter - There is no proven physical or mental benefit to a female having a litter.

Mating is natural and necessary - We tend to ascribe human emotions to our dogs, but they do not think emotionally about sex or having and raising a family. Unlike humans, their desire to mate or breed is entirely physical, triggered by the chemicals called hormones within their body. Without these hormones – i.e. after neutering or spaying – the desire disappears or is greatly reduced.

Male dogs will behave better if they can mate - This is simply not true; sex does not make a dog behave better. In fact, it can have the opposite effect. Having mated once, a male may show an increased interest in females. He may also consider his status elevated, which may make him harder to control or call back.

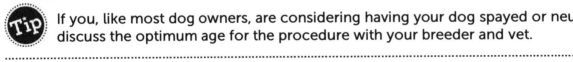 If you, like most dog owners, are considering having your dog spayed or neutered, discuss the optimum age for the procedure with your breeder and vet.

Pregnancy

Regardless of how big or small the dog is, a canine pregnancy lasts for 58 to 65 days; 63 days is average. This is true of all breeds of dog from the Chihuahua to the Great Dane. Sometimes pregnancy is referred to as *"the gestation period."*

It is recommended to take a female for a pre-natal check-up after mating when the vet should answer any questions about type of food, supplements and extra care needed, as well as informing the owner about any physical changes likely to occur in your female.

There is a blood test available that measures levels of *relaxin*. This is a hormone produced by the ovary and the developing placenta, and pregnancy can be detected by monitoring relaxin levels as early as 22 to 27 days after mating. The levels are high throughout pregnancy and then decline rapidly after the female has given birth.

A vet can usually see the puppies (but not how many) using Ultrasound from around the same time. X-rays carried out 45 days into the pregnancy show the puppies' skeletons and give the breeder a good idea of the number of puppies. They can also help to give the vet more information, which is particularly useful if the female has had previous whelping problems.

Signs of Pregnancy

- After mating, many females become more affectionate. However, a few may become uncharacteristically irritable and maybe even a little aggressive!

- The female may produce a slight clear discharge from her vagina one month after mating

- Three or four weeks after mating, some females experience morning sickness – if this is the case, feed little and often. She may seem more tired than usual

- She may seem slightly depressed and/or show a drop in appetite. These signs can also mean there are other problems, so you should consult your vet

- Her teats will become more prominent, pink and erect 25 to 30 days into the pregnancy. Later on, you may notice a fluid coming from them

- After about 35 days, or seven weeks, her body weight will noticeably increase

- Many pregnant females' appetite will increase in the second half of pregnancy

- Her abdomen will become noticeably larger from around day 40, although first-time mums and females carrying few puppies may not show as much

- Her nesting instincts will kick in as the delivery date approaches. She may seem restless or scratch her bed or the floor

- During the last week of pregnancy, females often start to look for a safe place for whelping. Some seem to become confused, wanting to be with their owners and at the same time wanting to prepare their nest. Even if the female is having a C-section, she should still be allowed to nest in a whelping box with layers of newspaper, which she will scratch and dig as the time approaches

If your female becomes pregnant – either by design or accident - your first step should be to consult a vet.

In terms of litter size: generally, the larger the dog, the bigger the litter; Cocker Spaniels and Miniature Poodles are small to medium-sized dogs. Typical litter sizes could be anything from two or three to seven pups. The number varies, according to the age of the dam and sire, size of the gene pool and even the dam's diet. Young and older females tend to have smaller litters.

False Pregnancies

As many as 50% or more of unspayed females may display signs of a false pregnancy. In the wild it was common for female dogs to have false pregnancies and to lactate (produce milk). This female would then nourish puppies if their own mother died.

False pregnancies occur 60 to 80 days after the female was in heat - about the time she would have given birth – and are generally nothing to worry about for an owner. The exact cause is unknown; however, hormonal imbalances are thought to play an important role. Some dogs have shown symptoms within three to four days of spaying; these include:

- Making a nest
- Mothering or adopting toys and other objects
- Producing milk (lactating)
- Appetite fluctuations
- Barking or whining a lot
- Restlessness, depression or anxiety
- Swollen abdomen
- She might even appear to go into labour

Try not to touch your dog's nipples, as touch will stimulate further milk production. If she is licking herself repeatedly, she may need an E-collar to minimise stimulation. To help reduce and eliminate milk production, you can apply cool compresses to the nipples.

Under no circumstances should you restrict your Cockapoo's water supply to try and prevent her from producing milk. This is dangerous as she can become dehydrated.

Some unspayed females may have a false pregnancy with each heat cycle. Spaying during a false pregnancy may actually prolong the condition, so better to wait until it is over to have her spayed.

 *False pregnancy is not a disease, but an exaggerated response to normal hormonal changes. Even if left untreated, it almost always resolves itself.*

However, if your dog appears physically ill or the behavioural changes are severe enough to worry about, visit your vet. He or she may prescribe *Galastop*, which very effectively stops milk production and quickly returns the hormones to normal. In rare cases, hormone treatment may be necessary. Generally, dogs experiencing false pregnancies do not have serious long-term problems, as the behaviour disappears when the hormones return to their normal levels in two to three weeks.

Pictured are seven English Cockapoo puppies aged six weeks.

Pyometra

One exception is **Pyometra**, a serious and potentially deadly infection of the womb, caused by a hormonal abnormality. It normally follows a heat cycle in which fertilisation did not occur and the dog typically starts showing symptoms within two to four months.

Commonly referred to as *"pyo,"* there are **open** and **closed** forms of the disease. Open pyo is usually easy to identify with a smelly discharge, so prompt treatment is easy. Closed pyo is often harder to identify and you may not even notice anything until your girl becomes feverish and lethargic. When this happens, it is very serious and time is of the essence. Typically, vets will recommend immediate spaying in an effort to save her life.

Signs of Pyometra are excessive drinking and urination, with the female trying to lick a white discharge from her vagina. She may also have a slight temperature. If the condition becomes severe, her back legs will become weak, possibly to the point where she can no longer get up without help.

Pyometra is serious if bacteria take a hold, and in extreme cases it can be fatal. It is also relatively common and needs to be dealt with promptly by a vet, who will give the dog intravenous fluids and antibiotics for several days. In most cases this is followed by spaying.

Should I Breed From My Cockapoo?

The short and simple answer is: **NO, leave it to the experts!** The rising cost of puppies and increasing number of dog owners are tempting more people to consider breeding their dogs. Producing healthy, happy Cockapoos with good temperaments doesn't just happen; it is a learned skill.

Due to several genetic diseases that can and do affect this hybrid, any responsible person who is considering breeding Cockapoos needs an extensive knowledge of genetic disorders affecting Cocker Spaniels and Poodles, and the relevant health tests prior to breeding. The suitability of a mate with regards to health and temperament then has to be fully researched.

Any good breeder also has to be prepared to part with a four-figure sum before a single pup is born. Good care, health screening and stud fees come at a cost and, although Cockapoos are expensive, they do not usually arrive in large litters. Don't enter into this thinking you will make a lot of money. If you do it properly, you won't.

You can't just put any two dogs together and expect perfect, healthy puppies. Ethical and successful breeding is much more scientific and time-consuming than that. Inexperience can result in tragic health consequences, poor specimens of the breed, the loss of pups - or even the mother.

Sometimes a C-section (Caesarean section) may be necessary. These are carried out when the mother is unable to birth the pups naturally – and timing is critical. Too early and the pups may be underdeveloped or the mother can bleed to death; too late and the pups can die.

Breeding Costs

Breeding healthy Cockapoos to type is a complex, expensive and time-consuming business when all the fees, DNA and health tests, care, nutrition and medical expenses have been taken into account. Here's a list of considerations to do it properly:

- ❧ Eye tests – both Cocker Spaniel and Poodle
- ❧ Familial Nephropathy (FN) test on an English Cocker Spaniel parent
- ❧ Patella Luxation – Toy Poodles, also American Cocker Spaniels
- ❧ Hip Dysplasia – Cocker Spaniels and Miniature Poodles
- ❧ Stud fees
- ❧ Pregnancy – ultrasound scan, worming, extra food and supplements for the mother
- ❧ Equipment – whelping box, vet bed, thermometer, feeding bottles, heat mat, hibiscrub, etc.
- ❧ Birth – vet's fees
- ❧ Puppies – vaccinations and worming, puppy food, coloured collars

And these are just the basics! These four-figure costs are considerable and swallow up a large chunk of any profit you thought you might make. And if there is a problem with the mother, birth or puppies and you rack up vet's bills, you can actually make a loss on a litter.

Jessica's Advice

Approved Canadian breeder Jessica Samson, of Legacy Cockapoos, Ontario, tells a cautionary tale to explain how she first got involved with breeding: "My love affair with Cockapoos started in the 1990s when I received my first Cockapoo, a beautiful sable girl who I named Samantha.

"I quickly fell in love with her many wonderful qualities. Sadly, I was told, like many people, that *"hybrid dog"* means *"hybrid vigor"* and that my dog would be healthier than any purebred dog because of this.

"WRONG! This is a half-truth. While combining two different breeds does limit the amount of genetic disorders passed on, any genetic disorder carried by both parent breeds can be passed onto

their offspring. Unfortunately, Samantha developed Progressive Rod Cone Atrophy (prcd-PRA) and this meant she went completely blind at a young age when her retinas detached.

"This is a well-known disorder in both Cockers and Poodles. I also had a friend with a Cockapoo from the same breeder, but different litter, that also developed prcd-PRA."

Pictured is Jessica's F2 female, Nessa, who was born white as snow before her wavy fleece coat changed to a rich dark apricot.

"Imagine my frustration and anger to learn that this is a hereditary disorder that had been passed on from their parents due to bad breeding practices. This experience spurred me into researching Cockapoos and their breeders. I was shocked that I could find no breeders doing any health/DNA testing/screenings of any kind on their Cockapoo parents in Canada at that time.

"As far as I could tell, 90% of "breeders" were backyard breeders with a Cocker and a Poodle looking to make a quick buck! And the other 10% wanted you to be impressed with their breeding dog's fancy purebred registration papers - which mean nothing for a hybrid puppy.

"No one really seemed to care about the genetic soundness of their dogs. Shouldn't hybrid dogs be held to the same health standards as purebred dogs? I thought so and so started this wonderful life-fulfilling adventure of breeding Cockapoos.

"All our breeding dogs are pets first and foremost and remain in our home or in their guardian home their entire lives. They are never re-homed when they are no longer suitable for breeding. We only breed a few litters a year to ensure we have time to care for each puppy born to us properly - the health and happiness of our dogs comes first and foremost.

"Sound health and temperaments come first for us. We believe that strong genetics, not *"hybrid vigor,"* makes healthy dogs."

....

Ask Yourself This...

1. **Did you get your Cockapoo from a good, ethical breeder?** Dogs sold in pet stores and on general sales websites are seldom good specimens and can be unhealthy.

2. **Is your dog, and his or her close relatives, free from a history of eye trouble?** Have you got the relevant eye certificates for your dog and seen those for his or her parents? Progressive Retinal Atrophy Progressive Rod Cone Degeneration (prcd-PRA) can be passed on to Cockapoo puppies if the parents aren't clear, as can Glaucoma and other eye problems.

3. **Is your dog, and his or her close relatives, free from other health issues?** Hip Dysplasia, Patella Luxation, von Willebrand's Disease, PFK (American Cockapoos) and Familial Nephropathy (English Cockapoos) are just some of the illnesses which Cockapoo puppies can inherit. Have you had your breeding dog and the stud dog DNA-tested and are you 100% sure your breeding dog is free from them all? Also, an unhealthy female is more likely to have trouble with pregnancy and whelping.

4. **Does your Cockapoo have a good temperament? Does he or she socialise well with people and other animals?** If you can't tell, take your dog to training classes where the instructor can help you evaluate the dog's temperament. Dogs with poor temperaments should not be bred from, regardless of how good they look and what sort of coat they have.

5. **Has your dog a healthy, low shedding coat and were the parents' coats similar?** If you are breeding for consistency, the coat is an important factor as many potential owners choose Cockapoos for their hypoallergenic characteristics.

6. **Does your dog conform to the standard/type?** Although there is no Kennel Club or AKC breed standard, as the Cockapoo is a hybrid not a purebred, the Cockapoo Club of GB has a strict Code of Ethics and promotes a breeding standard, as does the American Cockapoo Club. Do not breed from a Cockapoo which is not a good specimen, hoping that somehow the puppies will turn out better. They won't. Talk with experienced breeders and ask them for an honest assessment of your dog.

7. **Is your female two years old or older and at least in her second heat cycle?** Females should not be bred until they are fully physically mature, when they are able to carry a

litter to term, and are robust enough to whelp and care for a litter. Even then, not all females are suitable. Some are simply poor mothers who don't care for their puppies - which means you have to do it – others may not be able to produce enough milk.

8. **Do you know exactly what type of Cockapoo you are going to produce – F1s, F2s, F3s, F1bs? What size?**

9. **Do you understand COI and its implications?** COI stands for Coefficient of Inbreeding. It measures the common ancestors of a dam and sire and indicates the probability of how genetically similar they are. In the UK, the COI should remain below 6.25%, according to the Cockapoo Club of GB.

10. **Are you financially able to provide good veterinary care for the mother and puppies, particularly if complications occur?** Health can be expensive, and that's in addition to routine veterinary care and the added costs of pre-natal care and immunisations for puppies. What if your female needs a C-section, or the puppies need emergency treatment, can you afford the bills?

11. **Have you got the indoor space?** The mother and puppies will need their own space in your home, which will become messy as new-born pups do not come into this world housetrained. It should also be warm and draught-free.

12. **Do you have the time to provide full-time care for the mother and puppies if necessary?** Caring for the mother and new-borns is a 24/7 job for the first few weeks. You can't simply go out and leave mother and pups unattended.

13. **Will you be able to find good homes for however many puppies there should be and will you be prepared to take them back if necessary?** This is an important consideration for good breeders, who will not let their precious puppies go to any old home. They want to be sure that the new owners will take good care of their Cockapoos for their lifetime.

Pictured is a beautiful litter of one-week old F1 English Cockapoo puppies from fully health-tested parents, bred by Pat Pollington, of Polycinders Cockapoos, Devon, UK. Pat has bred dogs since 1980 and Cockapoos since 2004. Note the consistent appearance of the puppies.

If you are determined to breed from your Cockapoo, and breed properly, you must first learn a lot. If you are in the UK, search the Cockapoo Club of GB's list of approved breeders at: www.cockapooclubgb.co.uk – ask one who lives nearby if she would become a mentor. In the USA visit www.americancockapooclub.com for their list of approved breeders near you.

Regardless of where you live, you can visit online Cockapoo forums where other owners are willing to share their experiences. If you have provisionally selected a breeder, ask other owners if anyone has one of their puppies.

Whatever generation of Cockapoos you are interested in, make sure you are very familiar with the parent breeds of Cocker Spaniel and Poodle (of whichever size) and the potential health issues.

....

Having said all of that, good breeders are made, not born. Like any expert, they learn over time. If you're serious, spend time researching Cocker Spaniels, Poodles and Cockapoos and their genetics and make sure you are going into it for the right reasons and not just for the money - ask yourself how you intend to improve the Cockapoo.

One useful resource is *"Book of the Bitch" by J. M. Evans and Kay White.* Another good way of learning more about breeding is to find a mentor, someone who is already successfully breeding.

By "successful," we mean somebody who is producing healthy, handsome Cockapoos with good temperaments, not someone who is making lots of money from churning out puppies.

While there is no universal Cockapoo club, there are some reputable organisations covering popular crossbreeds. In the USA there is GANA, the Goldendoodle Association of North America www.goldendoodleassociation.com and in the UK there is The Cockapoo Owners Club www.cockapooowners-club.org.uk - both of which have a Code of Ethics on their websites; good breeders meet these standards. But before you take a look, read *Why NOT To Breed* by the Doodle Trust at www.doodletrust.com/education/why-not-to-breed

Committed Cockapoo breeders aren't in it for the cash. They use their skills and knowledge to produce healthy, attractive, structurally sound pups with good temperaments that ultimately improve this wonderful crossbreed.

....

You may have the most wonderful Cockapoo in the world, but don't enter the world of canine breeding without the motivation and knowledge. Don't do it for the money or the cute factor – or to show the kids "The Miracle of Birth!" Breeding poor examples only brings heartache in the long run when health or temperament issues develop.

14. Cockapoo Rescue

Are you thinking of adopting a Cockapoo from a rescue organisation? What could be kinder and more rewarding than giving a poor, abandoned Cockapoo a happy and loving home for the rest of his life?

Not much really; adoption saves lives. The problem of homeless dogs is truly depressing, particularly in the USA. The sheer numbers in kill shelters there is hard to comprehend. Randy Grim states in "Don't Dump The Dog" that 1,000 dogs are being put to sleep every hour in the States.

According to Jo-Anne Cousins, former Executive Director at International Doodle Owners Group (IDOG), the situations leading to a dog ending up in rescue can be summed up in one phrase: *unrealistic expectations.*

Unrealistic Expectations

She said: "In many situations, dog ownership was something that the family went into without fully understanding the time, money and commitment to exercise and training that it takes to raise a dog. While they may have spent hours on the internet pouring over cute puppy photos, they probably didn't read any puppy training books or look into actual costs of regular vet care, training and boarding."

Another reason some Cockapoos end up in rescue is that people get one believing they are all **"hypoallergenic,"** only to discover later that the dog triggers allergies in one member of the family - there are no sure-fire guarantees. While researching this boo, I came across this advert on Preloved in the UK:

"F1 Cockapoo puppy nine weeks old, selling due to my allergic reaction to her. Mum is a cocker spaniel KC registered, dad is a miniature poodle, KC registered and PRA eye clear. F1 puppy, £750 ($975)."

Incredible to think that the puppy had only lasted a week in her new "forever" home. That lack of thought was also highlighted in a story that appeared in the Press in my Yorkshire home town. A woman went shopping on Christmas Eve in a local retail centre. She returned home £700 ($910) poorer with a puppy she had bought on impulse. The pup was in a rescue centre two days later. Common reasons for a dog being put into rescue include:

- A change in family circumstance, such as divorce or a new baby
- A change in work patterns
- Moving home
- An elderly owner has died or moved to a care home
- The dog develops health issues

Often, the **"unrealistic expectations"** come home to roost and the dog is given up because:

- He has too much energy, needs too much exercise, knocks the kids over and/or jumps on people - young dogs are often boisterous and sometimes lack co-ordination

- He chews or eats things he shouldn't

- He is growling and/or nipping. All puppies bite, it is their way of exploring the world; they have to be trained not to bite the things (such as humans) that they are not supposed to bite

- He needs a lot more exercise/grooming/attention than the owner is able or prepared to give. Cockapoos are "Velcro" dogs and require a lot of attention from the owner

- He makes a mess in the house - housetraining requires time and patience from the owner

- He costs too much to keep - the cost of feeding, vets' bills, grooming (unless you do it yourself), etc. are not insignificant

There is, however, a ray of sunshine for some of these dogs. Every year tens of thousands of people adopt a rescue dog and the story often has a happy ending.

The Dog's Point of View...

If you are serious about adoption, then you should do so with the right motives and with your eyes wide open. If you're expecting a perfect dog, you could be in for a shock. Rescue dogs can and do become wonderful companions, but a lot of it depends on you.

Cockapoos are people-loving dogs. Sometimes those that have ended up in rescue centres are traumatised. Some may have health or behaviour problems.

They don't understand why they have been abandoned, neglected or badly treated by their beloved owners and may arrive at your home with "baggage" of their own until they adjust to being part of a loving family again. This may take time.

Time and patience are the keys to help the dog to adjust to his new surroundings and family and to learn to love and trust again. Ask yourself a few questions before you take the plunge and fill in the adoption forms:

- Are you prepared to accept and deal with any problems - such as bad behaviour, chewing, timidity, aggression, jumping up or peeing/pooing in the house - which a rescue dog may initially display when arriving in your home?

- How much time are you willing to spend with your new dog to help him integrate back into normal family life?

- Can you take time off work to be at home and help the dog settle in at the beginning?

- Are you prepared to take on a new addition to your family that may live for another decade?

- Are you prepared to stick with the dog even if he develops health issues later?

Think about the implications before rescuing a dog - try and look at it from the dog's point of view...What could be worse for the unlucky dog than to be abandoned again if things don't work out between you?

Warning from The Doodle Trust

Cockapoos that have been badly treated or have had difficult lives need plenty of time to rehabilitate. Some may have initial problems with potty training, others may need socialisation with people and/or other dogs. And if you are serious about adoption, you may have to wait a while until a suitable dog comes up.

In the UK, the Doodle Trust rescues and rehome Doodles – Labradoodles, Goldendoodles, Cockapoos, Cavapoos and other Poodle crosses. They have a long list of "Things to Consider BEFORE Getting a Doodle," including:

- If you are just not a Poodle person, DON'T GET A DOODLE. All doodles have Poodle in them and if the word Poodle makes you cringe, then do not get a Doodle

- If you are allergic to dogs, DON'T GET A DOODLE. Doodles go through coat changes and even if you are not allergic to your Doodle's puppy coat, you may be allergic to his adult coat. Doodles are often deemed hypoallergenic by the media, but for most, this is not the case

- If you want a low-energy dog, DON'T GET A DOODLE. Most Doodles require at least 30-60 minutes of real exercise a day. Simply letting your Doodle out in the backyard is not exercise. There are plenty of low-energy dog breeds that would be a better fit if you aren't overly active

- If you can't devote time and money into training, DON'T GET A DOODLE. Doodles are intelligent and want to please you, but they are not born with manners

- If you want an independent dog, DON'T GET A DOODLE. Doodles thrive on human companionship and most are Velcro dogs. They need your attention and will demand it

- If you want a low-maintenance dog, DON'T GET A DOODLE. The look that attracts so many would-be Doodle owners requires a lot of time and money; there is major grooming involved

- If you want a dog *"for the kids,"* DON'T GET A DOODLE. Doodles need lots of time on a daily basis, keeping their minds stimulated and reinforcing their behaviours. Kids won't keep that commitment

The Doodle Trust adds: "Doodles are lively, enthusiastic and sometimes boisterous dogs that require a lot of time and attention. If you are out at work for much of the time or lead a busy life, a Doodle is NOT the right breed for you. "These are people dogs and they demand human companionship; they thrive as a much-loved family member. If left to their own devices for long periods, they will find their own amusement and could become destructive.

"Most Doodles love water and can be mud magnets, bringing in an enormous amount of dirt into your home. They are certainly not a breed for the house-proud. Some coat types require grooming on a daily basis in order to keep them matt-free. Many Doodles also need professional grooming on a regular basis in order to keep the coat manageable and this can be expensive. You should therefore consider grooming costs on top of food, insurance, toys, vaccinations, worming, etc. It all mounts up!

"Doodles are not necessarily compatible with small children and, in any case, it is unwise to leave any dog with small children.

"Most Doodles coming into rescue are large boys so there may be a considerable waiting period before we can match you with the right dog. Waiting times are further increased if you specify a certain colour and coat type and our dogs will always be matched to families by their suitability, rather than looks."

Long-Term Commitment or Fostering?

Adopting a rescue dog is a big commitment for all involved. It is not a cheap way of getting a Cockapoo. It could cost you several hundred pounds - or dollars. You'll have adoption fees to pay and often vaccination and veterinary bills as well as worm and flea medication and spaying or neutering. Make sure you're aware of the full cost before committing.

One way of finding out if you, your family and home are suitable is to volunteer to become a foster home for one of the rescue centres. Fosters offer temporary homes until a forever home becomes available. It's a shorter-term arrangement, but still requires commitment and patience.

Rescue groups and shelters have to make sure that prospective adopters are suitable and they have thought through everything very carefully before making such a big decision.

They also want to match you with the right dog - putting a young or high-energy Cockapoo with an elderly couple might not be the perfect match, for example. Or putting any Cockapoo with somebody who is out at work all day would also be unsuitable. Here are some of the details required on a typical adoption form:

- Name, address and details of all people living in your home
- Extensive details of any other pets
- Your work hours and amount of time you spend away from the home each day
- Whether you have any previous experience with dogs
- Type of property you live in
- Your reasons for wanting to adopt a Cockapoo
- Size of your garden (if you have one) and height of the fence
- If you have ever previously given up a dog for adoption
- Whether you have any experience dealing with canine behaviour or health issues
- Details of your vet
- If you are prepared for destructive behaviour/chewing/fear/aggression/timidity/soiling inside the house/medical issues
- Whether you agree to insure your dog
- Whether you are prepared for the financial costs of dog ownership
- Whether you are willing to housetrain and obedience train the dog
- Your views on dog training methods
- Where your dog will sleep at night

 *Despite the fact that so many dogs need rehoming, it's not just the dogs that are screened - you have to be vetted too. You will also have to provide*

references and agree to your home being inspected. And UK rescue organisations will not place dogs in homes where they will be left alone for more than about four hours at a time.

It may seem like a lot of red tape, but the rescue groups have to be as sure as they can that you will provide a loving, forever home for the unfortunate dog. It would be terrible if the dog had to be placed back in rescue again.

All rescue organisations will neuter the dog or, if he is too young, specify in the adoption contract that the dog must be neutered and may not be used for breeding. Many rescue organisations have a lifetime rescue back-up policy, which means that if things don't work out, the dog must be returned to them.

Training a Rescue Dog

A rescue dog has a lot to cope with already without having a lot of new experiences as possible. Here are some tips to help your new arrival settle in quicker:

- Learn everything you can ahead of time about the dog's background
- Is he housetrained?
- Is he used to children and other animals?
- How does the dog react around other dogs – with confidence or fear?
- Is he used to a crate? If not, don't introduce it until the dog is comfortable in your home, then take things slowly. Make everything about the crate a positive, pleasant experience for the dog
- If he's not used to a crate, pen off an area to contain him when necessary
- In the beginning, supervise him all the time he's not in his crate or pen until you're comfortable with his behaviour in the home and around family members and any other pets

- If you have other pets, introduce them on neutral territory in a gentle manner
- Enrol him in a training class, which is a great way to get to know your new dog's character and for him to learn manners and socialise with other dogs
- Don't overface him with too many new people, dogs or experiences in the beginning - take things slowly
- Don't smack for bad behaviour. Say NO! or ACK! in a firm, loud manner. If the bad behaviour persists, remove your attention and put him in a crate or pen
- BE PATIENT! Rescue dogs need time to adjust

Rescue Organisations

UK:

Cockapoo Club Rescue www.cockapooclubgb.co.uk
Cockapoo Owners Club UK (COCUK) Facebook www.facebook.com/groups/319345271608278
Cockapoo Me https://cockapoo.me/cockapoo-rescue-pages
The Doodle Trust www.doodletrust.com There are a number of ways to help this worthy cause.
You could get involved by donating money, volunteering to become a foster home, a home
checker or a fundraiser. Or you could help with transport; check out the website for details.
General dog shelters and rescue groups with dogs of all breeds, including Battersea Dogs' Home.

There are also general dog rescue websites, but you may find that these have more of certain types
of dogs, such as Staffies or German Shepherds. These include: www.homes4dogs.co.uk
www.greenleafanimalrescue.org.uk www.petfinder.com www.adoptapet.com

USA

Cockapoo Rescue on Facebook www.facebook.com/cockapoo.rescueme.org/
Rescue Collective http://doodlerescuecollective.com
There are numerous websites rescuing dogs of all breeds and mixes, such as
www.petsmartcharities.org and www.adoptapet.com. A website that lists all of the Poodle crosses,
including Cockapoos, from other websites around the USA at: http://poomixrescue.com.

 FACT *You cannot presume that website descriptions are 100% accurate. Ideas of
what constitutes a "medium" dog and what is a "small" or "large" dog may vary.
Some dogs may be mistakenly described as "Poodle mix and Cocker Spaniel" when they may
have other breeds in their genetic make-up.*

It does not mean they are necessarily worse dogs, but if you are attracted to the Cockapoo for its
temperament and other assets, make sure you are looking at a Cockapoo.

Tip *DON'T buy a dog from eBay, Craig's List, Gumtree or any websites selling old cars,
washing machines, golf clubs etc. You might think you are getting a cheap dog, but you
could well end up regretting it.*

If the dog had been well bred and cared for, it is
highly unlikely he would be on a general ads
website, and you may well have health or
behavioural issues, due to poor breeding or
environment, at some point in the future.

If you haven't been put you off with all of the
above..... Congratulations, you may be just the
family or person that poor homeless Cockapoo is
looking for! If you can't spare the time to adopt -
and adoption means forever - consider fostering. Or
you could help by becoming a fundraiser to
generate cash to keep these very worthy rescue
groups providing such a wonderful service.

However you decide to get involved, Good Luck!

Saving one dog will not change the world
But it will change the world for one dog

With thanks to The Doodle Trust for their assistance with this chapter.

15. Caring for Older Cockapoos

If your Cockapoo has been well looked after and had no serious illnesses, she could live well into her teens. Several breeders thought that 15 to 17 years of age was not unusual. One even knew of a Cockapoo living to the ripe old age of 20.

Lifespan is influenced by genetics and also by owners; how you feed, exercise and generally look after your dog will all have an impact on her life. Cockapoos can remain fit and active well into their teens. But eventually all dogs – even Cockapoos – slow down.

Approaching Old Age

However fit your ageing Cockapoo is, at some point, she will start to feel the effects of ageing. After having got up at the crack of dawn when a puppy, you may find that she now likes to sleep in longer in the morning. She may be less keen to go out in the rain and snow.

Physically, joints may become stiffer, and organs, such as heart or liver, may not function as effectively. On the mental side - just as with humans - your dog's memory, ability to learn and awareness will all start to dim.

Your faithful companion might become a bit grumpier, stubborn or a little less tolerant of lively dogs and children. You may also notice that she doesn't see or hear as well as she used to. On the other hand, your old friend might not be hard of hearing at all. She might have developed that affliction common to many older dogs of *"selective hearing."*

Our 12-year-old Max had bionic hearing when it came to the word *"Dinnertime"* whispered from 20 paces, yet seemed strangely unable to hear the commands *"Come"* or *"Down"* when we were right in front of him!

Pictured is Toby, who is 16 years young. He is an F2 and was in the first litter ever bred by Jessica Sampson, of Legacy Cockapoos. He is owned by Jessica's mother, Caroline Leitch. Toby's silver sable colouring and long beard mean that he is sometimes mistaken for a Schnauzer!

You can help ease your mature dog into old age gracefully by keeping an eye on her, noticing the changes and taking action to help her as much as possible.

This might involve:

❧ A visit to the vet for supplements and/or medications

❧ Modifying your dog's environment

❧ A change of diet

❧ Slowly reducing the amount of daily exercise

Much depends on the individual dog. Just as with humans, a dog of ideal weight that has been active and stimulated all of her life is likely to age slower than an overweight couch potato.

Keeping Cockapoos at that optimum weight is challenging - and important – as they age. Their metabolisms slow down, making it easier to put on the pounds unless the daily calories are reduced. At the same time, extra weight places additional, unwanted stress on joints and organs, making them have to work harder than they should.

FACT ❯ *We normally talk about dogs being old when they reach the last third of their lives. This varies greatly from dog to dog and bloodline to bloodline. A dog is classed as a "Veteran" at seven years old in the show ring. Some Cockapoos may remain active with little signs of ageing until the day they die, others may start to show signs of ageing at seven or eight years old.*

Physical and Mental Signs of Ageing

If your Cockapoo is in or approaching the last third of her life, here are some signs that her body is feeling its age:

- She has generally slowed down and no longer seems as keen to go out on her walks — or if she does want to go, she doesn't want to go as far. She is happy pottering and sniffing - and often takes forever to inspect a single clump of grass! Some are less keen to go outside in bad weather

- She gets up from lying down and goes up and down stairs more slowly. She can no longer jump on to the couch or bed; all signs that joints are stiffening, often due to arthritis

- Grey hairs are appearing, particularly around the muzzle (it's harder to tell on dogs with lighter coats)

- She has put on a bit of weight

- She may have the occasional "accident" (incontinence) inside the house

- She urinates more frequently

- She drinks more water

- She has bouts of constipation or diarrhoea

- The foot pads thicken and nails may become more brittle

- One or more lumps or fatty deposits (lipomas) develop on the body. Our old dog developed two small bumps on top of his head aged 10 and we took him straight to the vet, who performed minor surgery to remove them. They were benign (harmless), but always get them checked out ASAP in case they are an early form of cancer - they can also grow quite rapidly, even if benign.

- She can't regulate body temperature as she used to and so feels the cold and heat more

- Hearing deteriorates

- Eyesight may also deteriorate – if her eyes appear cloudy she may be developing cataracts, so see your vet as soon as you notice the signs. Just as with humans, most older dogs live quite well with failing eyesight

- Your dog has bad breath (halitosis), which could be a sign of dental or gum disease. Brush the teeth regularly and if the bad breath persists, get her checked out by a vet

- If inactive, she may develop callouses on the elbows, especially if she lies on hard surfaces – this is more common with large dogs than small ones

It's not just your dog's body that deteriorates; her mind does too. It's often part of the normal ageing process. Your dog may display some, all or none of these signs of *Canine Cognitive Dysfunction:*

- Sleep patterns change; an older dog may be more restless at night and sleepy during the day. She may start wandering around the house at odd times, causing you sleepless nights

- She barks more, sometimes at nothing or open spaces

- She stares at objects, such as walls, hides in a corner, or wanders aimlessly around the house or garden

- Your dog shows increased anxiety, separation anxiety or aggression - although aggression is not common in older Cockapoos

- She forgets or ignores commands or habits she once knew well, such as the Recall and sometimes toilet training

- Some dogs may become clingier and more dependent, often resulting in separation anxiety. She may seek reassurance that you are near as faculties fade and she becomes a bit less confident and independent. Others may become a bit disengaged and less interested in human contact

Understanding the changes happening to your dog and acting on them compassionately and effectively will help ease your dog's passage through her senior years. Your dog has given you so much pleasure over the years, now she needs you to give that bit of extra care for a happy, healthy old age. You can also help your Cockapoo to stay mentally active by playing gentle games and getting new toys to stimulate interest.

Helping Your Dog Age Gracefully

There are many things you can do to ease your dog's passage into her declining years.

As dogs age they need fewer calories and less protein, so many owners switch to a food specially formulated for older dogs. These are labelled *Senior, Ageing* or *Mature.* Check the labelling; some are specifically for dogs aged over eight, others may be for 10 or 12-year-olds.

If you are not sure if a senior diet is necessary for your Cockapoo, talk to your vet the next time you are there. Remember, if you do change brand, switch the food

gradually over a week or so. Unlike with humans, a dog's digestive system cannot cope with sudden changes of diet.

Years of eating the same food, coupled with less sensitive taste buds can result in some dogs going off their food as they age. If you feed a dry food, try mixing a bit of gravy with it; this has worked well for us, as has feeding two different feeds: a morning one of kibble with gravy and the second tea-time feed of home-cooked rice and fish or chicken. Rice, white fish and chicken – all cooked – can be particularly good if your old dog has a sensitive stomach.

If you are considering a daily supplement, Omega-3 fatty acids are good for the brain and coat and glucosamine and various other supplements are available to help joints. Our dog gets a squirt of Yumega Omega 3 and half a small scoop of Joint Aid in one of his daily feeds.

We had one dog that became very sensitive to loud noises as he got older and the lead up to Bonfire Night was a nightmare. (November 5th in the UK, when the skies are filled with fireworks and loud bangs). Some dogs also become more stressed by trips to the groomer's as they get older.

There are medications and homeopathic remedies, such as melatonin which has natural sedative properties, to help relieve such anxieties. Check with your vet before introducing any new medicines.

One of the most important things you can do for your Cockapoo is regular tooth brushing throughout her life. Not only is toothache painful and unpleasant, it can be traumatic for dogs to have teeth removed under anaesthetic or when they start to lose weight due to being unable to eat properly.

If your old friend has started to ignore your verbal commands when out on a walk – either through *"switching off"* or deafness - try a whistle to attract her attention and then use an exaggerated hand signal for the Recall. Once your dog is looking at you, hold your arm out, palm down, at 90 degrees to your body and bring it down, keeping your arm straight, until your fingers point to your toes.

Hand signals worked very effectively with our Max. He looked, understood ......and then decided if he was going to come or not - but at least he knew what he should be doing! More often than not he did come back, especially if the visual signal was repeated while he was still making up his mind.

Weight - no matter how old your Cockapoo is, she still needs a waist! Maintaining a healthy weight with a balanced diet and regular, gentler exercise are two of the most important things you can do for your dog.

Environment - Make sure your dog has a nice soft place to rest her old bones, which may mean adding an extra blanket to her bed. This should be in a place that is not too hot or cold, as she may not be able to regulate her body temperature as well as when she was younger. She needs plenty of undisturbed sleep and should not be pestered and/or bullied by younger dogs, other animals or young children. If her eyesight is failing, move obstacles out of her way, and/or use pet barriers to reduce the chance of injuries.

Jumping on and off furniture or in or out of the car is high impact for old joints and bones. She will need a helping hand on and off the couch or your bed - if she's allowed up there - or even a little ramp to get in and out of the car.

We bought an expensive plastic ramp for one old dog as she became hesitant to jump in or out of the car. However, this proved to be a complete waste of money, as she didn't like the feel of the non-slip surface on her paws and after a couple of tentative attempts, steadfastly refused to set a paw on it. We ended up lifting the dog in and out of the car and donating the ramp to a canine charity!

Exercise - Take the lead from your dog, if she doesn't want to walk as far, then don't. But if your dog doesn't want to go out at all, you will have to coax her out. ALL old dogs need exercise, not only to keep their joints moving, but also to keep their heart, lungs and joints exercised and to help keep their minds engaged with different places, scents, etc.

Ears - Older Cockapoos often seem to produce more ear wax, so it's important to check inside the ears regularly. If necessary, use clean damp cotton wool to clean out the inner ear and pluck extra ear hair if it's getting waxy

....

Time to Get Checked Out

If your dog is showing any of these signs, get her to the vet for a full check over:

🐾 Excessive increased urination or drinking can be a sign of something amiss, such as reduced liver or kidney function, Cushing's disease or diabetes

🐾 Constipation or not urinating regularly could be a sign of something not functioning properly with the digestive system or organs

🐾 Incontinence, which could be a sign of a mental or physical problem

🐾 Cloudy eyes, which could be cataracts

🐾 Decreased appetite – often one of the first signs of an underlying problem

🐾 Lumps or bumps on the body - often benign, but can occasionally be malignant (cancerous)

🐾 Excessive sleeping or a lack of interest in you and her surroundings

🐾 Diarrhoea or vomiting

🐾 A darkening and dryness of skin that never seems to get any better - this can be a sign of hypothyroidism

🐾 Any other out-of-the-ordinary behaviour for your dog. A change in patterns or behaviour is often your dog's way of telling you that all is not well

....

What the Experts Say

Rebecca Mae Goins, of MoonShine Babies Cockapoos, Indiana, USA, has worked as a Pet Care Technician as well as a Companion Animal Hygienist since 1993, so she knows a thing or two about elderly dogs. She has bred Cockapoos since 2006. Here's our interview:

At what age would you say a Cockapoo becomes a senior- i.e. time to look at changing to a senior diet? "I personally would say seven to nine years old is when you start looking for your Cockapoo to require a lower calorie diet, because they will start to slow down and both Cockers and Poodles can get a little chubby when they get older."

What do you feed your older Cockapoos? "I feed Royal Canin Mini from Puppy Formula to Adult. When it comes to my older Cockapoos, I switch them to Royal Canin Weight Care or Royal Canin Mature, whichever is best for the Cockapoo in need of the diet change."

Do you feed any supplements to your older dogs - or anything else which helps them as they age? "I feed all my Cockapoos NuVet Plus supplements from puppyhood to adult. When they get older, I switch the seniors to NuJoint Plus, which contains all that is needed to help with the ageing joints."

Pictured is Rebecca's service dog, Scarlett.

Are there any health issues particular to older Cockapoos? "Well since Cockapoos are a mixture of Cocker Spaniel and Poodle, you have to look at both breeds. In general, Cockapoos are a hearty breed. If the parent dogs are health tested and have no health issues, then the puppies should follow suit. But even the pups of healthy parent dogs should be health tested to make sure nothing has been missed.

"There are a lot of issues that can happen to both breeds when they age, such as Luxating Patellas and several eye disorders, but the most common is Progressive Retinal Atrophy (PRA). Ear infections can occur due to the long droopy ears, and some Cockapoos have the hair that grows in the ear canal like the Poodle. If not removed by your groomer or vet, it can cause yeast and bacterial infections. Older Cockapoos can also develop lumps which will need to be looked at immediately."

How about behavioural changes? "With ageing Cockapoos, behavioural changes can happen as with any ageing dog. They can forget the training they have learned, so you will need to keep a steady schedule during your Cockapoo's lifetime so that there are fewer chances for a lapse in manners. Always be aware of behavioral changes, because this can sometimes mean that there is an underlying issue, in which case you need to make an appointment with your vet."

Do you have any tips you can pass on to owners of older Cockapoos? "Yes, as a breeder, rescuer and owner of Cockapoos I have dealt with a lot of older Cockapoos. The best advice I can give you with your ageing Cockapoo is: LOVE them and cherish every moment you have with them.

"Always watch the way they react to make sure you do not miss anything that needs veterinary care. Regularly groom them to keep their skin and coat in good condition, and feed quality foods and supplements. Have daily play times to exercise them and daily rub downs and petting sessions to make sure there are no sores, aches and pains or lump and growths.

"Join a Cockapoo online forum or Facebook group for support from other Cockapoo owners. Sometimes you can find local groups who will meet at parks or meeting areas to provide support and socialisation for you and your Cockapoo."

Here's the same interview with Jessica Sampson, of Legacy Cockapoos, Ontario, Canada:

"Many Cockapoos start to slow down between the ages of nine to 10, but some may show no signs of slowing down until 12 to 14 years of age. This is a good indication that it may be time to switch to a senior diet.

"I feed all my dogs, from puppies to seniors, an *All Stages* diet: Dick Van Patten's Natural Balance. I have had great success with this and my Cockapoos live a long healthy life of 16 to 18 years on average. I follow the careful advice of my veterinarian and she has never seen reason to change any of my dogs to a senior diet, as they have all been very healthy and their nutritional needs have always been met by the diet we feed.

"If you feed your dog an excellent quality food, there really is no need for vitamin or supplements, unless your veterinarian recommends otherwise. Follow your vet's advice. We feed all our dogs, regardless of age, a good quality canine probiotic, as good health starts from the inside.

"Cockapoos generally maintain their good health but, as with all breeds, arthritis can be an issue in older dogs, as well as cataracts and hearing loss.

"In terms of behavioural changes, your Cockapoo will sleep more throughout the day. You will notice he is also not as spry as he once was, but should remain the same happy affectionate dog you know and love. Some elderly dogs may have less tolerance and may become agitated or snappy if they are in pain (this is not normal behaviour). If this is the case, consult your vet as to the course of action to take for pain management.

"An active dog is a healthy dog! My advice to owners is to keep up with regular walks and activities. If your Cockapoo seems like or she has less energy, adjust your walk and play time to a more suitable level. I have had 16-year-old Cockapoos who have had no trouble keeping up on a two-hour hike in the woods!

"Make more regular visits to your vet and follow his or her advice. Elderly dogs' health can change quickly, so making regular vet visits will help identify any changes in your dog and help you to take the right course of action to maintain your dog's health and comfort through his or her senior years."

Jeanne Davis, Wind Horse Offering, Maryland, USA, adds: "I don't actually have any personal experience with elderly Cockapoo's, as I have only been breeding them for eight years. In terms of age, I have had people contact me who have said that their Cockapoo lived for 15 years, others say 18."

Pictured, courtesy of Jeanne and with plenty of life to look forward to, is Champ by Wind Horse Offering's Stud Muffin out of Wind Horse Offering's Lily.

"I would say that any dog has to stay active, properly fed and warm. As far as feeding goes, I am not one for any special supplementation, as long as the food that I am feeding is nutritious and palatable. However, it is important to keep Cockapoos' teeth clean so that they don't get gum disease and then start having tooth problems."

The Last Lap

Huge advances in veterinary science have meant that there are countless procedures and medications that can prolong the life of your dog, and this is a good thing. But there comes a time when you do have to let go.

If your dog is showing all the signs of ageing, has an ongoing medical condition from which she cannot recover, is showing signs of pain, mental anxiety or distress and there is no hope of improvement, then the dreaded time has come to say goodbye. You owe it to her.

There is no point keeping an old dog alive if all the dog has ahead is pain and death. We have their lives in our hands and we can give them the gift of passing away peacefully and humanely at the end when the time is right.

Losing our beloved companion, our best friend, a member of the family, is truly heart-breaking. But one of the things we realise at the back of our minds when we got that gorgeous, lively little puppy that bounded up to meet us like we were the best person in the whole wide world is the pain that comes with it. We know that we will live longer than them and that we'll probably have to make this most painful of decisions at some time in the future.

It's the worst thing about being a dog owner.

If your Cockapoo has had a long and happy life, then you could not have done any more. You were a great owner and your dog was lucky to have you. Remember all the good times you had together. And try not to rush out and buy another dog straight away; wait a while to grieve for your Cockapoo.

Assess your current life and lifestyle and, if your situation is right, only then consider getting another dog and all that that entails in terms of time, commitment and expense.

A dog coming into a happy, stable household will get off to a better start in life than a dog entering a home full of grief.

Whatever you decide to do, put the dog first.

....

16. (Wo)Man's Best Friend

With their intelligence, happy dispositions, empathy and love of humans, Cockapoos have developed a reputation as excellent therapy and service dogs.

They bring joy to the elderly and ill as well as providing a lifeline for people with disabilities. They assist children in the autistic spectrum and can also help youngsters overcome speech and emotional difficulties.

....

Therapy Dogs

There is a difference between a therapy and a service or assistance dog; and Cockapoos are suitable for training as either. A therapy dog visits settings such as retirement and nursing homes, hospitals, hospices and schools, where they are handled and petted to help provide a calming influence.

Scientific evidence has shown that being around and stroking dogs can provide comfort and reduce stress levels. In the UK, therapy dogs are also known as PAT dogs (Pets As Therapy); further information can be found at: www.petsastherapy.org

The history of the first-ever therapy dog dates back to World War II when a female Yorkshire Terrier was found on the battlefield in New Guinea. She was adopted by US Corporal William Wynne who named her Smoky *(pictured)*. She became the first therapy dog when William was hospitalised for a jungle disease and his friends brought the little Yorkie into the hospital to cheer him up as he was recovering.

Smoky immediately became so popular with the other wounded soldiers that the commanding officer, Dr Charles Mayo (who founded the Mayo Clinic), allowed her to go on ward rounds and to sleep on William's hospital bed.

Smoky also helped engineers to get communications up and running at an airbase in the Philippines. She dragged a telegraph wire tied to her collar under a runway and through a 70-foot-long pipe just eight inches high.

Smoky's use as a therapy dog continued for 12 years, during and after World War II. She died in 1957 aged about 14.

Wider use of therapy dogs is attributed to American nurse Elaine Smith, who noticed how well patients responded to visits by a chaplain and his Golden Retriever. In 1976, Smith started a programme for training dogs to visit institutions. She later formed Therapy Dogs International, which today has more than 24,000 registered dog and handler pairings.

Service dogs provide a wide range of tasks. They are specifically trained to help people who have disabilities such as visual, mobility or hearing impairments, mental illnesses - including PTSD - seizures and diabetes.

Mary Gosling is co-founder of the British Cockapoo Society. She is also deaf. After a difficult time, her life has been transformed by her Hearing Dog, Harley Here is their very moving story, written in Mary's own words for The Cockapoo Handbook:

Mary and Harley's Story

"Before becoming deaf, I was a fairly normal single Mum, living with my teenage daughter. She was gearing up for her GCSE exams and so that was the big thing going on. I had spent time living in Spain and was just readjusting back to living in the UK. When I became deaf, it literally happened out of the blue; without any warning or apparent reason.

"I had gone to bed one night feeling fine - my hearing was normal, no headache, earache etc., but when I woke up the next morning, I was completely deaf. I literally couldn't hear a thing.

Photo: Harley.

"My daughter was having a school exam that morning, so I tried to pretend that everything was fine. I didn't say anything to her, and took her in a cup of tea as usual. I couldn't ring anyone for help because obviously, I couldn't have heard them talking. I couldn't ring the doctor or friends.

"I became very anxious and started crying and my daughter asked me what the matter was. She then took over and got me to hospital.

"I was in hospital for about two weeks. I had nearly every test you can think of - blood tests, MRI scans - to see if I had some sort of tumour - lumbar punctures and hearing assessments. But all the time I was there, I couldn't hear and it wasn't improving.

"Eventually, they told me that my hearing had gone, and it was going to be permanent. I was one of the people to suffer from Sudden Hearing Loss and they don't know why - it can be viral, but they are not sure.

"Of course, I was devastated. All of the things we take for granted were gone. I couldn't hear the TV or radio, listen to music, hear my family talk to me, phone family or friends. Everything changed. I became quite good at lip-reading, but I couldn't hear people talk to me in the shops or hear what people were saying in a group conversation, I just couldn't follow what was going on.

"I felt isolated, even when I was with people, and soon depression set in. I just didn't know how to cope. I felt my life was over and didn't know what the future held. At 45 years of age, this wasn't supposed to be happening.

Hearing Dogs for Deaf People

"My daughter saw an advert for Hearing Dogs for Deaf People, a national UK charity that breeds and trains dogs to be Assistance Dogs for deaf adults and children, and mentioned it to me.

"That was the start of a long and on-going relationship I have had with this great charity. Hearing Dogs take puppies through socialisation and then on to learning what is called *"soundwork"* so they can alert their human recipient when the doorbell goes, the phone rings, or the fire alarm goes off, etc. It really is a wonderful charity. I also love dogs, which helps.

"So, we got in touch and went along to see them at their headquarters in Buckinghamshire, England. I went through an assessment where the charity gets to know you, sees how much help you need, what your personal circumstances are, what you can hear - or not hear - and so on.

"Deafness is not a standard thing; different people can hear different tones and sounds. Some people may be able to hear more than others, so each recipient of a Hearing Dog has a dog that is specifically trained for them.

"Unfortunately, there is a long waiting list of several years, and it took a long time before I got my own Hearing Dog, Harley **(pictured)**, a wonderful Cockapoo who has really changed my life.

"It takes about 18 months to two years to get pups from birth to being fully-fledged Hearing Dogs. They are first given the normal socialisation process, where they live with a volunteer family, get used to all the day-to-day sounds, experiences etc. that a well-grounded dog needs to cope with. They are introduced to babies, children, taken on buses and trains and so on.

"They then have to learn the basic obedience skills and, if they are deemed suitable, they go on to the final stage of learning; the all-important *soundwork.* Not all dogs pass this training. Those that don't are called *"The Fallen Angels,"* and they are placed with a loving family to be a much-loved family pet.

"Harley brought me companionship and restored my confidence. I didn't have to worry about missing a text from family or friends, as he would jump up and alert me about it. And at night, I didn't have to worry if the fire alarm went off, as I knew he would wake me up if I was sleeping. I didn't have to worry if someone was speaking to me in a shop - Harley would let me know!

"I'd previously had a couple of experiences where someone in a supermarket had literally barged into me with their trolley because I hadn't moved when they had asked to get past me in the aisle - I just hadn't heard them! This doesn't happen now. Everyone in the local shops knows Harley, he is a bit of a local star.

"On one occasion Harley saved me from serious injury. I was crossing the road when a car jumped the traffic lights and Harley just stopped; he wouldn't move at all, despite me telling him to walk on. By the time I realised why he had deliberately stopped me, I realised the car was inches away from my legs.

"I have some other health issues, and Harley is wonderful at helping me cope with the effects of those. He is amazing. He now opens the door, brings shoes, helps me undress - he takes my socks off and gives them to me or will put them in a basket. He takes trousers off - this is where his size lets him down. He tries to pick them up off the floor, but ends up standing on them because his legs are so short! He may only be a small dog, but his heart is huge, and he always tries his best to do what is needed or to help."

"I'm now in a sheltered housing (assisted living) bungalow, and the property has an emergency cord system you can pull if you are not well or if there is a problem. Pulling the cord triggers an alert system and someone will ring you and speak over an intercom to check you if you need assistance.

"Obviously, this is no good for me because I wouldn't be able to hear anyone if they rang, so Harley has now been taught to bark when they speak. They now know that if the alarm is pulled and he barks, it's a real emergency. He does this on top of all the other help he gives. I really don't know what I would do without Harley now. I rely on him for his help, his companionship; he gives me the confidence to get out in the world.

"I am now a volunteer for the Hearing Dogs charity, and fundraise for them as much as I can. It costs about £40,000 to raise and train each dog and to provide lifelong support for the dog and its human recipient, so every penny raised is so important.

"When we set up the British Cockapoo Society, we were determined that a big part of our remit was going to be to help raise money for Hearing Dogs. We hold competitions online, have a club shop selling items and money is donated to the charity. We produce and sell a yearly Cockapoo calendar, again with profits going to the charity.

"Every penny counts and I know that these dogs are changing people's lives for the better."

Mary is pictured here with her Harley on the right and another Cockapoo Hearing Dog, coincidentally also called Harley.

....

Hearing Dogs for Deaf People – This charity has helped thousands of UK people with hearing impairments since it was set up in 1982. It currently has some 1,000 Hearing Dogs, generally Labradors, Cocker Spaniels, Poodles, Golden Retrievers and Cockapoos. The charity has a network of helpers and is always looking for new volunteers, foster carers and fundraisers. People can sponsor a puppy and keep up to date with his or her progress for as little as £3 a month. For more information, visit www.hearingdogs.org.uk

The British Cockapoo Society was set up August 2013 by Mary and Diana Hoskins, who have since been joined by Jane Phillips. The BCS has several thousand members and continues to grow. The club's aims include to:

- Provide information and encourage prospective owners to purchase puppies bred from DNA health tested parents
- Give advice on finding breeders who are working to good standards
- Encourage responsible dog ownership by advocating training using non-aversive techniques and by supporting rewards-based training methods.

For more information, visit www.britishcockapoosociety.com or the charity's Facebook page at www.facebook.com/britishcockapoosociety

....

Raising Assistance Cockapoos

In the United States, Cockapoos have worked as service and therapy dogs for decades. Rebecca Mae Goins, of MoonShine Babies Cockapoos, Indiana, first came across them when she was a teenager visiting relatives in assisted living.

She said: "There would be visiting teams of handlers going from room to room; some would have dogs some would have cats, but this sparked an interest for me.

"As an adult, I chose to go to school to be a Pet Care Technician, and Companion Animal Hygienist. At that time in my life, I was very active and was raising and showing Chows. In 2006, my sister gave me the best birthday present - a lovely American Cocker Spaniel, Stella Luna. She came after a very hard hit to my health and opened the door to what I now know to be my calling: breeding, raising and training Cockapoos to help others,

"Our Poodle, Sirius, was to come a few months later as a gift from my mother, and MoonShine Babies Cockapoos was created. Since then, we have not stopped providing happy, healthy and loved Cockapoos to the world as assistance dogs, loved pets and family members. Many of our Cockapoo pups have gone into assistance and service homes."

Why Cockapoos Make Such Good Assistance Dogs

"Cockapoos are a very wise choice for an assistance dog, be it Therapy (TD), Service (SD) or Emotional Support Dog (ESD). They are loyal and smart, easy to train and eager to please. Plus, the low-shed coat means less dander, and that makes them the perfect choice for work in public where you may encounter people with pet allergies.

"I have found that children and adults of all ages with mental and physical special needs benefit from the companionship of an assistance dog - and none better than the happy, loving Cockapoo.

"Here in the US, we have a few different types of assistance dogs. Therapy Dogs assist with companionship and healing in hospitals, nursing and rehab facilities and schools, and Emotional Support Dogs assist individuals who suffer from mental disabilities, and these dogs can have access to any public areas.

"I have an F3 Cockapoo, Katie Scarlett – *pictured* - who is my Emotional Support Dog for bipolar disorder and multiple sclerosis.

"I also have an adult son with autism, and he benefits from the support of his Service Dog/Emotional Support Dog, a wonderful American Cocker Spaniel called Stella Grace. She has opened so many emotional doors and is such a caring and attentive dog. She can even alert people to emotional changes and sugar levels, and has alerted to seizure activity. Both will become mothers for future assistance pups.

"At MoonShine Babies, we raise all of our Cockapoo pups with the same training and socialisation techniques used for assistance dogs, and many of our pups go into service homes to help those in need.

"We are a breeder of the Pets for Vets program which provides assistance dogs to wounded military veterans suffering from PTSD (Post-Traumatic Stress Disorder) and for whom the dog will become that special companion and protector.

"In the US, we have many options for training service and therapy dogs. There are foster homes where the pups are cared for before they go on to the professional trainers. The foster parents train the dog to a certain point before sending him or her on to the owner/handler to complete the process.

"The other option is where the dog is raised and trained by the owner/handler. This is my preference, because the pup can form a strong bond with the owner/handler and that bond is what counts when you need a service or therapy dog.

"All dogs have to start off with basic manners and obedience training. During this time, they learn the necessary skills to prepare them for the task training, which is where they go out in public places and learn to become a disciplined, calm, well trained, socialized assistance dog.

"When it comes to ID tags and badges, it is recommended to have an *"In Training"* badge for those who have not yet completed training, to let people know this is a work in progress.

"After training, you can either acquire or assemble your Assistance Dog badge and vest or harness. Then, when you have issues with people in public that ask you for your proof that your dog is indeed a assistance dog - and sadly this will happen - always remember that, in the US, the ADA (American Disabilities Act) www.ada.gov/service_animals_2010.htm supports you.

"It is not required for the assistance dog to wear a vest or ID Badge, but it is recommended to avoid confusion. By the way, beware of companies who say 'Register your service dog for $$....'

"To sum up, you cannot go wrong with a Cockapoo as an assistance dog. They will do their job with love and pride."

For further information on therapy and service dogs in the USA, visit the Cockapoo registry at www.americancockapooclub.com or: www.ada.gov/regs2010/service_animal_qa.html

https://petpartners.org or www.assistancedogsinternational.org or www.therapydoginfo.net or www.nsarco.com.

....

With sincere thanks to Rebecca and Mary for sharing their stories

List of Contributors

Diana Hoskins and Mary Gosling, co-founders of the British Cockapoo Society
www.britishcockapoosociety.com

Dave and Linda Zarro, former President and Vice President of the American Cockapoo Club
https://americancockapooclub.com also of Sugar and Spice Cockapoos, South Carolina, USA
www.sugarandspicecockapoos.com

Barb Turnbull, The Doodle Trust www.doodletrust.com

Jo-Anne Cousins, IDOG Rescue www.idogrescue.com

Dr Sara Skiwski, Western Dragon holistic veterinary practice, San Jose, California, USA
www.thewesterndragon.com

Mike Payton, Cockapoo HQ www.cockapoohq.com

Breeders (in alphabetical order)

Chloe and Pat Pollington, Polycinders Cockapoos, Tiverton, Devon, England
www.polycinders.co.uk

Eileen Jackson, Brimstone Cockapoos, Christchurch, Cambridgeshire, England
www.facebook.com/Brimstone-Cockapoos-248762248828364

Jackie Stafford of Dj's Cockapoo Babies, Rusk, Texas, USA www.cockapoobabies.com

Jeanne Davis, Wind Horse Offering, Earleville, Maryland, USA www.windhorseoffering.com

Jessica Sampson, Legacy Cockapoos, Beaverton, Ontario, Canada www.legacycockapoos.com

Julie Shearman, Crystalwood Cockapoos, Devon, England www.crystalwoodpuppies.co.uk

Karol Watson Todd, KaroColin Cockapoos, Sleaford, Lincolnshire, England
www.facebook.com/karol.watsontodd

Rebecca Mae Goins, MoonShine Babies Cockapoos, Indiana, USA www.moonshinebabiescpoo.com

Owners

All the puppy parents of Karol Watson Todd, and Ann Draghicchio, Arleen Stone King, Beth Ratkowski, Caroline Littlewood, Judy and Greg Moorhouse, Nigel and Julie Houston, Stacy Robinson and Tiff Atkinson

Useful Contacts

British Cockapoo Society www.britishcockapoosociety.com

The Cockapoo Club of Great Britain www.cockapooclubgb.co.uk

Cockapoo Owners Club (UK) www.cockapooowners-club.org.uk

American Cockapoo Club www.americancockapooclub.com

American Cockapoo Club breeders' list http://www.americancockapooclub.com/breeders.asp

Cockapoo Club of America www.cockapooclub.com

Breeders Online (UK) www.breedersonline.co.uk/dogs/cockapoo.asp

The Doodle Trust (UK) www.doodletrust.com

Doodle Rescue Collective (USA) http://doodlerescuecollective.com

Cockapoo internet forums and Facebook groups are also a good source of information from other owners, including:

http://ilovemycockapoo.com/forum.php

http://cockapoocrazy.proboards.com

www.cockapooclubgb.co.uk/cockapoo-club-chat.html

Association of Pet Dog Trainers UK www.apdt.co.uk

Association of Pet Dog Trainers USA www.apdt.com

Canadian Association of Professional Pet Dog Trainers www.cappdt.ca

Useful information on grain-free and hypoallergenic dog foods www.dogfoodadvisor.com

Helps find lost or stolen dogs in USA, register your dog's microchip www.akcreunite.org

Checking the health of a puppy's parents or a mate (USA) - www.k9data.com

Disclaimer

This book has been written to provide helpful information on Cockapoos. It is not meant to be used, nor should it be used, to diagnose or treat any medical condition. For diagnosis or treatment of any animal medical problem, consult a qualified veterinarian.

The author is not responsible for any specific health or allergy conditions that may require medical supervision and is not liable for any damages or negative consequences from any treatment, action, application or preparation, to any animal or to any person reading or following the information in this book.

The views expressed by contributors to this book are solely personal and do not necessarily represent those of the author. References are provided for informational purposes only and do not constitute endorsement of any websites or other sources.

Copyright

Pet Care Tracker

Vet's Name: _ _ _ _ _ _ _ _ _ _ _ _   Groomer's Name: _ _ _ _ _ _ _ _ _ _ _

Vet's Phone: _ _ _ _ _ _ _ _ _ _   Groomer's Phone: _ _ _ _ _ _ _ _ _ _ _

Day Care: _ _ _ _ _ _ _ _ _ _ _   Holiday Sitter: _ _ _ _ _ _ _ _ _ _ _ _

Pet's Name	Date	Vet Visit	Groomer	NOTES

Printed in Great Britain
by Amazon